China in the New Era:
Interviews with Politicians and Academics from the Former Soviet Union and Eastern Europe

Editor-in-Chief: Jiang Hui
Associate Editor-in-Chief: Xin Xiangyang
Compiled by Li Ruiqin, Yu Haiqing, etc.

CONTENTS

Foreword

Overviews

The Important Contributions of the People's Republic of China to Scientific Socialism Over 70 Years   3
Jiang Hui

Socialism with Chinese Characteristics for a New Era from the International Perspective   19
Xin Xiangyang

Interviews

"China Is Providing an Inspirational Approach" in the Search for the Prospects of Socialism   39
– An Interview with Hans Modrow, the Last Premier of the Former German Democratic Republic from the Socialist Unity Party
Interviewed by Li Ruiqin, Wang Jianzheng

China in the New Era Has a Pioneering and Enterprising Spirit   59
– An Interview with Raif Dizdarević, Former Yugoslavian Leader
Interviewed by Qiao Ruihua, Peng Yuchao

China's Experience from an International Perspective   82
– An Interview with Megyessy Peter, Former Hungarian Prime Minister
Interviewed by Tang Fangfang

Unsurmountable Significance of China's Reform Experience for the World   101
– An Interview with Leonid Danylovych Kuchma, Former Ukrainian President
Interviewed by Li Xiaohua

The Road Taken by China Bears on the Destiny of Socialism in the World   119
– An Interview with Adrian Nastase, Former Prime Minister of Romania
Interviewed by Liu Xinxin

China in the New Era

A Prosperous World Requires a Prosperous China   129
– An Interview with Anatoly Tozik, Former Vice Premier of Belarus
Interviewed by Kang Yanru

**Adhering to the Socialist Road in the Process of Reform and Opening up Is China's
Key to Success**   140
– An Interview with Gennady Zyuganov, Chairman of the Central Committee
of the Communist Party of the Russian Federation
Interviewed by Chen Airu

**Socialism with Chinese Characteristics for a New Era Has Blazed a Trail for the
Rejuvenation of World Socialism**   161
– An Interview with Thürmer Gyula, Chairman of Hungarian Workers' Party
Interviewed by Yu Haiqing

China Is a Successful Socialist Country in the World   186
– An Interview with Toma Ioan, Secretary of the Central Committee of the
Former Romanian Communist Youth League
Interviewed by Lei Xiaohuan

Ukraine and Other Countries Should Learn from China's Experience   203
– An Interview with Petro Symonenko, First Secretary of the Central Committee
of the Communist Party of Ukraine
Interviewed by Kang Yanru

China's Rise Has Profoundly Changed the World Landscape   216
– An Interview with Zoran Jolevski, Former Defense Minister of Macedonia
Interviewed by Zhou Miao, Liu Xiaolan

**Socialism with Chinese Characteristics Has Brought Vigor and Vitality to World
Socialism**   232
– An Interview with Sylwester Szafarz, Former Polish Consul General in Shanghai
Interviewed by Qiao Ruihua

**The CPRF's Interest in and Research and Evaluation on Xi Jinping Thought on
Socialism with Chinese Characteristics for a New Era**   248
– An Interview with Dmitry Novikov, Vice-chairman of the CPRF
Interviewed by Kang Yanru , Li Xiaohua

China Seeks a Just Global Order in the New Era   260
– An Interview with Srgjan Kerim, Former Foreign Minister of Macedonia
Interviewed by Zhang Li

Contents

The Unique Advantage of Socialism with Chinese Characteristics and Its World Significance   275
– An Interview with Vladimir Petkovski, the First Macedonian Ambassador to China
Interviewed by Song Lidan

Comments on the Failure of European Socialism and the Success of Socialism with Chinese Characteristics   287
– An Interview with Frank Schumann, Director of the Edition Ost Verlag in Berlin
Interviewed by Li Ruiqin, Wang Jianzheng

FOREWORD

Jiang Hui

Translated by Xie Shengzhe

Finalized by Wang Qiuhai

In the 1970s-80s, a wave of reform rose in socialist countries in the world. In this reform wave that swept all these countries in the world, the Soviet Union and the socialist countries in Eastern Europe abandoned the leadership of communist parties guided by Marxism and Leninism as well as the basic principles of scientific socialism. Capitalism achieved complete resurgence in the countries in the Soviet Union and Eastern Europe and resulted in a centennial, historic and epochal tragedy in the history of the development of socialism in the world, which shocked the globe. Curtains fell for the socialist "reform" in the countries in the Soviet Union and Eastern Europe after the leadership of communist parties was abolished, the socialist system failed and fell, the Soviet Union disintegrated, nations divided, and the countries were trapped in total crisis. After the drastic changes in Eastern Europe and the disintegration of the Soviet Union, socialism in the world faced an extremely stern situation. In the field of theoretical study, the arguments such as the "failure of socialism" and the "end of history" made a great noise. Under such a morbid circumstance, there was unprecedented pressure and challenge confronting the existing socialist countries, and particularly China, a major power in the east. People questioned whether these countries could adhere to socialism, go through the rocky times and continue to develop. In effect, the future of socialism in the world is closely intertwined with that in China.

The Communist Party of China (CPC), which represents the socialist forces in the world, adheres to Marxism and the objective laws of the development of human history and socialism. It draws from the experiences and lessons in the successes and failures of socialism. It persists in reform and opening up, courageously makes innovations in theory and practice, and gradually forms the path, theory, system and culture of socialism with Chinese characteristics by adapting Marxism to China's conditions and the realities of modern times, and popularization of Marxism. The Deng Xiaoping Theory integrates the basic principles of Marxism and Leninism with the practice of contemporary China and the features of the times. It sheds light on the basic questions about building, consolidating and developing socialism in China. And it contributes to the gradual formation of the routes, guidelines and policies in building socialism with Chinese characteristics, and opens up a new era for the development of socialist undertakings. The Theory of Three Represents inherits, develops and reflects the development changes in contemporary world and China and reflects the new requirements of the work of the CPC and the state. It deepens people's understanding of what socialism is, how to build it, what kind of Party to build and how to build it. It has helped the Chinese Communists accumulate precious new experience in governing the Party and the state, and successfully brought socialism with Chinese characteristics into the 21st century. The Scientific Outlook on Development represents the important achievement in adapting Marxism to Chinese conditions and epitomizes Marxist world outlook and methodology on development. It provides deep understanding of and answers to the important issues of what kind of development China should achieve in the new situation and how to achieve it. It has successfully adhered to and developed socialism with Chinese characteristics from a new historical starting point. Ever since the 18th CPC National Congress, the Party and the state have proposed a series of new concepts, thoughts and strategies in various areas of their work, which drove historic changes to occur in the undertakings of the Party and the state with historic achievements achieved. Chinese communists have kept pace with the times, and provided systematic answers, both theoretical and practical, to two critical questions of this new era: What is the socialism with Chinese characteristics that we should uphold and develop? How are we to achieve it? And, thus, they have established the Xi Jinping Thought on Socialism with Chinese Characteristics for a New Era. China has achieved great victory in reform and opening up and droved socialism in the world into the new era of socialism with Chinese characteristics.

China enters a new era and this attracts the general attention of the people who see hope in socialism in the world. When the important dates arrived for the Chinese people to celebrate the 40th anniversary of reform and opening up and the 70th anniversary of the founding of the People's Republic of China, 30 years had passed for the drastic changes in Eastern Europe. Certain leaders in the regions of the former Soviet Union and the Eastern Europe personally experienced the failure of socialism in Europe. And they have paid attention to and witnessed the historic leap of China's reform and opening up over a long period of time. The situation caused them to give high attention to socialism with Chinese characteristics and to think over the future and destiny of socialism in the world. Egon Krenz, the last leader of the communist party and state of the former German Democratic Republic, believed that Socialism with Chinese Characteristics for a New Era was of great significance to the contemporary world. He wrote that China could become a textbook that caused other countries in Asia, Africa and Latin America to think over how they should shape the present and future of their own countries. He held that the role of pioneer in human progress was played by the Revolution of 1789 in France in the 18th century, by the October Revolution in Russia in the 20th century, and will be played by the People's

Republic of China in the 21st century. As Lenin and his comrades made the new country a great socialism in 1917, China, with its plans, has hard pioneering work to do in the 21st century.[1] China successfully opened up a new path for socialist modernization, which not only has very important and far-reaching meaning for the great rejuvenation of the Chinese nation but also constitutes an important event in the development histories of Marxism and of socialism in the world.

General Secretary Xi Jinping said the success of scientific socialism in China had great significance for Marxism, scientific socialism and world socialism. Socialism with Chinese characteristics has played a crucial historical role in promoting the development of world socialism in each important point in history. It is the most accomplished and vital component of world socialism in the 21st century. The editors have focused on and deeply studied the thoughts and theoretical research results of Communist leaders in the former Soviet Union and Eastern European countries because their thinking had distinctive and important meaning in both theory and reality. Based on their personal experience, these former Communist leaders compared the developments of world socialist movements before and after the drastic changes in Eastern Europe and the disintegration of the Soviet Union. They reflected on the reasons for the drastic changes and explored the kernel and essence of the new thoughts in China in the new era. Their conclusions drawn with their distinctive points of view deserve careful consideration. They believe that people must understand the role of the Communist Party of China when understanding the "China phenomenon"; lifting several hundred million people out of poverty is a "historical monument" on the Chinese path in human history; to create the "China miracle" with the Chinese path is a superior mode of social development in the 21st century; building a community with a shared future for mankind and launching the Belt and Road Initiative (BRI) are the new contributions of China to a more scientific and reasonable new international order; the thought

---

1 Egon Krenz, *China, Wie Ich Es Sehe*, translated by Wang Jianzheng, World Affairs Press, 2019, p. 5.

of President Xi Jinping will play a more and more important role in the world, etc. These thoughts reflect their high hopes that Socialism with Chinese Characteristics for a New Era can contribute to the rejuvenation of world socialism and exert significant influence on the contemporary times, and also express the deep and rich feelings of Communist leaders and left theorists in the former Soviet Union and Eastern European countries for Marxist socialism. These are both vigorous support for China to advance and a particular manifestation of Marxist internationalism.

Socialism with Chinese Characteristics for a New Era supplies successful paradigms to the development of world socialism. It also opens up a new path for developing countries to shake off poverty and advance toward modernization. Besides, it provides Chinese wisdom and experience for the reasonable orientation of contemporary world and the solution of the issues of the mankind. It won deep recognition and praise from the Communist leaders in the former Soviet Union and Eastern European countries. In the 21st century, China provides its solution to the exploration of the mankind in building a better social system, and the cause of socialism with Chinese characteristics with the CPC at the core of leadership will exert greater influence on the world. In a certain sense, socialism with Chinese characteristics represents the future of world socialism. It is the epitome of the Four Matters of Confidence, namely the confidence in the path, theory, system and culture of socialism with Chinese characteristics. And it is the historical commitment of the CPC to its socialist undertakings and to the mankind's social development and civilization progress. According to the grand blueprint drawn at the 19th National Congress of the CPC, China will develop into a great modern socialist country that is prosperous, strong, democratic, culturally advanced, harmonious and beautiful; it will become a global leader in terms of comprehensive national strength and international influence; and the Chinese nation will stand among the nations of the world with a more positive attitude by the middle of the 21st century. Socialism with Chinese Characteristics for a New Era will become a well-deserved mainstay in the rejuvenation of world socialism with its great achievements in an all-round way.

Overviews

The Important Contributions of the People's Republic of China to Scientific Socialism Over 70 Years

Jiang Hui[1]

Translated by Xie Shengzhe

Finalized by Wang Qiuhai

During the 70 years since the founding of the People's Republic of China in 1949, the Chinese people, under the leadership of the Communist Party of China, have written a world-changing epic on the broad path of socialism. The Chinese nation made a great leap forward in which it rose up and became rich and strong. In this brilliant historical process, socialism with Chinese characteristics underwent preparation, creation, development and improvement. With it, scientific socialism, which has a history of over 170 years, has found a practical and workable path of realization in this major power in the East with nearly 1.4 billion population. Upon the start of a new era, socialism with Chinese characteristics shows great historical significance in the development history of scientific socialism, world socialism and human society. "It means that scientific socialism is full of vitality in 21st century China, and that the banner of socialism with Chinese characteristics is now flying high and proud for all to see,"[2] which indicates that Socialism with Chinese Characteristics

---

1   Jiang Hui, vice president of the Chinese Acaderny of Social Sciences (CASS), a member of the CPC leadership group of CASS, and director of the Institute of Contemporary China Studies at CASS.

2   Xi Jinping, *Secure a Decisive Victory in Building a Moderately Prosperous Society in All Respects and Strive for the Great Success of Socialism with Chinese Characteristics for a New Era*, People's Publishing House, 2017, p. 10.

for a New Era has become a leading banner of scientific socialism in the 21st century. It also has become the mainstay of the development of world socialism and the leading force in the development and progress of human society.

I. The success of the People's Republic of China Over 70 years has successfully answered the historical issue of "what socialism is and how to build it". This gives scientific socialism, which has a history of over 170 years, strong vigor and vitality

How to build socialism in a country with a relatively backward economy and culture after the victory of a revolution is a crucial historical issue in the history of the development of socialism. Marx and Engels once envisaged a victory of socialist revolution in developed countries simultaneously and the construction of a new society on the basis of a higher level of productive forces. They also pondered over the path of development of countries with a relatively backward economy and culture, such as Russia, and proposed the assumption that these countries could leap over the Caudine Forks of capitalism. However, as they did not have any experience in building socialism in their life, their ideas were mostly predictive or the "bringing out" of the historical issues. After the victory of the October Revolution (1917) in Russia, Lenin made many creative explorations on how to build socialism in a country with a relatively backward economy and culture. He proposed and implemented new economic policies, carried out industrialization, developed advanced culture, and strengthened the construction of the ruling party, resulting in initial success. This can be evaluated as a "solution" to historical issues. After that, the Soviet Union launched large-scale socialist development for several decades and made great achievements while also committing serious mistakes. In the end, their explorations failed with the disintegration of the Soviet Union. It can be said that it took the Soviet Union about 70 years to explore the way of building socialism, but they "deviated from the course" and ended in the complete change of the social system.

The preparation, creation, development and improvement of socialism with Chinese characteristics during the 70 years since the founding of the People's Republic of China constitute the "solution to" the historical issue of how to build socialism in a country with a relatively backward economy and culture. This process of great history-making is divided into the two historical periods – before and after the start of the reform and opening up. Comrade Xi Jinping pointed out, "The two phases – at once related to and distinct from each other – are both pragmatic explorations in building socialism conducted by the people under the leadership of the Party."[1] From the founding of the People's Republic of China till the start of the reform and opening up, our party led the people in socialist revolution and construction. It arduously explored a path of socialist development suitable to the situations in China. Although it experienced serious detours and made serious mistakes, China, in general, has comprehensively established a basic socialist system, realized the greatest and deepest social transformation in history and formed original theories and achieved great feats and laid a political and system foundation for all the progress and development of contemporary China. It supplied precious experience, theoretical preparation and material basis for the establishment of socialism with Chinese characteristics later. In the period of more than 40 years after the start of the reform and opening up, from the beginning of a new period to the start of the new century and from a new starting point to entering a new era, socialism with Chinese characteristics saw a great leap-forward from establishment and development to improvement. The constant exploration and successful answer to the historical issue of "what socialism is and how to build it" has injected strong vigor and vitality into the scientific socialism with a history of over 170 years. Our party has reached an unprecedented level in mastering the laws of socialist development and unprecedented standard in leading the Chinese people in the

---

1　Xi Jinping, "Several Questions on Adhering to and Developing Socialism with Chinese Characteristics," *A Selection of Important Documents from the 18th CPC National Congress*, Vol. I, Central Party Literature Press, 2014, p. 111-112.

historical creation of socialist revolution, construction and reform. Since the 18th CPC National Congress, socialism with Chinese characteristics has entered a new era marked by the CPC's efforts in comprehensively promoting scientific socialism in theory, practice and system. It is not only of theoretical and practical significance, but also is important for the world today. Thus, China has made monumental contribution to successfully resolving the historical issues of socialism during the 70 years since the founding of the People's Republic of China.

Over the past 70 years, China successfully resolved the historical issue of "what socialism is and how to build it". The most fundamental reason is that it has found a correct path, namely the path of socialism with Chinese characteristics. This path has been opened up from scratch by several generations of the CPC members who led the Chinese people in arduous struggle, and it is a successful path in the long-term exploration according to the national conditions of our country, a broad path for the Chinese nation to stride ahead to catch up with the times and lead the development of the era. The path of socialism with Chinese characteristics is also one for independent innovation. Independence and self-reliance is the fine tradition of the CPC and also the important approach to running and maintaining the Party and the state. In order to make revolution, construction and reform in China, a large country with nearly 1.4 billion population and over 5,000 years history of civilization, the Chinese people have to find a path of their own. In the past, we followed conventions and imitated other nations. Again and again, we ran into a blank wall, became aware of the reality, and then practiced until making a breakthrough. In the end, we found this successful path. Both history and reality prove that no one nation or country in human history can achieve power and rejuvenation through relying on external forces or following others step by step. Only the path of socialism with Chinese characteristics can lead China to progress and bring welfare to the people. As Comrade Xi Jinping pointed out, "The sweeping social changes that China is undergoing are not simply the extension of China's historical and cultural experiences, the repetition of socialist practices by other countries, or the duplication of modernization endeavors elsewhere. Nor can they be readily slotted into the template devised by earlier writers of Marxist classics."[1] The path of socialism with Chinese characteristics is an original version created by the CPC. The CPC neither follows the old path of a rigid closed-door policy nor an erroneous path by abandoning socialism. It will resolutely take the path of socialism with Chinese characteristics.

The path of socialism with Chinese characteristics is a road to realize full development. Classical Marxist writers believe that the inherent requirement of a new society is to achieve the free and comprehensive development of man. Karl Marx envisioned a future society as "a more advanced form of society in which the free and comprehensive development of each person is taken as fundamental principle."[2] Socialism with Chinese characteristics fully follows this fundamental principle and tries to realize the comprehensive development of man and progress of the society. The path of socialism with Chinese characteristics is to adhere to the people-oriented principle under the leadership of the Communist Party of China, always taking the expectation of the people for a better life as its goal of struggle. It should advance the Five-point Strategy (of promoting economic, political, cultural, social, and ecological progress) and the Four-pronged Strategy (to complete a moderately prosperous society in all respects, to further reform, to advance the rule of law, and to strengthen Party discipline), constantly liberating and developing social productive forces so that people can share the fruits of development in various aspects, such as economy, politics, culture, society and ecology, and have a more direct and genuine sense of contentment, happiness and security. Moreover, comprehensive development of man and the common prosperity of all people

---

1 Xi Jinping, "Accelerating the Construction of Philosophy and Social Sciences with Chinese Characteristics," *A Selection of Important Documents from the 18th CPC National Congress*, Vol. II, Central Party Literature Press, 2018, p. 327.

2 *Complete Works of Karl Marx and Friedrich Engels*, Vol. 23, People's Publishing House, 1972, p. 649.

should also be constantly promoted.

The path of socialism with Chinese characteristics is key to realize the rejuvenation of the Chinese nation. Comrade Xi Jinping pointed out, "Having reviewed our historical experience and made painstaking efforts to probe our way forward in the past 30 years and more since the reform and opening-up process was started, we have finally embarked on the right path to achieve the rejuvenation of the Chinese nation and made impressive achievements in this pursuit. This path is one for building socialism with Chinese characteristics."[1] On this path, we are closer to the goal of the great rejuvenation of the Chinese nation than any time in history and more confident of realizing this goal than any moment in history. On this path, we have a clear timetable and roadmap, namely the strategic planning worked out at the 19th CPC National Congress: To build a moderately prosperous society in all respects in 2020, to basically realize socialist modernization in 2035, and to build China into a great modern socialist country that is prosperous, strong, democratic, culturally advanced, harmonious and beautiful by the middle of this century. By then, the Chinese nation will stand among the nations of the world with a more positive attitude.

II. During the 70 years since the founding of new China, we have continuously deepened our understanding of the laws of socialist development, and formed the guiding ideology of the Party and the state to keep pace with the times

Friedrich Engels said, "Ever since socialism became a science, it has been

---

1 Xi Jinping, "The Chinese Dream, a Path to National Rejuvenation," *A Selection of Important Documents from the 18th CPC National Congress*, Vol. I, Central Party Literature Press, 2014, p. 83.

required that people treat it as such. Namely, they are required to study it."[1] The word "study" here mentioned by Engels was in fact the requirement that Marxists constantly explore and creatively employ the development principles of socialism. They should constantly promote theoretical innovation on the basis of the development of the times and in practice and thus constantly enrich the treasure-house of the theories on scientific socialism. Karl Marx and Friedrich Engels established the fundamental rationale and principles of scientific socialism, proposed its fundamental standpoint, outlook and method, and laid a foundation for their successors to carry on further exploration and theoretical innovation. Leninism was formed when Lenin led the Russian people in exploring socialist revolution and construction, which greatly enriched and developed scientific socialism. As a result, Marxism and Leninism became the guiding thought of Marxist political parties and socialist countries and also the theoretical foundation for promoting socialist undertakings.

In the past 70 years, the Communist Party of China has adhered to combining the fundamental principles of scientific socialism with the reality in the country. During different historical periods, the Party enriched and developed the theories on scientific socialism. The theories on socialist revolution and construction form an important component of the Mao Zedong Thought which can be found in his works *On the Ten Major Relationships* and *On the Correct Handling of Contradictions Among the People*. These works still have important and realistic value of guidance at present. Since the reform and opening up, the Deng Xiaoping Theory, the Theory of Three Represents, the Scientific Outlook on Development, and the Xi Jinping Thought on Socialism with Chinese Characteristics for a New Era have been formed successively in the historical process of the establishment, development and improvement of socialism with Chinese characteristics. These theories show

---

1 *Selected Works of Karl Marx and Friedrich Engels*, Vol. 2, People's Publishing House, 1995, p. 636.

consistency in evolution and keep pace with the times. They constantly endow socialism with Chinese characteristics with distinct practical, theoretical, national and contemporary characteristics.

As socialism with Chinese characteristics enters a new era, the understanding and mastering of the laws of socialist development becomes more profound and mature. For example, the proposals of the "Eight Clarifications" and "Fourteen Commitments" have enriched and developed the holistic and pioneering nature of socialism with Chinese characteristics. The CPC proposed the integrated development of the path, theory, system and culture of socialism, which expanded the scientific system of socialism with Chinese characteristics. It proposed the thought on people-centered development and deepened the theory of the essence of socialism. It also proposed that the main social contradictions in our country have undergone historical transformation, which has enriched the theory of the primary stage of socialism and developed the theory of the development stage of socialism. In the new era, it comprehensively deepened reform and enhanced the theory of driving force of socialism. It promoted the modernization of national governance system and capacity, and enriched and developed the theory of socialist modernization. It pushed forward the "Five-point Strategy" and the "Four-pronged Strategy", and improved the theory of the comprehensive development of socialism. It implemented the new concepts of innovative, coordinated, green, open and inclusive development, and expanded the theory behind the approach and goal of the development of socialism. It adhered to the overall leadership of the CPC and proposed the important judgment on the "Two Mosts" of the CPC's leadership. Namely, the leadership of the Communist Party of China was the most essential feature of socialism with Chinese characteristics and the most advantageous feature of the system of socialism with Chinese characteristics. It also enriched and developed the theory concerning the construction of ruling party in a socialist country. It expounded the inevitable trend of the historical development of human society and proposed new thoughts on scientifically understanding of the relationship between two major social systems. And it enriched the theory of correctly handling the relationship between socialism and capitalism. It proposed and promoted constructing "a community with a shared future for mankind". And it enriched and developed the theory of Marxism on future society, etc. These new philosophies, thoughts and strategies with important theoretical significance and distinctive significance of times are important innovation and comprehensive development of scientific socialism which greatly have deepened people's understanding of the laws of socialist development.

III. The past 70 years have witnessed the great superiority of the socialist system and the construction of socialism superior to capitalism

On the basis of the historical materialism and their analysis of the fundamental contradictory of the capitalist society, founders of scientific socialism believed that the social system for the future in which socialism replaces capitalism has its advanced nature and superiority. But in reality, socialist system is built in countries with relatively backward economy and culture. How to demonstrate and realize the superiority of socialist system in reality, when rivaling with developed capitalism, has become an important historical issue that Marxists had to face in a world of "two systems on one globe" during the century after the October Revolution in Russia. It is also a difficult question that needs to be explored and solved. The mode of socialism in the Soviet Union once demonstrated great advantages of socialist system in reality. However, it also had many shortcomings. Later, the aim of reforms in the socialist countries was to make great efforts to remove shortcomings and demonstrate the superiority of socialist system in a better way. After the disintegration of the Soviet Union, socialist countries in reality, represented by China, continued to explore and look for the solution to this difficult historical question.

In the 70 years since the founding of new China, socialist system has evolved from establishment to consolidation and development and from system reform to innovation and improvement. As it keeps making historical achievements, it also constantly demonstrates the superiority and huge advantage of the socialist system. After its founding, the People's Republic of China established a basic socialist system through socialist transformation and thus made a great leap forward from a feudal system that lasted for several thousand years to a people's democratic system and a socialist system. In the beginning of the reform and opening up, Comrade Deng Xiaoping said, "The socialist revolution has greatly narrowed the gap in economic development between China and the advanced capitalist countries. Despite our errors, in the past three decades we have made progress on a scale which old China could not achieve in hundreds or even thousands of years."[1] This was the initial demonstration and powerful proof of the huge superiority of socialist system in China. Reform was the "second revolution" in China. It was in essence the self-improvement and development of socialist system so as to exhibit vitality in reform and innovation and more efficiently demonstrate its superiority. General Secretary Xi Jinping pointed out that the practice of reform and opening up showed us, "Improving and developing the Chinese socialist system is key to China's progress. It provides a strong guarantee for unlocking and developing productivity, for releasing and enhancing social vitality, for maintaining the vigor of the Party and the country."[2] Through constant reform and innovation, the CPC made socialist system with Chinese characteristics more efficient than capitalist system so that it has more comparative advantage in competition. Since the start of the reform and opening up, socialism with Chinese characteristics has achieved brilliant feats that attracted the attention of the whole world. The superiority of socialist system has been proved convincingly in the great effort of realizing national prosperity, people's happiness and national rejuvenation.

---

1 Deng Xiaoping, "Uphold the Four Cardinal Principles," *Selected Works of Deng Xiaoping*, Vol. 2, People's Publishing House, 1994, p. 167.

2 Xi Jinping, "The Speech at the Conference Celebrating the 40th Anniversary of Reform and Opening Up," *People's Daily*, December 19, 2018.

Since the 18th CPC National Congress, our party, through deepening reform in an all-round way, has constantly developed and improved the socialist system with Chinese characteristics and improved its ability in effective governance through applying socialist system with Chinese characteristics. The CPC not only has embarked on a successful development path different from that of western countries but also established a set of successful institutions different from those in western countries. The system demonstrates distinctive advantages, ranging from the leadership of the Communist Party of China, rallying all forces that can be unified, possessing strong mobilization power and concentrating effort and resources to deal with important issues, to effectively promoting social fairness and justice, etc. In the new era, our party adheres to comprehensively deepening reform and building a systematic, scientific, standardized and effective system. This has given full play to the superiority of China's socialist system. Through comprehensively deepening reform, our party has constantly developed and improved the system with socialism with Chinese characteristics and constantly enhanced its ability in effective governance through employing socialist system with Chinese characteristics. Specifically speaking, China's economic system effectively promotes the unification between efficiency and fairness, its political system effectively guarantees that the people are the masters of the country, its cultural system constantly promotes the flourishing and prosperity of socialist culture, its social management system comprehensively guarantees and improves the people's livelihood, and its ecological system effectively realizes the harmonious coexistence between man and nature and sustained development. As General Secretary Xi Jinping pointed out, "As socialism progresses, our institutions will undoubtedly mature, the strengths of our system will become self-evident, and our development path will assuredly become wider and exert greater influence on the world."[1] Socialist system with Chinese characteristics

---

1   Xi Jinping, "Several Questions on Adhering to and Developing Socialism with Chinese Characteristics," *A Selection of Important Documents from the 18th CPC National Congress*, Vol. I, Central Party Literature Press, 2014, p. 111.

will become more mature and set. China will constantly build its socialism that is superior to capitalism. It will make contribution to scientific socialism in the area of system and institution with its distinctive institutional achievements. It has also provided a new choice for other countries in the construction of social system, constantly enriching and innovating civilized system for the world.

The sharp contrast between the "Effective Governance of China" and the "West's Disorder" in the present world fully proves the superiority and advantage of socialist system with Chinese characteristics. In western countries, huge wealth disparity, failure in social governance, constant party strife, ever-growing protectionism and populism, and the rampant terrorism all show the failure and governance ineffectiveness in the West system. At present, many foreign theorists have profoundly revealed the crises of capitalism in system, institution and value, which actually is the prominent manifestation of the structural contradictions in capitalist system. In contrast, China shows "unique excellent performance". Through comprehensively deepening reform, it has promoted the socialist system with Chinese characteristics to make it more mature and finalized. It has created a full set of institutional systems that are more complete, stable and effective, for the development of the CPC and the state, the happiness and welfare of the people, the harmony and stability of the society, and the long-term peace and security of the country. Its superiority has won recognition and affirmation of many men of insight in the world. Socialism with Chinese characteristics has made remarkable achievements that have attracted the attention of the whole world, providing convincing proof of the superiority of socialism in China in achieving wealth and strength of the country, the happiness of the people, and the rejuvenation of nation.

In the beginning of the reform and opening up, Comrade Deng Xiaoping predicted with full confidence that, "Our system will improve more and more with the passage of time. By absorbing the progressive elements of other countries, it will become the best in the world."[1] Today, socialist system with Chinese characteristics shows strong vigor and vitality and keeps developing and improving itself. As Comrade Xi Jinping pointed out, "This requires constant reforms and innovations to ensure that Chinese socialism is more efficient than capitalism in releasing and developing the productive forces, stimulating and strengthening the vigor of society and promoting a well-rounded development of the person, and the arousing of greater enthusiasm, initiative and creativity among the people, create more favorable conditions for social development, and show a better edge in competition, thus fully displaying its advantages."[2]

IV. In the past 70 years, new China has made great contributions to human progress and pushed world socialism into a new stage

The Communist Party of China always takes it as its mission to make new and greater contribution to the mankind. The 70 years from the founding of new China witnessed a historical process in which people of China devoted themselves to the prosperity of the country, the happiness of the people and the rejuvenation of the Chinese nation. It is also a historical process in which socialist China kept making contribution to the progress of the mankind. Comrade Mao Zedong said in 1956, "China is a large country. Its population accounts for one quarter of the whole world. But its contribution to the mankind is not in line with the proportion of population."[3] So in order to make its due contribution to the progress of mankind, China needs to change its backward situation and build itself into a flourishing

---

1   Deng Xiaoping, "On the Reform of the System of Party and State Leadership," *Selected Works of Deng Xiaoping*, Vol. 2, People's Publishing House, 1994, p. 337.

2   Xi Jinping, "Align Our Thinking with the Guidelines of the Third Plenary Session of the 18th CPC Central Committee," *A Selection of Important Documents from the 18th CPC National Congress*, Vol. I, Central Party Literature Press, 2014, p. 550.

3   Mao Zedong, "Learning from Historical Lessons and Opposing Great Power Chauvinism," *Collected Works of Mao Zedong*, Vol. 7, People's Publishing House, 1999, p. 124.

and prosperous socialist country. The founding of the People's Republic of China created political basis and institutional guarantee for China to go global. The enormous achievements that China made in various economic and social areas strengthened socialist forces in the world and greatly promoted the progress of the mankind. Since the reform and opening up, it has been the inherent requirement for socialist China to make more contributions to mankind. When meeting with foreign guests in 1978, Comrade Deng Xiaoping said, "Not only China should develop itself and realize the four modernizations of agriculture, industry, national defense, and science and technology, but it should also make more contributions to the mankind as it develops. This is the way to judge whether or not we are a real socialist country." [1]More than 40 years of reform and opening up not only greatly changed China but also deeply changed the world. Today, China is advancing closer to the center of the world. It positively promotes building "a community with a shared future for mankind" and makes new and greater contribution to the peace and development of the world. It offers Chinese wisdom and solution for the exploration of a better social system for the mankind. General Secretary Xi Jinping pointed out, the success of scientific socialism in China is of great significance to Marxism, scientific socialism and world socialism.

China has made great contributions to the common development of the world. The Communist Party of China brings benefits not only to the Chinese people but also to the people in the world. It promotes building a new order for international economy and politics, pushing for the healthy development of economic globalization, and resolving the difficulties in the world that confront human society. China follows a new development philosophy and contributes the new outlook of "scientific development, peaceful development, inclusive development, and win-win development" to the development of human society. It advocates constructing

---

1　Literature Research Office of the CPC Central Committe Ed., *Deng Xiaoping Thought Chronology (1975-1997)*, Central Party Literature Press, 1998, p.70.

"a community with a shared future for mankind" and proposes new principles for international order and new visions for the development of human society. It advances the Belt and Road Initiative in a down-do-earth manner to bring tangible benefits to the people of all countries and regions along the route and promotes the common development and prosperity of all the countries.

China has made great contributions to world socialism. Over the past 30 years, the world socialist movement has gone through a process from the low ebb caused by the drastic changes in Eastern Europe and the disintegration of the Soviet Union to seeking revitalization at the beginning of the 21st century. At each important historical point, socialism with Chinese characteristics played a crucial historical role in world socialist movement. Toward the end of the 1980s and the beginning of the 1990s, socialism was hit hard by the drastic changes in Eastern Europe, the disintegration of the Soviet Union, and the downfall of the Communist Party of the Soviet Union (CPSU). The views of the "failure of socialism" and "the end of history" caused a temporary clamor. But China stood up to the tremendous pressure and challenge. It held the banner of socialism firmly and defended and saved socialism. At the beginning of the 21st century, international financial crisis triggered the crisis of the entire capitalism. Socialism with Chinese characteristics made the balance of power between the two systems change in favor of socialism. It developed and rejuvenated socialism. In recent years, a de-globalization trend has appeared in the USA and other major western countries. This indicates that the power of capitalism to control the world has decreased significantly and become incompetent. As it promotes economic globalization to develop in a more just and rational direction, China has become the mainstay in the new development of world socialist movement, leading and shaping the world socialism in the 21st century.

China has made tremendous contributions to the development of human civilization. With a broad mind of openness and inclusiveness that seeks common grounds while reserving difference, China positively promotes the prosperity of the civilizations of all countries and the progress of the mankind. Comrade Xi Jinping repeatedly emphasized, "Civilizations have become richer and more colorful with exchanges and mutual learning."[1] Through continuous and unremitting efforts, China advocates that all countries go beyond cultural estrangement through cultural exchanges, cultural conflict through mutual learning, and cultural superiority through cultural coexistence. In the present world, although cliches such as clash of civilizations and superiority of civilizations pop up from time to time, China always advocates that cultural diversity is the inexhaustible driving power of the progress of the mankind. It works together with the international community to promote mutual respect and harmonious coexistence of different civilizations. Thus, it turns the mutual learning of different civilizations into a positive force for the construction of "a community with a shared future for mankind". And it helps to let all kinds of civilizations created by human beings complement each other and be woven into a colorful picture. Through the communication and dialogue between different civilizations, the CPC is introducing the Chinese civilization to the world. It makes the traditional Chinese concepts such as "great harmony in the world", "harmony among nations" and "working together with one heart" become important elements in promoting world peace and development and building a just and reasonable international order. These concepts are playing an important role in constructing "a community with a shared future for mankind".

China is the largest socialist country in the world and the Communist Party of China is the largest Marxist political party in the world, both of which persist unswervingly in adhering to and developing socialism. The success of the CPC is also the success of scientific socialism. The victory of the socialism with Chinese characteristics is also the victory of scientific socialism. The great rejuvenation of the Chinese nation will definitely result in the revitalization of world socialism.

---

1 "The Speech of President Xi Jinping at the UNESCO Headquarters," *People's Daily*, March 28, 2014.

Socialism with Chinese Characteristics for a New Era from the International Perspective

Xin Xiangyang[1]

Translated by Xie Shengzhe

Finalized by Wang Qiuhai

Socialism with Chinese characteristics has entered a new era. It means that the Chinese nation, which underwent long afflictions from modern times, has made a great leap forward, risen up and become rich and strong. It has ushered in a brilliant prospect for realizing the great rejuvenation of the Chinese nation. It also means that scientific socialism has presented strong vigor and vitality in China in the 21st century. It held up high the great banner of socialism with Chinese characteristics in the world. It means that the path, theory, system and culture of socialism with Chinese characteristics are undergoing constant development, thus boosting developing countries to achieve modernization and providing brand-new choices for the countries and nations in the world that hope to speed up development and, at the same time, retain their independence. It has contributed Chinese wisdom and Chinese roadmap to resolving the issues of the mankind. These indicate that socialism with Chinese characteristics in the new era stands in a time in which the great banner of socialism flies high and the great ideal of scientific socialism is full of vibrancy.

---

1   Xin Xiangyang, research fellow and deputy director of the Academy of Marxism, Chinese Academy of Social Sciences.

I. The competition between socialism and capitalism has never stopped since the October Revolution in Russia

Such competition was determined by the times. On September 29, 2017, General Secretary Xi Jinping noted at the 43rd Collective Learning Session of the Political Bureau of the CPC Central Committee, that although tremendous and profound changes have occurred in our times, comparing with the times when Karl Marx lived, we are still in a historical period as specified by Marx from the perspective of the 500 years of world socialist movement. What is this historical time like? It is a time when capitalism still dominates and also a time when socialism is replacing capitalism and will finally prevail over capitalism and advance towards communism.

The October Revolution in Russia ushered in a new era in human history which has a fundamental feature: two predominant social systems, namely capitalism and socialism, coexist on earth. And at the same time, intense competition between them is going on through the comparison of attractiveness, superiority and vitality. Over a century, such competition has been going on intensely which can be divided into the following several stages:

The first stage lasted from the end of the October Revolution till the beginning of the Second World War, during which the competition was between the emerging Soviet socialist countries and capitalist countries. After the October Revolution in 1917, capitalist countries clamored that they would "strangle Bolsheviks in their cradle". Fourteen imperialist countries laid siege to the Soviet Union and numerous revolts broke out, led by Anton Ivanovich Denikin, Aleksandr Vasilyevich Kolchak, Nickolai Nickolayevich Yudenich, Lavr Kornilov and others. Soviet socialism was therefore, for a moment, in extreme danger. On February 21, 1918, the Council of People's Commissars adopted an act written by V. I. Lenin, entitled *The Socialist Fatherland in Danger*. The council thus decided: The country's entire manpower and resources should be devoted to the revolutionary cause of defense. All Soviets and revolutionary organizations should be ordered to defend every position to their last drop of blood. All grain and food stocks, as well as all valuable properties that were in danger of falling into the enemy's hands, should be unconditionally destroyed. Soviet Russia suffered innumerable sacrifices. By the end of the 1920, Soviet Russian socialism finally lifted imperialist siege and subdued the domestic insurrection and successfully defended socialist system. In the 1930s, Soviet socialism showed great vitality while capitalist countries fell into the Great Depression in 1933. Many people in capitalist countries longed for socialism. After the crisis struck capitalism in 1933, thousands of people queued up and requested to emigrate to the Soviet Union at the US Citizenship and Immigration Services.

The second stage of competition occurred from the end of the Second World War till the end of the Cold War between socialism and capitalism. A large number of socialist countries emerged after the Second World War and formed the socialist camp. The Cold War started from 1946, when the socialist camp, represented by the Soviet Union, and the capitalist camp, represented by the United States, engaged in contest. Through military blockade, economic containment, and ideological suppression, the capitalist camp eventually caused the disintegration of the Soviet Union.

The third stage lasted from the end of the Cold War to the present and the competition was between socialism with Chinese characteristics and the capitalist camp. After the Cold War ended, capitalist countries thought that they had won a global victory and proposed the theory of the end of history and the theory of the failure of communism. They attempted to peacefully include China into the capitalist system through new liberalism and economic globalization. However, socialism with Chinese characteristics keeps growing stronger through cooperation and competition with capitalism. For many consecutive years, China has contributed 30 percent to world economic growth and become its major stabilizer and driving power. With these facts, China proclaims the debacle of the theory of the end of history and the wrongness of the historical view that all countries will eventually end up with the western system. The competition between socialism with Chinese characteristics entered a new era.

The competition between these two systems over a century shows the following features: First, capitalist countries have always tried to suppress socialism with strong military power. After the Soviet Union disintegrated, the Warsaw Treaty Organization (WTO) terminated with it. But the North Atlantic Treaty Organization (NATO) still exists and has strengthened its military presence. One of the important reasons why the US can exercise the so-called "long-arm jurisdiction" in the present world is that it has military bases across the globe. At present, US has 374 overseas military bases in over 140 countries and regions with 300,000 soldiers. On March 28, 1999, Thomas Friedman published an article entitled "A Manifesto for the Fast World" at the *New York Times*, in which he wrote, "The hidden hand of the market will never work without a hidden fist. McDonald's cannot flourish without McDonnell Douglas, the builder of the F-15. And the hidden fist that keeps the world safe for Silicon Valley's technologies to flourish is called the US Army, Air Force, Navy and Marine Corps." Second, capitalism tried to control the economic lifeline of socialist countries by means of unfair economic rules. As some scholars stated, by the end of 2000, the highest proportion of foreign capital holding reached 97 percent and the lowest exceeded 50 percent in the banking industry in Eastern Europe. The so-called social transformation was nothing but replacing the tanks and missiles of the Soviet Union with the banks and McDonalds of the US. The people there not only lost their original social welfare but also suffered the manifold exploitation of western capital. Finally, capitalism used ideological propaganda to attack socialist system. Early in the 1920s, the mass media of capitalist countries attacked the Soviet Russia as "a cruel gorilla", trying to turn the "peaceful economic development" in the Soviet Russia into the "peaceful disintegration of the Soviet regime".[1] From the beginning of the Cold War, western countries kept supporting

---

1 *The Complete Works of Lenin,* Vol. 32, People's Publishing House, 1958, p. 447.

the peaceful evolution of socialist countries in an attempt to win without a war. After the Soviet Union disintegrated in 1991, western countries have always looked on socialism with Chinese characteristics as "being freak" and put many labels on China, such as "one-party autocracy" and "a totalitarian state".

II. The new era is a time of Intense competition between the two systems: socialism with Chinese characteristics and capitalism

(I) In such an era, western countries represented by the US have always been hostile to socialism with Chinese characteristics. They condemned it as "state capitalism", "new bureaucratic capitalism" and "despotic authoritarianism"

Since June, 2018, important politicians in the US have repeatedly condemned China Model. In his remark at the graduation ceremony of the United States Naval Academy in June, 2018, US Secretary of Defense James N. Mattis said, "The Ming Dynasty appears to be their model, albeit a model of a more muscular manner, demanding other nations to become tribute states, kowtowing to Beijing; espousing One Belt, One Road, when this diverse world has many belts and many roads; and attempting to replicate, on the international stage, their authoritarian model… while using predatory economic means to let other countries accumulate huge debts." On June 18, 2018, US Secretary of State Michael R. Pompeo delivered a speech of 30,000 words at the Detroit Economic Club. He indicated that global economy must return to the American model. In particular, people must get rid of China's influence in Africa and let Africa take the American model rather than the China Model. In his eyes, the China model had neither democracy nor the rule of law. On October 4, 2018, US Vice President Mike Pence made a long speech on the US government's policy on China at the Hudson Institute in Washington. He condemned with both ignorance and arrogance China as moving in the direction of controlling and suppressing their own people in recent years. He also ridiculously criticized China's credit system building. i.e. By 2020, China's rulers would attempt to implement an Orwellian system, namely the so-called "social credit point" with a premise of controlling almost every aspect of people's life. All the accusations made by American politicians were targeted to China's social system. On February 5, 2020, President Donald Trump swore that the USA would never become a socialist country when he made his state-of-the-union message at the US Congress.

(II) In such an era, market economy can be different on the basis of social system. Market economy includes both socialist market economy and capitalist market economy

Former president Jiang Zemin made it clear, "What we undertake is socialist market economy. The word 'socialist' cannot be spared. It is not 'paint a snake with feet', something unnecessary. It is the finishing touch which clearly defines the nature of our market economy."[1] General Secretary Xi Jinping also clearly pointed out that, "to develop market economy under the condition of socialism is a great pioneering task of our party. A key factor for the huge success achieved in China's economic development is that we have brought into play both the advantages of market economy and the superiority of socialist system. We have developed market economy under the leadership of the Communist Party of China and socialist system. Under no circumstances should we forget the attribute 'socialist'. The reason why our system is socialist market economy is that we must adhere to the superiority of our system and effectively prevent the shortcomings of capitalist market economy."[2] Ours is socialist market economy which is fundamentally different from capitalist market economy. Our market economy stresses "benefiting others as well as ourselves" whereas capitalist market economy "takes from the less to give to the more". Our market economy lays stress on fairness and trading

---

1 *Jiang Zemin on Socialism with Chinese Characteristics (Special Articles)*, Central Party Literature Press, 2002, p.69.

2 *Excerpts from Xi Jinping's Treatise on Socialist Economic Construction*, Central Party Literature Press, 2017, p.64.

according to fair international rules while capitalist market economy stresses the maximization of their own profits. The latter often has double standards so that they apply their standards when they are favorable to them and refuse to apply them when they are unfavorable to them even when these standards are laid down by themselves. Contradiction or even conflict occurs between the two systems in the process of economic globalization. One important manifestation is that it prohibits normal investment and acquisition by Chinese enterprises like Huawei in the name of state security. In recent years, the United States has become more concerned about the rapid development of China's high technology industry and the changing trend of core competitiveness between China and the United States. The common understanding in the United States is that the US needs to protect its competitive advantage in the area of high technology through trade and investments. It needs to prevent Chinese enterprises and government from obtaining US technology. In November 2017, the US-China Economic and Security Review Commission published its 2017 annual report. In the recommendation section, it was clearly suggested to restrict the investment of China's state-owned capital in the United States and the investment of China's high-tech industries in the US. In the middle of February, 2020, Secretary of State Michael R. Pompeo warned the Hungary government while visiting the country that, the deployment of Huawei's equipment would cause difficulty in the cooperation between Hungary and the US. During his visit to Slovakia, he indicated that it is necessary to prevent China from making Slovakia depend on China and manipulating Slovak political system through economic and other means. The US wanted to be ensured that its friends and partners recognize that security risks exist in the procurement of Chinese commodity. During his visit to Poland, he indicated again that, if Poland gave up its cooperation with China, it would be beneficial for the US to deploy military bases in the country. It was extremely unfair and immoral to use state power to suppress the rights and interests of Chinese enterprises in their regular development and to intervene in economic activities by political means. But in essence, capitalist market economy runs without any morality.

(III) In such an era, western countries have set up various invisible barriers to China's market economy by using economic, industrial and high-tech policies to restrict China's development

On one hand, western countries do not recognize China's market economy status, accuse China of "state capitalism", impose restrictions on Chinese enterprises' overseas investments, and implement tariff policies to suppress China's market economy, such as the US tariff policy of US$200 billion implemented on September 24, 2018, on the other hand, implicit rules and obstacles have been set up to ban high technology trade with China in an unfair way in which China is treated as a non-market economy. From the Coordinating Committee for Multilateral Export Controls (CoCom) established in Paris 70 years ago to the Wassenaar Arrangement on Export Controls for Conventional Arms and Dual-Use Good and Technologies (WA) 20 years ago, the main policy had been the prohibition of high technology transfer to China. CoCom was set up secretly in November 1949 under the proposal of the United States. It was an unofficial international institution in the field of international trade founded by western developed countries after the Second World War for the purpose of restricting its members to export strategic materials and high technology to the socialist countries. Its embargo list included more than 10,000 items in three major categories: weapons and military equipment, sophisticated technology products and rare materials. Not only socialist countries were listed as the targets of embargo by CoCom but also some nationalist countries, with a total of thirty. Established in 1952, the CoCom was the enforcement agency for the embargo against China. Its organizational structure included: 1. an advisory group as the supreme policy-making body consisting of high-level government officials of its member countries, 2. the regulating committee set up in 1950, which was the enforcement agency that imposed the embargo on the countries of Soviet Union and Eastern Europe. And 3. The China Committee. The purpose of the CoCom was to implement the embargo policy against the socialist countries.

The prohibited products fall into three main categories, including weapons and military equipment, products of sophisticated technology and strategic products. The industrial list under the embargo had four categories: 1. item I was strictly prohibited, such as weapons and atomic energy materials. 2. item II were those under quantity control, 3. item III were those under monitoring and surveillance, and 4. a list for China, namely the special embargo list against China in international trade, which included over 500 more items than the products in the lists applicable to the Soviet Union and the countries in Eastern Europe. In 1983, the 10,000-ton cargo ship "Veteran Communist" under a Soviet shipping company loaded several dozens of boxes of parts and components for five-axis numerical control machine tools when it left Shibaura, Japan. The Soviet Union purchased these numerical control machine tools for improving the propulsion performance of the submarine as well as the propellers on its new aircraft carrier model then under construction. This was the sensational "Toshiba-Kongsberg Incident". During the negotiations, a Toshiba employee said, "Except for Toshiba, no capitalist country had the guts to do so!" In December 1985, Hitori Kumagai, one of the participants in signing the secret agreement between Japan and the Soviet Union and an employee of Wako Koeki, a small Japanese trading firm located in Moscow, resigned in a dispute with his employer, and angrily disclosed the Incident to Gunnell Torq, chairman of the CoCom in France. The chairman immediately asked the Japanese side to investigate the matter. By early 1987 the Americans, after further investigation, had reliable evidence that the Soviet Union had acquired precision machine tools from Japan. Under the pressure from the United States, Japan's Metropolitan Police Department raided Toshiba, seized all the secret documents and arrested those involved. In the several months that followed, the US government and the American public became furious, repeatedly condemning Japan and imposing sanctions on Toshiba. Prime Minister Nakasone Yasuhiro had to apologize to the United States and Japan spent 100 million *yen* publishing a full-page "repentance ads" in more than 50 American newspapers.

With the dramatic changes in Eastern Europe and the disintegration of the Soviet Union, the CoCom announced its formal dissolution on April 1, 1994. But soon, a new CoCom, or the WA, appeared on the stage. Under the manipulation of the United States, 33 countries, mainly western countries, signed the Wassenaar Arrangement on Export Controls for Conventional Arms and Dual-Use Good and Technologies in Vienna, Austria, in July 1996, and decided to implement the new control list and information exchange rules from November 1, 1996. The Wassenaar Arrangement also contains two control lists: one is the list of dual-use goods and technologies, covering nine categories of advanced materials, material processing, electronic devices, computers, telecommunications and information security, sensing and laser, navigation and avionic instruments, ships and maritime equipment, and propulsion systems. The other deals with technologies and goods with a purely military objective, covering 22 categories of weapons, ammunition, equipment and combat platforms. China is also included in the embargoed countries. In 2005, the US government fined Boeing US$ 47 million for allegedly selling nine civilian aircrafts equipped with gyroscope chip technology to China from 2000 to 2003, which violated US export controls and could be used to significantly improve missile guidance accuracy. That is to say, it is difficult for China to acquire foreign high technology through free trade, an integral part of the market economy.

III. How can socialism with Chinese characteristics win comparative advantage over capitalism in the new era?

In November 2013, General Secretary Xi Jinping made an explanation to the plenary session on the Decision of the Central Committee of the CPC on Some Major Issues Concerning Comprehensively Continuing the Reform: "What has helped our Party inspire the people, unify them and pull their strength together over the past 35 years? What have we been relying on to stimulate the creativity and vitality of our people, realize rapid economic and social development and win a competitive advantage over capitalism? The answer has always been reform and opening up."[1] Indeed, the achievement has been made through opening up, the courage to emancipate the mind and the establishment of Marxist dialectical and strategic thinking.

(I) To find and make good use of all kinds of contradictions in the capitalist camp

In a talk with leading officials of the central authorities on March 3, 1990, Comrade Deng Xiaoping pointed out, "In this world there are plenty of complicated contradictions, and some deep-seated ones have just come to light. There are contradictions that we can use, conditions that are favorable to us, opportunities that we can take advantage of – the problem is to seize them at the right moment."[2] The contradictions between the western countries are significant and numerous. At present, the international situation is undergoing major changes unseen in a century and relations between the Western countries are undergoing major adjustments. Trump's "America First" has resulted in huge conflicts between the US and other developed capitalist countries, such as Japan and those in Europe. On February 16, 2020, German Chancellor Angela Merkel delivered a speech at the Munich Security Conference, where she blasted the "arbitrary actions" of the United States, saying that multilateral organizations should not be easily damaged. The US Commerce Department has made an assessment that European cars were posing a threat to American national security. Merkel said she did not understand why Americans see German cars as a threat to national security. "These cars are made in the United States and South Carolina has the largest BMW plant in the United States," she noted. "It's not in Bavaria, it's in South Carolina." This indicates that Germany and the United States have conflicting interests in many areas. We should make good use of these contradictions and strengthen the strategic cooperation between "Made

---

1 *Xi Jinping: The Governance of China*, vol.1, Foreign Language Press, 2018, p. 86.
2 *Selected Works of Deng Xiaoping* Vol.3, People's Publishing House, 1993, p. 354.

in China 2025" and Germany's "National Industry Strategy 2030". On February 5, 2019, the Federal Ministry of Economy and Energy of Germany officially announced "National Industry Strategy 2030" in Berlin, which aims to provide targeted support to key industrial sectors, improve industrial output, and ensure the competitiveness of German industry in Europe and even the world.

(II) To thoroughly study and understand the characteristics of changes and new forms of the fundamental contradictions in contemporary capitalist society

Contemporary capitalism has taken on new characteristics. On one hand, capitalism still leads the world in productivity. It has a strong capacity to ease class conflicts, make self-adjustments and repair its system. It still has a capacity and space to transfer and reverse crises and has a strong control over the world economic and political order. On the other hand, the fundamental contradictions of capitalism are deepening and many new problems have emerged. As General Secretary Xi Jinping pointed out, "Many Western countries continue to experience economic downturn, increasing polarization and deepening of social contradictions, which indicates that the inherent contradiction between the socialization of production and the private possession of the means of production in capitalism still exists but the forms and features of its manifestation are different now."[1] What are the differences? First, the socialized production features high degree, large scope and scale. For example, the Boeing 787 represents the highest standard of the civil aircraft industry. It is the product of a US-led global partnership involving Japan, Canada, Brazil and other countries. The production of this model was contracted to 43 Tier-1 suppliers in ten countries, involving tens of thousands of companies. Second, the private possession of production means is highly concentrated. As a listed company on the New York Stock Exchange, Boeing's equity is mainly held by 1,140 financial

---

1 Xi Jinping, *A Speech at the Symposium on Philosophy and Social Sciences*, May 17, 2016, People's Publishing House, 2016, p. 14.

institutions and funds. These financial institutions and funds are controlled by a very small number of people. We should take advantage of this change to participate in the socialization process of international division of labor. For example, we have already participated in the production of Boeing's passenger aircraft. We also need to participate in various financial institutions and fund companies by engaging in the equity acquisition and even moving into management.

(III) To maintain the true character of the socialist system in the course of cooperation with capitalism. What can be changed must be changed, and what cannot be changed must remain unchanged

It should be stressed that building a "community of shared future for mankind" does not mean eliminating the differences between the socialist and capitalist systems. The building of such a community emphasizes that all countries and social systems are faced with common problems that need to be solved. There are not only common interests, but also non-traditional security problems. For example, the gap between the rich and the poor in the world is becoming increasingly serious, the momentum of global economic growth is seriously insufficient, hegemonism and power politics occur repeatedly, regional hot issues emerge one after another, as well as terrorism, cyber security, major infectious diseases and climate changes. The competition between the two systems is to answer which system can solve these problems in a way that is better, less costly and more suitable to the interest of all mankind. In the new era, we must always emphasize that the leadership of the CPC is the most essential characteristic and the greatest strength of socialism with Chinese characteristics. We should also emphasize self-confidence in the road, theory, system and culture of socialism with Chinese characteristics and demonstrate the advantages of our system.

(IV) To improve our ability to regulate socialist market economy, bring its efficiency into full play and curb its disadvantages

General Secretary Xi Jinping attaches great importance to improving the ability to manage socialist market economy. In November 2015, he pointed out that, when confronted with extremely complex economic situation at home and abroad and diverse economic phenomena, we need to engage in in-depth study of the important views of the fundamental principle and methodology of Marxist political economics, which can help us master the scientific methods of economic analysis, understand the process of economic activities and rules of social and economic development, as well as to improve the ability to control socialist market economy. First of all, attention should be paid to preventing the emergence of interest groups. In his speech at the Second Plenary Session of the Fifth Plenum of the 18th CPC Central Committee on October 29, 2015, General Secretary Xi Jinping stated the most fundamental precautious approach: "All Party members, especially leading officials, should bear in mind the provisions in the Constitution of the CPC: The Party has no special interests of its own other than those of the working class and the broad masses of the people. If a person has his or her own self-interest, he or she may do anything outrageous. There shall be no political interest groups of any kind within the Party, nor any political interest groups that collude with other people within and outside the Party to trade power for money. The CPC Central Committee is firm in its fight against corruption to prevent and eliminate the influence of such illegal interests on intraparty political life and restore the Party's sound political ecology. The earlier, the more resolutely and thoroughly this work is done, the better the result will be."[1] Secondly, we must prevent the commodity exchange from infiltrating into the Party. On one hand, we should enhance the political, epochal, principled and militant nature of the party's political life, consciously resist the erosion of the practice of commodity exchange on the party's life, and create a good political ecology with clean and upright atmosphere. On the other hand, we should prevent the officials from falling victims to interest groups. Leading officials should be strictly self-disciplined, guard against "being rounded up and hunted" by interest

---

1 *Excerpts from Xi Jinping's Treatise on Strengthening Party Discipline and Rules*, Central Party Literature Press, China Fangzheng Press, 2016, pp.30-31.

groups. They must use power justly, cautiously and in accordance with the law and follow principles, boundaries and rules in social interaction.

(V) To strengthen national capacity-building and break through the ceiling of economic development

The ceiling of economic development involves many aspects, which mainly include limited market capacity, insufficient human resources and difficulties in industrial upgrading and transformation. However, firstly, China's 1.4 billion people are breaking through the ceiling of market capacity in its development. Large population and strong consumption power mean a huge market potential. By the time it achieves the goal of building a moderately prosperous society in an all-round way by 2020, China, a major developing socialist country with an ancient civilization and a long history, will become one of the largest countries in the world in terms of the overall size of its domestic market. At the Central Economic Work Conference in 2019, it was clearly stated that "China's market size is among the largest in the world and has a greater potential in the future. People should work hard to meet consumption demand, improve product quality, and speed up the development of service industries, such as education, childcare, elderly care, medical care, culture and tourism. They should improve consumption environment, implement the policy of special additional deductions for personal income tax, and increase consumption power to let people eat safe food, dress well and use daily necessities comfortably."[1] In the new era, people's growing need for a better life is more extensive and of higher quality, which provides a strong driving force for economic and social development. Secondly, China has abundant human resources, which provide a powerful talent guarantee for economic and social development. Out of a population of 1.4 billion, we have a workforce of over 900 million of which more than 100 million people have received a higher education and have professional skills. This is our greatest resource and advantage. On October 24,

---

1 *People's Daily*, December 13, 2019.

2018, Premier Li Keqiang was invited to give a report on the economic situation at the 17th National Congress of the China Trade Union. "China has the largest pool of human resources in the world, which is a huge potential for development," he said. "The quality of the workforce continues to improve and the number of highly-skilled personnel is growing. As long as we motivate initiative, spontaneity and creativity of millions of workers, there will be no difficulties that we cannot overcome."[1] Finally, these resources can help to continuously upgrade China's industrial structure and get rid of the ceiling in transformation and upgrading. In the 1930s, the Soviet Union completed its industrial upgrading from light industry to heavy industry. Because of its stress on the development of heavy industry, the Soviet Union had a solid economic and technological foundation. During the Soviet Union's great patriotic war against Nazi Germany, the Soviet Union produced 40,000 aircrafts, 30,000 tanks, 120,000 artillery pieces and 150,000 machine guns every year. From the 1950s and 1960s, the Soviet Union intended to turn the industrial structure dominated by heavy industry into a more reasonable one. As a result, it developed high technology, represented by Sputnik, a man-made satellite. When the Soviet Union formulated the Ninth Five-Year Plan (1971-1975), it determined that the focus of economic work was to transform input-induced economic growth into productivity-induced economic growth. But the change never came and its second industrial transformation and upgrading failed to be realized, leading to various problems in the Soviet economy. After the World War II, Japan completed the reconstruction of heavy chemical industry, expanded coal and steel production capacity and finished other industrial upgrading tasks, which led to an entire economic recovery. In the 1980s, the Japanese industry was further transformed and upgraded, and the output of semiconductors exceeded that of the United States. Japan held half of the world's top 10 semiconductor companies ranked by total revenue. With the improvement of the standard of the

---

1 *People's Daily*, October 25, 2018.

manufacturing industry, Japan's exports to the United States and Europe rose sharply and the country became a first-class manufacturing power. However, from the 1990s, Japan's industrial structure transformation and upgrading encountered major challenges. Until now, it is still in a difficult transition. And many industries in Japan are showing signs of decline. China is a country that can continuously break through the ceiling of industrial upgrading in all aspects. China has basically completed the transformation and upgrading from an agricultural society to an industrial society. It has entered a new era. China's output of major agricultural products has leapt to the forefront of the world. It has established the most complete modern industrial system and achieved many successes in technological innovations and major construction projects. China is shifting from high-speed growth to high-quality development, advancing from an industrial society into information society. China has implemented the "Internet Plus" Action Plan which led to the rise of innovation and entrepreneurship in the whole society. China's big data, smart technology, mobile technology and cloud computing industries have seen vigorous development and the proportion of information economy keeps rising in the China's gross domestic product (GDP).

(VI) To strengthen cooperation with other developing countries

China, just like other developing countries in Asia, Africa, Latin America and elsewhere in the world, has a long history and splendid civilization. They all have same or similar experience of struggles for national independence and liberation, are all faced with the common development goals and tasks and share the common interest in the pursuit of peace, development and cooperation. All these have enabled China and other developing countries to reach consensus on major issues concerning world peace and development. The financial crisis has made the international landscape move more obviously towards multi-polarization. Therefore, it is all the more necessary for us to follow the trend, coordinate our positions and strengthen cooperation with other developing countries, so as to promote the realization of this trend. In particular, in the face of provocations from some Western countries, we should steadily hold on to our position, further deepen cooperation between China and other developing countries, and establish an appropriate "international united front".

(VII) To enhance capacity building of four major channels

The first channel is the channel to the outer space. At the General Assembly of Academicians of the Chinese Academy of Sciences (CAS) and the Chinese Academy of Engineering (CAE) on May 30, 2016, General Secretary Xi Jinping noted that space technology has profoundly changed mankind's understanding of the universe and provided an important driving force for the progress of human society. At the same time, there are still many unknown mysteries to be explored in the vast space. So, it is necessary to promote an all-round development of space science, technology and application. The second channel is the channel to the ocean. China must greatly improve its ability to protect its maritime rights and interests, vigorously develop its marine industry, and build itself into a maritime power as quickly as possible. The third channel refers to passages on land. Relying on the construction of the Belt and Road Initiative, we should vigorously build roads and railways leading to Central Asia and Europe. The fourth channel refers to the network system. The information revolution has enhanced human brain power, brought about another substantive leap in productivity, and has had a profound impact on the development of international politics, economy, culture, society, ecology and military. We should lose no time in building the strongest digital economy in the world. These four major channels will enable China to develop a more powerful and all-round network system and the ability to explore space and the ocean.

Interviews

"China Is Providing an Inspirational Approach" in the Search for the Prospects of Socialism

– An Interview with Hans Modrow, the Last Premier of the Former German Democratic Republic from the Socialist Unity Party

Interviewed by Li Ruiqin[1], Wang Jianzheng[2]

Translated by Xie Shengzhe

Finalized by Wang Qiuhai

Hans Modrow

Hans Modrow was born on January 27, 1928 in Jasenitz, Pomerania, Germany (now Western Pomerania, Poland).

From 1949, Hans Modrow began to participate in the activities of the Free German Youth (FDJ), working as a fitter at the Henningsdorf Machinery Works. After the Berlin Wall was erected, Modrow served as first secretary of the district administration of the Socialist Unity Party of Germany (Sozialistische Einheitspartei Deutschlands, SED) in Berlin-Köpenick and later as secretary in the SED's district leadership in Berlin. In this period, he received a Ph.D. in economics. From 1971 to 1973, Modrow was the head of the SED's department of agitation and, then until

---

1 Li Ruiqin, research fellow of the Academy of Marxism, Chinese Academy of Social Sciences.

2 Wang Jianzheng, senior advisor of China Institute for International Strategic Studies.

1989, SED's first secretary in Dresden. From November 13, 1989 to March 18, 1990, Modrow served as premier of the German Democratic Republic (GDR) for four months.

Modrow took office after the GDR announced the fall of the Berlin Wall and the opening of the border between East Germany and West Germany on November 9, 1989. At the time, German reunification was already under way. As the last communist premier of the GDR, Modrow personally experienced the whole process of German reunification. He was both a witness and a "direct participant". The primary task that he faced was to carry out a large amount of work on how to implement the reunification.

On November 28, 1989, the then Chancellor Helmut Kohl of the Federal Republic of Germany put forward a 10-Point Plan for German reunification. From December 19 to December 20, 1989, Chancellor Helmut Kohl paid a visit to the GDR and the leaders of the two sides agreed to establish a contractual community centered on economic cooperation. On February 1, 1990, Hans Modrow, chairman of the Council of Ministers of the GDR, proposed a "four-step program" for the reunification of Germany. On February 7, 1990, the government of the Federal Republic of Germany (West Germany) proposed to the German Democratic Republic (East Germany) that negotiations begin immediately on monetary union and economic reform. On February 13, Hans Modrow and Helmut Kohl held a talk in Bonn. The two sides indicated that they would achieve the goal of German reunification within Europe. The two countries also agreed on the establishment of a committee of experts on monetary union. On February 13, 1990, the foreign ministers of the United States, the Soviet Union, the United Kingdom, France and Germany agreed in Ottawa to hold a "two-plus-four" meeting of foreign ministers to discuss and resolve the "external issues" related to the reunification.

On March 18, 1990, the final results of the last election were released in the German Democratic Republic. The Alliance for Germany, which advocated that German reunification be achieved as quickly as possible, won a surprising and unexpected 48.15 percent of the vote. It took 193 seats in the upcoming 400 seats at the 10th People's Chamber of the GDR. The Social Democratic Party won 21.84 percent of the vote and 87 seats. The Party of Democratic Socialism, the renamed successor of the SED, won 16.33 percent of the vote and 65 seats, ranking third. Thus it failed to join the government and became an opposition party. Hans Modrow, the candidate of the Party of Democratic Socialism, left office. Lothar de Maizière, chair of the Christian Democratic Union (CDU), became premier. Technically speaking, the last GDR premier was Lothar de Maizière. From then on, the pace of the German reunification accelerated. The Berlin Wall was formally dismantled and the currencies were unified. The proposal of joining the Federal Republic of Germany was adopted in East Germany which withdrew from the Warsaw Treaty Organization. On October 1, 1990, the East German CDU merged into the West German CDU in Hamburg with Lothar de Maizière as deputy chairman and Helmut Kohl as chairman.

On October 3, 1990, the German Democratic Republic "joined" the Federal Republic of Germany and the GDR ceased to exist. After 45 years of separation, the two Germanies were "quickly" reunified.

Later, Hans Modrow became the honorary chairman of the Party of Democratic Socialism in Germany. In addition, he had been a member of the German Bundestag and the European Parliament for many years since 1994. And now he remains chairman of the Council of Elders of the Left Party. He wrote a number of books on history and current politics, such as *Perestroika, As I See It (Die Perestroika, Wie Ich Sie Sehe,* whose Chinese version was published by Central Compilation & Translation Press on September 18, 2012), and *Talks about Cuba: Anvil or Hammer (Gespräche über Kuba: Amboss oder Hammer)*, co-authored with Volker Hermsdorf.

Modrow has visited China many times. His first visit to China was in January 1959. He attended the 10th World Socialism Forum in Beijing in November 2019.

Modrow was the last communist premier of the GDR. During the 30 years since the drastic changes in Eastern Europe and the reunification of Germany, he has visited China many times, witnessed the history of China's reform and opening up, continuously followed and studied the development of socialism with Chinese characteristics for a long time, and contemplated on the rise and fall of socialism in the world. Especially in recent years, he has accepted the invitation of the Chinese Academy of Social Sciences to participate in the World Socialism Forum for a number of times. His observation of and reflection on the undertakings of the Chinese people and the socialism with Chinese characteristics in the new era are characterized by calm and sober rationality. And his views are worth studying and learning from.

Interview Summary

With his rational and prudent thinking characteristic of the German people, Modrow studied socialism with Chinese characteristics in the new era under the background of this complex and everchanging world and the evolution of world socialism. In his view, it was Gorbachev's perestroika (restructuring) that led to the "demise of the GDR" and the "reunification of the two Germanies". The so-called perestroika was in effect the destruction of the existing political system. The Communist Party of China (CPC) takes the existing system as the engine to drive social change and relies on and cooperates with other political parties to achieve the country's development. Contemporary China "is providing creative answers to various current and future problems". Its steady, prudent and rational policies are playing a positive role in world politics. And "China is providing an inspirational approach" in the search for the prospects of socialism. In view of the deep-rooted anti-communist ideology in Europe since the dramatic changes in Eastern Europe and the disintegration of the Soviet Union, Modrow believes that Europe still regards China's development with the outdated ideology, which is the source of certain media's prejudice against socialist China. Socialist China is the hope of world socialism. But, at the same time, it also faces the tremendous pressure and challenge that capitalism still has the upper hand and world socialism has not yet come out of the low ebb.

I. Gorbachev's so-called "Perestroika" made world socialism reach a low ebb

Q: Nice to meet you, Mr. Modrow! Thank you for coming to the 10th World Socialism Forum of the Chinese Academy of Social Sciences and joining me in this interview. It has been 30 years since the drastic changes in Eastern Europe and the reunification of Germany. You are the last communist premier of the GDR. Would you please talk about the historical process of German reunification?

A: In 1990, the GDR bade farewell to world history. This is a great loss for the German people who built this country for 40 years and had complete confidence in its future.

The GDR was founded due to the dominance of the anti-Hitler coalition that had achieved great success in the World War II. In the agreements concluded at Tehran (1943), Yalta (1945), and Potsdam (1945), the leading powers of the anti-Hitler coalition determined the postwar order in Europe. Later, political confrontation took shape with the Soviet Union on one side and western countries on the other, and the Cold War began. The most obvious sign in Europe was the division of Germany into two countries. And in Asia, the People's Republic of China was founded.

The Federal Republic of Germany, which saw itself as the sole legal successor to the German Empire, set the goal of freeing the GDR from the "yoke of the Communist Party" at the very beginning of the Cold War. The goal was achieved in 1990 because the Soviet Union, headed by Gorbachev, had carried out perestroika.

The Soviet Union's perestroika, which began in 1985, abandoned not only the Warsaw Treaty Organization but also Eastern Europe and the GDR. When I first took office as premier of the GDR in November 1989, the country was already in turmoil and "the journey to its doom had begun." I set foot on an irresistible "trend that was surging forward" and proposed a three-step plan for the prospect of the reunification of the two German countries, the main aim of which was to ensure as much as possible the fundamental rights and property of the citizens of the GDR. Many goals were achieved except the basic principles. For example, we had hoped that it would be better if a unified Germany was militarily neutral rather than for the North Atlantic Treaty Organization (NATO) forces to be stationed on the territory of the GDR. While the GDR withdrew from the Warsaw Treaty Organization, the Federal Republic of Germany should withdraw from NATO as well.

Clearly Gorbachev was not mature enough as he believed the verbal assurances of Western politicians that NATO would not expand eastward. He failed to demand that the West put its commitments into a written agreement. Today, NATO has reached Russia's borders. German soldiers are "defending" the Baltic countries against the so-called "Russian invaders". German soldiers have once again arrived where the Reich Wehrmacht had reached in 1941 during World War II. The reunification of Germany and the drastic changes in Eastern Europe marked the failure of European socialism.

Q: Looking back from the perspective of the contemporary world, how do you evaluate the reunification of Germany?

A: Looking back at the historical development of the past 30 years, people must be aware with sobriety that the so-called "German reunification" in 1989-1990 was, in effect, a by-product of the US strategic offensive to change the postwar order in Europe. Together with the ruling class of the Federal Republic of Germany, the United States has pushed the Russians out of Central Europe and back into their own territory.

Germany has proved itself that it was and still is, a loyal servant of the United States. Germany has even acted against its own economic interests, not only participating in the sanctions ordered by the United States but also exposing its great-power ambitions in Europe. The German government's strategic choice is beneficial to the interests of the United States but harmful to the national interests of Germany. The balance of power in Europe that Bismarck hoped to establish in 1871 has now come to nothing. The collective security system created in the Cold War during the 1970s and 1980s no longer exists. The German government only follows America's lead and has increased its military spending to €72 billion. Left-wing forces have been severely weakened in Germany and on the European continent. In the last European Parliament elections in 2019, the Party of the European Left lost 20 percent of their seats in the parliament in Brussels. The Left Party in Germany obtained only 5.5 percent of the vote in its own country.

II. China is the most successful socialist country in the world

Q: Thank you for your historical review and reflection. You have been to China both before and after the reunification of Germany. Why do you think China has become the most successful socialist country in the world?

A: Before we talk about the new era, I would like to tell a story in the past first.

My first visit to the People's Republic of China was a long time ago. From November to December 1959, I, as secretary of the Central Committee of the Free German Youth, led a five-member delegation to investigate the youth work in China and participated in the construction of the Miyun Reservoir on the outskirts of Beijing. The experience and ideas we brought back to Berlin were very rich and diverse. It was in May 1988, almost 30 years later, that I set foot on the land of China again, where I saw a country taking on a completely new look.

Now people are asking, "Why can China become the most successful socialist country in the world?" Certainly not because the CPC never makes any mistake – it has made mistakes during the "Long March" of revolution since the founding of the People's Republic of China 70 years ago, just like all other countries. As long as you set foot on a new frontier, it is inevitable that you will encounter ups and downs.

I think the reasons are as follows: First, China has always been able to learn from its own mistakes. Second, the CPC has always adhered to the principles of Marxism. Even when Marxism has fallen out of its sight – please allow me to take the liberty of using the wrong moments of the "Cultural Revolution" and the "Great Leap-Forward" as examples – the party leadership has been able to return to the Marxist stand and, as always, to analyze bourgeois economics effectively in a Marxist way. Third, among the Chinese communists was Deng Xiaoping, a gifted strategist. As it is known in the West, he initiated the policy of reform and opening up. And he perceived that, in order to promote socialism, the potential energies of the capitalist system must be made use of more than ever before. The meaning of socialism is to guarantee the peace, dignity and well-being of the people. In other words, as Deng Xiaoping said: "Poverty is not socialism. Socialism means eliminating poverty. Unless you are developing the productive forces and raising people's living standards, you cannot say that you are building socialism."

Q: How do you think the different paths of reform in China and the Soviet Union have affected the cause of socialism?

A: We can compare the results of two different reform directions in China and the Soviet Union. While the reform policies of the Communist Party of China achieved obvious success, Gorbachev's so-called "perestroika" turned out to be a disaster, whether or not he had intended to implement reform policies in the beginning. What Gorbachev achieved was not obvious: The shelves were empty. The so-called "perestroika" is in fact the destruction of the existing political system. On the opposite, the Communist Party of China regards the existing system as the engine to drive social changes. Reform does not exclude political parties, but relies on and works with them to achieve national development. There is a world of difference between the two states.

China owes its development to socialism with Chinese characteristics, which has been initiated by Deng Xiaoping. Now, China has entered a new era of socialism with Chinese characteristics. Hundreds of millions of Chinese people have lifted themselves out of poverty and become rich and the number is still growing. This fact is unprecedented in world history. India, another country in Asia with a population of more than one billion, started out in a similar way to the beginning of the founding of the People's Republic of China, but it still has the world's largest impoverished neighborhoods. Today, slum areas, such as those in Mumbai, which exist in India and many other countries, are long gone in China.

The development of the People's Republic of China has not been plain sailing or without any bumpy roads. But what cannot be ignored is that China has kept exploring the causes of its backwardness, spotting its own mistakes, and correcting them as it goes along the road ahead. We were and are impressed by China's courage to explore a new path and embark on a new journey. The Communist Party of China is not only attempting to serve the people, but also to know how they feel and act with them. These were precisely what we lacked in our policies in the last days of the GDR.

The remarkable achievements of socialism in China have proved that it is wrong for the west to claim from 1989 to 1990 that the socialist thought has come to an end. Socialism is not dead. It is the Soviet model in Europe that has failed. In Europe, capitalism means an emotional way of intrigue, highlighting selfishness and the law of the stronger while China attaches more importance to the power of the collective. Although the rights and needs of individuals should also be taken into account, the interests of the majority in society should come before those of the minority or some individuals. What socialist China has shown to the world represents the trend of the future development of mankind.

Q: You compared the great achievements of China's reform and opening up with the perestroika of Mikhail Gorbachev in the Soviet Union. It is very convincing. In the great course of reform and opening up, China is constantly drawing lessons from both positive and negative aspects in the history of the world socialist movement. It has blazed a path of socialism with Chinese characteristics. Please share your understanding of Xi Jinping Thought on Socialism with Chinese

Characteristics for a New Era.

A: Speaking of Xi Jinping Thought on Socialism with Chinese Characteristics for a New Era, I think that it comes from an analysis of China's reality, from Marxist theory, from the creative development of Mao Zedong's experience, and from the understanding and appreciation of Deng Xiaoping's thoughts. The achievements of socialism with Chinese characteristics can play an exemplary role. The new thoughts for the new era are based on the understanding and creative application of Marxism, which have further developed Marxist theories.

In the contemporary world and China, Xi Jinping is not only a venerable successor but also the true leader of this country of more than one billion people. He is the leader of the world's largest political party, which is providing creative solutions to current and future problems.

There are talented strategists and thinkers in other parts of the world. Their ideas could also have led humanity forward, if they could have moved the people. As Lenin once described, only when a program becomes a guide to action and is accepted by the public as a code of conduct for daily life can ideas bear fruit. But all these will not come from nowhere. Society must be organized, or there will be anarchy. It requires a political force to implement ideas and turn them into reality. It should be able to organize, educate, guide and direct the people in a concentrated and flexible manner. We should not expect to achieve success overnight but should have perseverance and patience. This is what political parties are for. And the Communist Party of China has played just such a role. In an era when the world is experiencing political turbulence and there is a lack of trust in international relations, Beijing has always been a predictable factor. China's example is an inspiration to parties and countries seeking autonomy because they know that China is an honest and reliable partner.

The Communist Party of China, with its General Secretary Xi Jinping in particular, has drawn lessons from its own history as well as the history of the Soviet Union. They creatively inherit and develop the traditional theory of Marxism and constantly explore new solutions to the challenges today and in the future. They are doing this not only at home but also at the international level. If we talk about world socialism today, we cannot expect to find a one-size-fits-all model. However, in the search for answers to the prospects of socialism, Chinese characteristics are an important paradigm of the new era. I often take Cuba as an example to strengthen my faith. Cuba takes China's experience as an impetus to its own revolutionary process, which has brought it huge benefits. Cubans see ideas from Beijing as an inspiration not a model.

III. China's steady, prudent and rational policies have played a positive role in the world political affairs

Q: What impact do you think a successful socialist China will have on the world and world socialism in the future?

A: There is not only one voice in the contemporary world. Many Western politicians and others still influenced by outdated ideological thinking would not readily acknowledge the fact that China has made great achievements. However, Xi Jinping's report at the 19th CPC National Congress is already widely known. People have to recognize the results listed in the report and various targets proposed by Xi Jinping for the coming decades. All this marks a milestone in socialism with Chinese characteristics in the new era. The goals and tasks that China will achieve by 2049 are well-known in Europe. It's going to be a tremendous project. In order to achieve these objectives effectively, the most important prerequisite is a peaceful environment – both domestically and internationally. If the Communist Party of China also makes a great effort in this regard, it will be able to fend off the charges of aggression and militarism and issue a proper rebuttal to the clamor for war from other countries.

The Chinese people have little doubt that the roadmap announced by Xi Jinping will be followed. This will also bring bright prospects to socialism on other continents. The appealing, humanitarian Chinese socialism will inspire people around the world to explore their own socialist path. They will give more and more support to China's development, while waging a determined struggle against the imperialists in their own countries.

Q: What role do you think China is playing in the contemporary world and the international order?

A: The present international order is in a stage of change and there are obvious threats to human life. Capitalist society, it is asserted, is descending into chaos. In his masterpiece *Capital*, Marx has described very pertinently, "Capital is said by a Quarterly Reviewer to fly turbulence and strife, and to be timid, which is very true; but this is very incompletely stating the question. Capital eschews no profit, or very small profit, just as Nature was formerly said to abhor a vacuum. With adequate profit, capital is very bold. A certain 10 percent will ensure its employment anywhere; 20 percent certain will produce eagerness; 50 percent, positive audacity; 100 percent will make it ready to trample on all human laws; 300 percent, and there is not a crime at which it will scruple, nor a risk it will not run, even to the chance of its owner being hanged. If turbulence and strife will bring a profit, it will freely encourage both."[1] The turbulence and strife, as described in the *Capital*, encourage the profit seekers, which is the root cause of many conflicts. The world today is full of such examples, which are too numerous to mention.

War, as always, is another means for politics to extend its power. Capital is also very likely to fall in this way. Therefore, the existence of a great military power with socialist characteristics is of great significance to constraining the bloodthirsty imperialist powers. In formulating and carrying out foreign policy, China seeks balance and mutual trust and does not actively intervene in conflicts. The steady, prudent and rational policies carried out by Beijing are playing a positive role in world politics.

---

1   Karl Marx, *Capital*, Vol. 1, People's Publishing House, 1975, p. 829.

IV. "China is providing an inspirational approach" in the search for the prospects of socialism

Q: Thank you for sharing your views. Could you please talk about the significance of China holding high the banner of socialism to world socialism?

A: Karl Marx used to believe that socialism would spread around the world rather than being limited to particular countries. The October Revolution led by Lenin ushered in the socialist revolution and construction in Soviet Russia alone. After the World War II, some countries followed the lead of the Soviet Union on the path to socialism. Indeed, the Soviet Union attached great importance to this development, hoping that Eastern European countries would follow its example as "pioneers of human progress".

In the late 1980s, the Soviet model failed in the Soviet Union and Eastern Europe. This was also a result of violating Lenin's theory. On the basis of absorbing the wealth of European thought and his own revolutionary experience, Lenin developed Marxism and founded Leninism, which incorporated the reality of his own country. Lenin's successors inherited his theory but departed from his historical method of carrying out revolution and construction with the reality of his own country taken into account. And they "reversely transplanted" the Soviet development model to other countries, the result of which proved to be very disastrous. So at least socialists need to learn the lesson that the "one-country model" will not work for all countries.

In 1998, I spoke with Volodia Teitelboim, general secretary of the Chilean Communist Party, about rethinking the prospects of socialism. We achieved the following consensus: In the search for the prospects of socialism, China is providing an inspirational approach. President Xi Jinping stated that, as a big country, we cannot afford any drastic mistake on issues of fundamental importance. Indeed, the Chinese people do not need guardians or other people telling them what to do about their country's future, as they know better than foreigners what is not perfect yet. In his work *"Left-Wing" Communism: An Infantile Disorder*, Lenin has made a very appropriate statement: Frankly acknowledging a mistake, ascertaining the reasons for it, analyzing the conditions that have led up to it, and thrashing out the means of its rectification – that is the hallmark of a serious party. The Communist Party of China is exactly such a party which is navigating China into a safe port.

If we can draw a lesson from the fall of socialism in Europe, it is that every country has its own unique conditions and must always take into account its own characteristics on the road of building socialism. Therefore, there cannot be a one-size-fits-all model of socialism. Socialist countries can and must learn from and communicate with each other on how to apply theory to practice under existing conditions. If it is revolutionary change that people want to bring about and if it is a new society that people want to build, there are no ready drawings to copy. But the existence of an efficient and outstanding socialist China will be of great help and encouragement to world socialism in the future.

Q: Over the 30 years since the drastic changes in Eastern Europe, has world socialism got out of the low ebb?

A: Although socialist China has become a world power and some countries have put socialism on their flags, they still face the low ebb and hardship that Brecht once described. Capitalism is now leading humanity towards the abyss of self-destruction but it is still not easy to replace it.

At present, the socialism in Europe is in decline and the influence of the subsequent socialist organizations has been very weak. Even the social democratic parties in different countries, often seen as the "caretakers" of the "sick man of capitalism", are in retreat: they are no longer needed. Hope is one thing, reality is another.

In today's world, the rampant plundering of resources, the release of noxious air, the accumulation of garbage in the oceans, numerous wars and conflicts, the impoverishment of the people in different countries, and so on continue to spread. What is more, a number of politicians in high positions are hastening the decline with their self-destructive stupidity. The time is ripe for a decisive turn in world politics but that does not mean it will happen soon. As long as capitalist countries are successful in manipulating public opinion as they are now, reason cannot prevail.

Q: What can you predict about the role of socialism with Chinese characteristics in the revival of world socialism in the new era?

A: There is a dialectical relationship between China's achievements in socialist development and the changes in the world. Quantitative changes will not lead to a qualitative change of something new in a short time. I remember an answer given by Deng Xiaoping to a question raised by a European journalist in 1989. Deng was asked by a journalist to comment on the French Revolution in 1789. His answer was: It is too early to draw a final conclusion. Deng's response caused a roar of laughter in the whole room because 200 years is a long enough to draw a conclusion. However, Deng's answer is in line with the truth. His words show that, only through a long historical process, can people's social consciousness be changed continuously. The development and change of things are independent of people's will. In the autumn of 1961, the Central Committee of the Communist Party of the Soviet Union announced at the 22nd Congress that the Soviet Union would soon transition to a communist society. At that time, it was less than 50 years after the October Revolution, and the economic and political foundations for a socialist society had not yet been fully established after a world war. So, with the bitter lesson of the failure of Soviet socialism, history has refuted that unrealistic conclusion.

Therefore, it is necessary to take time to see when the world socialism will recover from the low ebb and what kind of development the world socialism, which is to be represented by socialism with Chinese characteristics, will experience in the future.

V. European anti-communist ideology is the root cause of the prejudice against socialist China

Q: How do you view the Western media's prejudice against socialism with Chinese characteristics?

A: I live in Central Europe. I think the German media's reports on China are biased. The reasons are obvious: First, the media's stance is anti-Communist. Second, the media is always Eurocentric, which means that whatever is happening in the world, including changes in China, is measured against European standards. There is an abnormal phenomenon in Europe that people do not see the world as it is. If the institutions and organizations in other countries have something different from the so-called European democracy, they will not be respected, but rather criticized.

In the 30 years after 1989 and 1990, many people were born in Germany. If a person in the former GDR who has experienced socialism has a positive impression of the GDR's socialism, he or she also has an absolutely positive impression of China. Half of the German people either have never lived in the time when East Germany and West Germany were independent of each other or have no clear memory of it. As a result, some German people have an anti-communist view, which is just covered up by economic pragmatism. China's economic strength is the most important factor why the country is respected and recognized. As for China's other policies – reduction of armed forces, scientific achievements and active participation in the international arena – they are seen more as Chinese propaganda. At the same time, they continue to blast the alleged "violation of human rights," "oppression of ethnics," "surveillance of public life" and "monitoring of the media in China"(These are all groundless accusations and refuted by the Chinese government). The views of most Germans are influenced by the images given by the German state propaganda machine.

Q: What is the root cause of the prejudice against China in the German media and some Western media?

A: Germany claims to be a country that "protects" freedom of expression. Article 5 of the Basic Law for the Federal Republic of Germany, namely the German constitution, stipulates, "Every person shall have the right to freely express and disseminate his opinions in speech, writing and pictures, and to inform himself without hindrance from generally accessible sources. Freedom of the press and freedom of reporting by means of broadcasts and films shall be guaranteed. There shall be no censorship." Of course, it's necessary to resort to media if one wants the freely expressed opinions to be conveyed to the majority of the people. *Der Spiegel*, a weekly news magazine, wrote as early as March 5, 1965, that freedom of the press was the freedom of the 200 richest people to say what they want. Only rich people have the freedom of speech. Little has changed so far.

Germany is a capitalist country and its programs have obvious anti-communist characteristics. Anyone who raises questions about the system, or in other words, questions the capitalist system, is openly condemned.

For example, Gesine Lötzsch, the former chairman of the Left Party in Germany, wrote in a newspaper article in early 2011, "How many roads leading to nowhere have the leftists found? A hundred or a thousand? Definitely not 10,000! That is exactly the problem! We always talk too much on the map. If we want to find the way to communism, we must hit the road ourselves and try it, whether in the position of the opposition party or in the government." This speech triggered a public outcry. Hermann Gröhe, the then CDU's general secretary, called the remark "scandalous desire for communism". And the words are "a slap in the face for all victims under this ideology that treats humans with contempt". "Whoever dreams of adopting Rosa Luxemburg's plan for the 'conquest of political power' twenty years after German reunification and propagating system change has learned nothing from the bloody history of communism." *Frankfurter Allgemeine Zeitung*, the leading bourgeois daily, ran a headline on January 5, 2011, "Gesine Lötzsch Defends Communism", which directly saw Gesine Lötzsch as an enemy. Such headlines are meant to doom pro-communist leftists to death so that hatred and anger can be appeased. The hostility to and fear of communism in the mainstream European media have not diminished after the failure of European socialism. The negative evaluation of socialist China in the Western media, including the German media, all comes from deep-rooted ideological prejudice.

Q: Thank you very much for your pertinent analysis, Premier Modrow. So how do you think people should understand some Western media's misinterpretation of China's Belt and Road Initiative?

A: The growing influence of socialist China on the world gives real grounds for fear of China in the west, which advocated "China threat theory".

Xi Jinping introduced the Belt and Road Initiative in Astana, which involves the international order. This initiative is not a threat signal and has nothing to do with the threat played up in the West, including Germany. However, some western countries still adopt a demagogic approach to publicize the "China threat theory". This can be seen in an analysis report released in the spring of 2019 by the Rhodium Group, a US research institution.

Around 2017, Brahma Chellaney, an Indian scholar, publicly denounced China's Belt and Road Initiative, which mainly focuses on infrastructure projects, as "debt-trap diplomacy". He alleged that China gave loans to poor countries so as to make them dependent on it and then achieve its own geostrategic goals. In this way, the Chinese navy secured access to foreign ports and boosted its military expansion. The US government immediately upgraded the concept of "debt trap" to the concept of war. In March 2019, US Secretary of State Michael R. Pompeo claimed that Beijing used "the debt trap which I referred to just a moment ago to put these countries in a place where it is not a commercial transaction, but a political transaction designed to bring harm and political influence in the country in which they're operating."

This is obviously hypocritical because the US and other western countries have been doing exactly what they call "political transaction" for decades. And it is America's own research institution that has exposed its hypocrisy. A survey on China's state banks, also made by Rhodium Group, came to a different conclusion, however. A commentary published in the *Frankfurter Allgemeine Zeitung* on May 6, 2019 said, "Among the 40 cases investigated, debt was forgiven in 16 cases, and debt repayment period was extended or suspension of debt repayment was agreed upon in 11 cases. On the one hand, the results demonstrate that Beijing is fully willing to engage in a dialogue if a country in debt has trouble repaying its debt. On the other hand, the large number of follow-up negotiations suggests that China-funded projects often prove financially unaffordable to debtor countries, leaving mighty China without the long end of the leverage if repayment lags behind. Ukraine, for example, once refused to deliver the promised grain and Venezuela exported far less oil to China than the amount agreed. So, there is no evidence that Beijing can gain a geo-strategic advantage." This conclusion is a strong refutation to the prejudice that the United States and other countries have always held. But the habitual disregard for the facts on the part of the US and the west will not change.

Johns Hopkins University in Baltimore has a China-Africa research team that has long studied China's financial flows around the world. In a report for *The New York Times*, the team noted that, of the 17 African countries currently in debt crisis, only 3 are debtor countries to China. These investigations have nothing to do with the West's interests or issues related to its own interests. The purpose of their survey is to find out the extent of socialist China's influence in the world and to formulate policies towards China based on their conclusions. The West has done its utmost to demonize China through propaganda.

Q: Thank you again for talking with us. Please conclude our interview with several sentences.

A: I want to stress that, despite the failure of European socialism, the People's Republic of China has succeeded in demonstrating that there is a social alternative to pure capitalism. When the Soviet Union celebrated the 70th anniversary of its great October Revolution in 1987, the light of its doom was already looming on the horizon. But today, China is so powerful that it has surpassed the Soviet Union in any historical period. I am confident that, by the time when the People's Republic of China celebrates its 100th birthday in 2049, it will fulfill the vision outlined by Xi Jinping at the 19th CPC National Congress.

China in the New Era Has a Pioneering and Enterprising Spirit
– An Interview with Raif Dizdarević, Former Yugoslavian Leader

Interviewed by Qiao Ruihua,[1] Peng Yuchao[2]

Translated by Xie Shengzhe

Finalized by Wang Qiuhai

Raif Dizdarević

Raif Dizdarević was former president of the Federal Assembly of the Socialist Federal Republic of Yugoslavia (SFRY), chairman of the Federal Presidium of the SFRY, and member of the Central Committee of the League of Communists of Yugoslavia. He is a renowned politician, diplomat, labor movement activist and statesman.

From 1974 to 1978, Raif Dizdarević was engaged in trade union work, serving as president of the Council of the Federation of Trade Unions of the Socialist Republic of Bosnia and Herzegovina and member of the presidium of the Central Council of the Federation of Trade Unions of Yugoslavia. From April 1978 to

---

1 Qiao Ruihua, assistant research fellow of the Academy of Marxism, Chinese Academy of Social Sciences.

2 Peng Yuchao, lecturer of School of European Languages and Cultures of Beijing Foreign Studies University.

April 1982, he worked as president of the Presidency of the Republic of Bosnia and Herzegovina. In 1974, he was elected member of the Central Committee of the Communist Alliance of Bosnia and Herzegovina and member of the Central Presidium of the Communist Alliance of Bosnia and Herzegovina. In 1984, he was elected to the Central Committee of the Communist Alliance of Yugoslavia.

From May 15, 1982 to May 15, 1984, Raif Dizdarević served as chairman of the Federal Assembly of Yugoslavia. From May 15, 1984 to December 30, 1987, he worked as Minister of Foreign Affairs of Yugoslavia. On December 31, 1987, he was elected vice chairman of the Federal Presidency of Yugoslavia and chairman of the Committee for the Protection of the Constitution of Yugoslavia, succeeding Hamdija Pozderac, also representative of Bosnia and Herzegovina, who resigned due to financial scandal. From May 15, 1988 to May 15, 1989, he worked as chairman of the Federal Presidency of Yugoslavia and chairman of the National Defense Commission.

Dizdarević has visited China many times and witnessed the various stages of China's exploration and development of socialism. In 1957, Dizdarević visited China for the first time, which coincided with the first anniversary of Chairman Mao Zedong's policy of "letting a hundred flowers blossom and a hundred schools of thought contend" for the prosperity of socialist culture. "The whole world was very interested in this policy of China," he recalled. For Yugoslavia at the time, this was a major event in the socialist camp and, at the same time, a hope that some unprecedented changes were happening – that the great China began embarking on its own socialist road.

In January 1983, Dizdarević led a delegation to China as chairman of the Yugoslavian parliament and had extensive exchanges with Chinese leaders. The two sides held in-depth discussions on the development and experience of the socialist system of Yugoslavia, the development road and status of Yugoslavia, and its involvement in international affairs. "There is no doubt that China was heading for an era full of changes", Dizdarević said with deep emotion.

After that, the relationship between China and Yugoslavia has developed steadily. In 1984, Chinese President Li Xiannian visited Yugoslavia. Two years later, chairman of the Yugoslavian Presidency led a delegation to pay a return visit to China. Dizdarević was involved in all meetings and talks in the above visits as Yugoslavia's foreign minister.

Yugoslavian leaders also met and talked with Deng Xiaoping, the chief architect of China's socialist reform, opening up and modernization, from whom they learned about China's long-term development strategy. Dizdarević wrote down what Deng Xiaoping said during the meeting, "We will adhere to the socialist road, revitalize economy through reform and opening up to the world. Development cannot be achieved without opening up to the world. We oppose hegemonism and maintain world peace. If a country with more than one billion people does not oppose hegemonism, it may become hegemonic itself. Our goal is to build a socialist society with Chinese characteristics." Deng kept reiterating that it was important for China to stay on the path of socialism and maintain world peace – that was China's way of contributing to the world. Deng Xiaoping also made very positive comments on the development of China-Yugoslavia relations.

After 1988 when a full-scale crisis broke out in Yugoslavia, Dizdarević tried his best to maintain the solidarity and unity of the federation and opposed nationalism and national separatism. But with the collapse of the Yugoslavian Communist Alliance, the civil war broke out in Yugoslavia, the Yugoslavian Federation fell apart, and he lost political influence. Since then, he has settled in Sarajevo where he wrote and published his memoir, *From the Death of Tito to the Death of Yugoslavia.*

Interview Summary

On the occasion of the 70th anniversary of the founding of the People's Republic of China, Dizdarević sent a congratulatory letter to China, sincerely congratulating China on its important contribution of global significance to the world, socialism and human progress in opening up a new development path for socialist recovery. He noted that the reform carried out by the Communist Party of China (CPC) and its leaders with the conviction of reforming and innovating and with extraordinary courage of action is of extensive and profound historical significance. All those who believe in communism and support socialist ideas will be grateful to the CPC.

As the principal leader of the former Yugoslavian communist party and state, Raif Dizdarević, an old man now, has visited China several times since 1957. He was received by Mao Zedong, Deng Xiaoping and other leaders, and witnessed the different stages of China's exploration and development of socialism. In recent years he pays close attention to China's development and deeply reflects on the development and changes in China.

I. A Retrospective analysis of the disintegration of Yugoslavia

Q: Nice to meet you, President Dizdarević. We are very happy to have you with us for an interview. As a witness of the development of socialism in Yugoslavia, would you please tell us about the exploration of a new socialist model in Yugoslavia at that time?

A: Yugoslavia gained its independence from the occupation of fascism through the war of national liberation. And then it followed its own path and established a new federal state. On the strategic level, Yugoslavia resorted to the road of socialist workers' autonomy and development, which led to its differences with the Soviet Union. From 1947 to the beginning of 1948, the differences between the Soviet Union and Yugoslavia were growing continuously. Yugoslavia insisted on its independence while upholding the principles of justice and recognizing its national destiny. At the same time, Yugoslavia was under pressure from the socialist camp led by the Soviet Union. Since then, Yugoslavia has undergone a series of profound changes, gradually getting rid of the dogmatic restrictions on the road of socialist development and broadening its understanding of the current situation and changes of the international community it participated in, thus it established the road and strategic principles of its state and social system. We concluded that the main threat in the socialist development was the bureaucratization of the system and that the main way to solve this problem was to develop workers' autonomy in an all-round way.

The strategic goal at that time was to establish the socialist autonomy system in the development of a new type of socialist democracy. In terms of foreign policy and international exchanges, Yugoslavia should break the blockade, formulate a positive policy of peaceful coexistence, and open itself up to the world. It supported anti-colonial revolutions and committed itself to developing international relations. Yugoslavia gained a good international reputation and increased its international influence. And Tito became one of the most important state leaders at the time. So, it was a "Renaissance" for the development of Yugoslavia. Not everything along the way was "honey and milk". There were still difficulties to overcome and doubts to be removed.

Q: Yugoslavia made remarkable achievements in its socialist development and was regarded as a regional power in the Balkans and even in the Near East. But it also disintegrated in the late 1980s and early 1990s. How do you see it?

A: Thank you for your question. It is a very good one. I think this is a question that many people are eager to know the answer: Given such a great feat that Yugoslavia has achieved, why did it fall apart? In fact, the Yugoslav economy fell into stagnation in the late 1970s. Soon there was a serious economic crisis. It was difficult for various sides to reach agreement on whether radical reform measures should be taken to develop a more comprehensive market economy. As time passed, the crisis deepened. It affected the overall situation in Yugoslavia and developed into a general social crisis. Domestic discontent was building up as a result of the crisis. The lack of solidarity among the country's leaders caused them to lose credibility with the people. Internal dissension had eaten away the Yugoslavian communist alliance and paralyzed the party both in thought and action. The alliance lost its leadership in carrying out reform and its role in social cohesion. At the moment, Nationalism has taken advantage of the situation and influenced the national policy, which has affected the behavior of some leaders and seriously damaged the unity of the country.

The Presidency, which I chaired at the time when the country was on the verge of collapse, was alert to the fact that a fateful moment had arrived and that Yugoslavia was facing the danger of not being able to survive as a socialist federation. So, the Presidency warned the public and took some intervention measures. But the tendency to divide within the federation stifled the impact of these interventions. Nationalism was the most primitive ideology which led the country down the tragic path of disintegration. Nationalism, the grave-digger of Yugoslavia, was welcomed by anti-communist outsiders, who pushed it into a wider space. In 1990, the congress of the Yugoslavian communist alliance was dissolved. The dissolution of Yugoslavia was now a foregone conclusion. As a builder of a system of civilization, Yugoslavia came to a tragic end.

Q: As a leader of the Socialist Federal Republic of Yugoslavia, how do you evaluate the development and changes in your country in the past 30 years after the drastic changes in Eastern Europe?

A: As is known to all, after the disintegration of Yugoslavia, it was divided into six independent sovereign states: Slovenia, Croatia, Bosnia and Herzegovina, Serbia, Montenegro and Northern Macedonia. I have lived in Sarajevo, the capital of Bosnia and Herzegovina, since the disintegration of Yugoslavia. Now, let me talk about my personal experience so that everyone can have a glimpse about the situation then.

For Bosnia and Herzegovina, a multi-ethnic country, there was a tragic situation following the disintegration of Yugoslavia. From 1992 to 1996, Bosnia and Herzegovina fell victim to the invasion of greater Serbianism and greater

Croatianism. In the four years of fighting, more than 100,000 people died and about two million became homeless. Sarajevo, the capital of Bosnia and Herzegovina, was under siege for 1,425 days, the longest one ever recorded in modern history, during which it was under constant bombardment. Some 500,000 shells were dropped on the city, killing more than 10,000 people and injuring more than 200,000. The war was stopped only with the intervention of the international community but left the country in a special state of division, which was recognized by the *Dayton Accords*.

The consequences of the war are still being felt and people are still living in the deep divisions caused by the war. In the post-war period, the authorities in Bosnia and Herzegovina took the form of a joint government with political parties from three ethnic groups, which further deepened the division between the ethnic groups. The separation between the ethnic groups and in the government has reached absurd proportions. In the first years of so-called transformation and privatization, the government of Bosnia and Herzegovina set up an economic system that could be said to be the most brutal of capital looting. In all enterprises and commercial institutions, there were financial frauds of capital robbing. As a result, public interests were destroyed. Over the past 30 years, Bosnia and Herzegovina was unable to escape the downward trend. Until now the economy of Bosnia and Herzegovina has not been able to recover to the level of 1990. Almost all of its economic indicators rank at the bottom of Europe. In 1980, for example, there were one million people employed in Bosnia and Herzegovina. Today, 40 years later, there are fewer than 800, 000.

Popular discontent is building up in Bosnia-Herzegovina. People grieve for what they once had but are now forced to lose. Nostalgic feeling is also growing, which is basically people's attitude to socialism. Of course, we can't say that everyone thinks the same way, but certainly the majority of people are nostalgic. In the face of widespread discontent and difficult circumstances in the country, there is a growing consensus among the forces planning a revolt against the government that the only form of resistance that is likely to work is to act together.

However, these forces were gradually splitting too. Fortunately, in this situation, there is still a critical voice against the government from the public, using modern communications, public forums and limited organizations. If you take all of these forms of resistance together, you will see a simmering discontent that will have a greater impact on the future. In addition, people are quickly migrating to western countries due to loss of confidence and even fear in the future of their country. And even though it has been 40 years since Tito's death, he is still a symbol of the times of prosperity and, for many, the spiritual support in their life.

II. China's achievements in modernization have attracted worldwide attention

Q: Thank you very much for sharing with us your comments of the socialist history of Yugoslavia. Now please tell us your views on socialism with Chinese characteristics.

A: China is the most populous country in the world. Naturally, there are deep-rooted and diversified traditions in China. This basic national condition determines China's many and different ways of dealing with problems. Compared with other countries, China is different in size, stage of development and historical tradition. Obviously, it cannot be included in any generalized model. If one looks at China's changes and ways of doing things in the same way as they look at Europe or the United States, it is obviously difficult to come up with an objective assessment.

In my opinion, many innovative interpretations and strategic differences exist under the general theme of socialism. The revival of socialism requires breaking the shackles of outlook and thinking, constant innovation, and the courage to seek truth. China is leading the way in this area. To fundamentally change people's outlook and thinking through reform is of great significance for China's miraculous development. China has set an example for the world and provided possible answers to the new questions of socialism at present and in the future.

Q: In your opinion, what concrete achievements have been made in building socialism with Chinese characteristics over the past 70 years?

A: I think the question can be understood as thus: What have the tremendous changes that China has realized and is carrying out brought to China itself? China's reform has cast away dogmatism. And what are the creative aspects of its striving spirit? Over the past 40 years since the reform and opening-up, China has made remarkable achievements that attracted the attention of the whole world. China has become the world's second largest economy and maintained the highest growth rates in all key development indicators. It has abundant foreign exchange reserves, the most extensive social security system, and the largest manufacturing sector. According to the 2010 data from the World Bank, the added value of China's manufacturing industry has surpassed that of the United States to become the world's largest and has remained so ever since.

In the 21st century, China has focused on developing high technology and advanced manufacturing industries and has launched its own space program. In 2017, the main revenue of the high technology industry reached US$2.2 trillion! As a country with the largest foreign exchange reserves, China has become the third largest foreign investor in the world through exporting capital to development and financing projects around the world. It is estimated that, since the introduction of reform and opening up, China's direct investment in the world has exceeded US$1.2 trillion. Different from the conditions imposed by the World Bank, the International Monetary Fund or other developed capitalist countries, China will introduce more favorable terms and prices, with no political or other conditions attached, which can be regarded as a new criterion in the world's investment and financing economic relations.

To return to the question, the short answer is that these and other Chinese achievements have real global significance and impact. No matter now or in the future, a world without China is inconceivable. This is true both for the world economy and for international relations as a whole.

Q: In your opinion, what are the benefits of China's achievements to the world?

A: As for the answer to this question as well as what are the pace, coverage and development prospects of this achievement, I think that the implementation and promotion of the Belt and Road Initiative can let us see the expected answers we want to see from our respective positions.

While showing intense interest in China's achievements over the last few decades, people of the world are also skeptical, asking questions about the future of the "China miracle" – can China achieve further development? How long can the development last?

Is the Belt and Road Initiative proposed by China in 2013 the answer of the country to the question above? The Initiative is unique for world development whose realization will significantly alter the world economic landscape, existing international relations and the distribution of global power if India's development is also included in the changes.

As the sponsor of the Initiative, one of the main makers of detailed rules, and the executor of the Initiative, China indicated that, in addition to the projects which connect the developed economies at both ends of Eurasia, such as Western Europe and China, and cover the continent from the Pacific to the Baltic Sea and then across Europe, the Belt and Road Initiative should also bring economic growth opportunities to all the countries in the vast regions along the Belt and Road. One of the main objectives of the Initiative is to create a vast free trade zone along the Belt and Road by signing free trade agreements.

The Initiative is expected to cover four billion people or 40 percent of global GDP and create millions of jobs. It has attracted wide attention around the world and many international organizations have shown great interest in it as well. UN Secretary-General António Guterres once mentioned at the Belt and Road Forum for International Cooperation that the Belt and Road Initiative, as a grand international project, represents the common vision for global development. Chinese President Xi Jinping indicated that China planned to invest US$150 billion in the project each year.

In introducing and interpreting the Initiative, China stresses "three principles": no interference in other countries' internal affairs; no pursuing of sphere of influence; no seeking of hegemony. This is a very advanced political philosophy.

I have paid particular attention to the Belt and Road Initiative when answering to this question because everything that has been said and done about this Initiative so far shows that it is of great geopolitical significance. Its realization will bring about significant changes to the world's economic landscape, the balance of forces in international relations and their respective influence. It will challenge mainstream solutions and existing practices in international relations and the privileged status granted to the United States by the Bretton Woods Accord that established the dollar as the world currency. The means by which the United States and the most developed countries in the West dominate the world economic order through the World Bank and the International Monetary Fund will also gradually collapse.

Through the development of the Belt and Road Initiative, China can ensure that it will continue to enhance its development strength. It will resolve the issues on the balanced development between countries and regions, enhance its international status and influence as a global power and raise its involvement and voice in international affairs. So far, 126 countries and 29 regions have signed cooperation documents on the Belt and Road Initiative with China.

In stressing the importance of the Belt and Road Initiative and the changes it will bring about, people should not forget the role that China itself has played. What will China face under this new background? China needs to forge ahead and explore for answers on a road full of interests, problems and confusions.

The world is paying great attention to and showing great interest in the development projects under the Belt and Road Initiative. In some parts of the world, questions are being asked – will China always follow the Initiative's basic principles, stick to the role it plays, and maintain the momentum of its admirable creativity? Most of these questions and interests are well-meant.

But not everyone is well-intentioned. There are people who raise questions and slanders, claiming that the Initiative is a form of "neocolonialism" in disguise. And some western countries are even convinced of it. The United States has tried to compete with the Belt and Road Initiative by promoting the "America's Indo-Pacific Economic Vision", using the old-fashioned tools of new loans and personal investment. There is nothing new about this. As mentioned above, in the process of promoting cooperation projects under "the Belt and Road Initiative", China is committed to secure the success of the Initiative. Every step in the process has been a powerful response to skepticism and discredit.

III. China has made positive contributions to maintaining world peace

Q: In your understanding, what impact will socialist China's achievements have on the international order?

A: Today, China has become the world's second largest economy. Its reform and the results that it has achieved have had a huge positive impact on the landscape of world order and international relations. And the general trend is that China's influence will continue to grow. The situation and relations in the world are deteriorating. Outdated elements of the Cold War have resurfaced or emerged in disguise. In the international arena, confrontation and competition have overshadowed dialogue, consultation and cooperation. And the arms race has once again blown its trumpet. The newly developed weapons of mass destruction are appalling. US President Donald Trump has ordered the shelving of a disarmament agreement that ended the Cold War. The flames of war have not been extinguished but are spreading. In the process of scrambling for the sphere of influence, the Balkans is the place where the great powers must wrestle. Conflicts and disputes become increasingly fiercer. I think, in this situation, the level of mistrust between the players has grown to the point where everybody seems to stand in front of an abyss or on thin ice. They seem to have lost trust in all.

After he took office, Trump's political views have had a negative impact on international relations, intensified the aggressiveness of the United States and strengthened the trend of rightwing politics around the world. In an increasing number of countries, neo-nationalist and neo-fascist organizations have emerged and gained power which was strengthened even in the parliaments of some countries. Trump's policies have undermined the positive consensus on global development. Global and regional agreements are important factors in the formation of a world system. But the United States' gradual withdrawal from multilateral agreements at the present stage has delivered a big blow on existing international organizations.

Take the World Trade Organization as an example. The US is trying to threaten the EU by starting a trade war and hitting it economically. "America First" is a policy of ruthlessly imposing American rule on the world in order to advance American interests. It undermines the principle of equality and mutual benefit, opposes globalism, and advocates and incites narrow nationalism rather than encouraging cooperation. It could lead many countries down the abyss of extreme nationalism.

Trump's foreign policy has a negative and stunning impact. It is not an act of state but a political means of dictatorship and threat relying on sanctions. Recently, Trump has even launched a trade war against China. People may forget that Trump, as the leader of a great power, talked about destroying North Korea and then threatened Afghanistan, Iran and Turkey, claiming to destroy their economies. Then he supported Israel's occupation of the Golan Heights, a Syrian territory, and declared it Israeli sovereign territory. While these threats and blusters, with the exception of the Golan Heights incident, may sound whimsical for the moment, we should not forget how the initiators of such farces went on stage to sow fear in the world. As a whole, this is essentially nothing more than a poorly disguised imperialist policy.

Trump's policies have caused infighting even between the United States and its closest allies. Against the general background of the overall deterioration of world relations, the divisions and rivalries between the United States and its allies have become a positive phenomenon. What influence will China have in such a global movement?

The reason why China has become the world's second largest economy and reached its current level of development is that China has always adhered to the principle of peaceful coexistence and has always been committed to strengthening peace and cooperation as the main theme of development. Chinese President Xi Jinping has pointed out that China aspires to have a more peaceful and prosperous life in the 21st century and China is willing to work with other countries to make our planet a better place.

Much has been said about China's achievements and its importance in the development of all countries in the world and international relations. China is an integral part of the global development process. China's influence is not limited to economic relations, which cannot be separated from politics and vice versa. China has an influence on the overall state and relations of the world. It is exerting its influence through expanded concrete forms of cooperation and effective development initiatives.

I think it is wise for China to counter the provocation, competition and confrontation from the Trump administration. China has responded decisively to the trade war, issuing reciprocal measures while engaging in ongoing negotiations with patience and perseverance, a Chinese style that people are familiar with. The impact of some achievements made by China on the world economy is very convincing. For example, the Belt and Road Initiative can strengthen China's presence in international relations. If the Initiative succeeds as expected, it will have a global significance. Generally speaking, President Xi Jinping's foreign activities, such as issuing statements, visiting foreign countries, signing agreements and contracts, is a ray of sunshine in the deteriorating world situation, as well as a strong response to Trump's policy.

Q: As you said, China has made great achievements in socialist development and is exerting a positive influence on the order of the international community. Then, how do you view the global significance and influence of Xi Jinping thought on socialism with Chinese characteristics for a new era?

A: From my perspective, President Xi Jinping has been playing an important leading role since he was elected as the top leader of the CPC in 2012 and has won a good reputation in the international arena. Xi Jinping himself is widely recognized as an outstanding statesman of this era. In the international community, most people have a positive impression of his international influence as he is regarded as a leader with a broad and global strategic vision, which is exactly what China needs for its current development.

Xi Jinping has visited 31 countries and international organizations in a short time after he became president since 2013. Most visits, including regular ones, aim at long-term interests and well-thought-out goals. President Xi Jinping's visits have covered major countries and regions in the world. He first visited neighboring countries, then countries with which China had previously had strained relations, then those in which there were potential problems, followed by countries with which China enjoys friendly cooperation and mutual understanding. He also visited all the important ones: he went to Russia more than once and also visited the United States, Britain, France, Germany, Japan, Australia, Kazakhstan and so on. He also visited the United Nations, the European Union and other international organizations. During each visit and at every international meeting, President Xi Jinping would outline China's development goals and principles and describe what China will achieve with its "policy of peaceful rise". No leader in any other country has visited so many countries, covered so much issues in his visits, and achieved so many goals in the same period. President Xi's initiative to build a community with a shared future for mankind has left a deep impression on the people of the world. It is undoubtedly beneficial to have a well-thought-out vision in specific and long-term projects at present.

What I would also suggest here is that, in international affairs, China can present itself as a more distinct and independent power. In the eyes of the world's public, there is sometimes a suspicion that China always votes in the same way as Russia in international affairs and organizations, especially when on UN Security Council resolutions. In the eyes of other countries, the two giants seem to have formed some kind of alliance or bloc. For this reason, people always see "Russia and China" as a group of countries and a community of interests who share the same views. But they often ignore the differences in political system, foreign policies, goals and interests between China and Russia. In fact, guided by the principle of peaceful diplomacy, China advocates the establishment of relations with no strings attached. The principle of mutual non-interference is stressed in international cooperation, especially in international economic cooperation. In the Belt and Road Initiative, China advocates its three principles: "no interference in other countries' internal affairs; no pursuing of sphere of influence; no seeking of hegemony." This is its strategic commitment to the development of international relations. The friendly relations between China and Russia are of great significance to the security and stability of the Eurasian continent as a whole. It is not surprising that China and Russia side with each other on certain issues. It is hard to avoid the suspicion that the two countries are voting the same way at the United Nations on international political issues, but it does not mean anything else. As a major country with the world's second largest economy, China is also expected to play a bigger role in international affairs.

IV. China has opened up a new course of world socialism

Q: In your opinion, 30 years after the drastic changes in Eastern Europe, has world socialism emerged from its stagnation?

A: Not really. The stagnation of socialism is not an isolated phenomenon. From a global perspective, it is a profound crisis. People's understanding and practice of socialism are distorted and dogmatized, which is the second stage of the crisis caused by the stagnation of socialism. Fallen regimes disappear – "frozen in time and space" – and some countries that consider themselves socialism no longer exist, no matter how advanced their socialism may have been. Gone, too, is the Soviet Union, which used to sit on one pole for decades in the struggle for hegemony between the two poles. It means the failure of dogmatic bureaucracy and socialism. The so-called "socialist bloc" of Eastern European countries is no more. The innovative practice of socialist thought fell into a crisis in Eastern Europe and suffered a major blow, which eventually became one of the important reasons for the disappearance of these socialist countries.

Tito pointed out in his speech at the sixth congress of the Communist Party in Yugoslavia in 1953, "It is clear that the Soviet system is degraded into bureaucracy. The Soviet Union is now under the appalling domination of bureaucracy where democracy and humanity are deprived by a distorted notion of socialism. What can spawn from it is only imperialist foreign policy." After the end of World War II, the development and status of Eastern European countries were subordinated to the model and interests of the Soviet Union. Such unhealthy relations within the international communist movement brewed crisis. I need to make it clear that the harsh criticism I make here does not mean that I hold a completely negative attitude about the Soviet Union. On one hand, the compulsory education and medical security system built by the Soviet Union had some positive and desirable elements that were in line with the interests of its citizens, on the other hand, the Soviet Union made great contributions and sacrifices for the victory of the anti-fascist war.

The upheavals in the socialist camp have had unfortunate consequences in all Eastern European countries – Reactionary regimes emerged in some countries, extreme right-wing forces in others, and even Neo-Nazism organizations and legal institutions in Poland, Hungary and other countries. In these countries, there are few serious left-wing parties with wide influence.

Q: In your understanding, what is the basis of the global revival of socialism?

A: To answer this question, we need to re-examine and grasp the concept of socialism in the ever-changing environment of today's world. Nowadays, the progress of science and technology has reached an unbelievable level, which was unimaginable in the past. Under the influence of scientific and technological progress, today's world is developing day by day, and its great and deep changes are also amazing. The question to be asked is – has the world ever seen such a dramatic transition? If we combine the basic conditions needed for the revival of socialism with this question, what answer will we get? Has the social class structure in the past changed during the process of revival and transformation? What is the more concrete meaning of socialism today? Is it a long-term world process?

As we all know, socialism was previously confined to a "camp" or the narrow concept of class. Socialism hopes to be fully awakened from its dogmatic slumber. It hasn't renewed itself in a right way. If socialism wants to be reborn in a new world environment, it is necessary to innovate and develop its concept. For example, how do you view the changes that conventional solutions bring to the framework? Every process, every positive thought, and every form of organization with progressive goals need to be examined, commented on, and supported, for all of them are part of the worldwide process of socialism.

Socialist thoughts and ideas are always derived from reflections about the status, rights, freedom and liberation of human beings in a society. These questions are particularly critical when it comes to the basis of the revival of socialism. Dogmatism and bureaucratic concepts ignore the basis and their progress and tend to treat these issues negatively in movement. In the development of the world and the process of exploring the path of democratic transformation, this has become an issue of fighting for progress. It often happens that under the pretext of "democracy" and "progress", the anti-communist forces and reactionary forces often engage in subversive activities within socialist countries or countries seeking social liberation.

What I want to express in the above is that the times we are in, the road we take, and the rebirth or revival of socialism we are seeking all require us to break the shackle of outlook and thinking, to innovate constantly, and to have the courage to seek truth. China sets an example in this regard. In my opinion, fundamentally changing people's outlook and thinking through reform is of great significance to China's miraculous development. China has set an example to the rest of the world, and with its efforts and its influence on international relations, it has provided referential answers to the new questions of socialism at present and in the future.

Q: What role do you think China plays in the global socialist movement? What is the significance of China holding high the banner of socialism for the socialism worldwide?

A: China's strategic commitment is that every socialist country should take its own path based on its national conditions and characteristics, be involved in international affairs independently, and make continuous contributions to innovating and practicing the concepts and roads of socialism. This is China's mission in the new era – to contribute to the cause of socialism. China's achievements under the guidance of this principle have enhanced its influence in the world and enabled it to play an important role in promoting development of socialism in the world in the future.

As I have already said in my previous answer, China's development has moved away from dogmatism and into innovative reform, which has produced incredible results. In the process of China's reform, it has got rid of the parochialism of dogma, emancipated their minds, and not only revived the forgotten values but also transformed them in an extensive and innovative way. For the overall process of socialism, China's development is a kind of great encouragement and inspiration. It is also a kind of important contribution and support to the rebirth of world socialism and the development of socialist ideology. Therefore, China's contribution is unique to socialism today.

These are the recent achievements of China's socialist development. China's reform is still deepening. It would be a big mistake to assume that this process is over. The initial achievements of China's reform cannot to be taken as the solution to all problems and the realization of all goals in China's social development. China needs to further emancipate the mind and innovate concepts in order to meet new challenges in institutional building and adapt to the practical requirements in its goals and visions. So far, China's contribution to socialism has fundamental significance. Even so, China's future contribution depends on the level of its involvement in international affairs and its future development.

V. Socialist China in the eyes of the people of the former Yugoslavia

Q: How do people in your country view socialism and how do they view China?

A: For us, our attitude towards socialism is shown by our living memory – our people personally experienced it during the time of the Socialist Federal Republic of Yugoslavia, ranging from solidarity, security, equality and harmony, benefits of life, to the development of the system of workers' autonomy and civil rights. What they felt most deeply was the sense of security in life brought about by material wealth and in particular, the improvement of autonomy and institutions. It is a nostalgic feeling as well as a livid memory of the inspiring socialist era. No matter how hard a regime tries to paint a false picture of that era and rewrite history, it cannot suppress the advanced ideas of that time, nor erase socialist ideas, because it really existed and had important significance and played a special role of promoting the advancement of society. Of course, the past of Yugoslavia can serve as a lesson for the exploration of China's path and for China to break away from dogmatism.

When it comes to how the people in our country view China, traditionally, our people see China as a comrade-in-arms in the war of national liberation and, therefore, have strong compassion about your country. Relations between China and Yugoslavia had suffered setbacks under the influence of the Soviet Union but this history is over. People in Bosnia and Herzegovina are more and more interested in the rapid development of China and in the growing, friendly and cooperative relations between the two countries. Our business sector shows increasing interest in investment, while China engages in the market of Bosnia and Herzegovina through economic activities and especially investment. The desire of the two countries to expand cooperation is also becoming clearer. In my view, there is bureaucracy in our current regime and a clear inadequacy in encouraging and creating conditions for the expansion of investment. Bosnia and Herzegovina has participated in the 17+1 Cooperation and the Belt and Road Initiative. I think the high level of enthusiasm on both sides will bring good results – our country greatly needs this kind of economic cooperation, because it already ranks near the bottom in Europe in terms of development.

Other forms of cooperation – cultural, educational, scientific and technological – are also being strengthened. The mutual visa exemption policy between the two countries has brought great convenience and attracted more Chinese tourists to Bosnia and Herzegovina and vice versa. This year, the frequent visits of the two countries' delegations have further created a positive atmosphere for cooperation, which will, in turn, promote further cooperation.

It must be pointed out that our people, facing all kinds of adversities and worries, lack a concrete understanding of the tremendous changes that China has undergone. The general public has only a sketchy understanding of China. But intellectuals, educational institutions and business circles have a deeper understanding of China. I think we should continue to open up more space and channels to promote mutual understanding, such as more artistic exchanges and cultural cooperation. The two sides should make joint efforts to deepen mutual understanding between the two countries. The work of the Chinese embassy in Bosnia and Herzegovina is of vital importance. China also needs to understand Bosnia and Herzegovina, the history of the country, and call for opening up channels of international cooperation through diplomatic relations.

VI. Suggestions for China's future development

Q: 2019 marks the 70th anniversary of the founding of the People's Republic of China. What are your suggestions for China's future development?

A: With high respect and heart-felt joy, I sincerely congratulate the People's Republic of China on making a major contribution of global significance to itself and the world as well as to socialism and human progress on the occasion of the 70th anniversary of its founding and also on opening up a new way of development for socialist revival. The reform, carried out by the CPC and its leaders with the conviction of reforming and innovating and with extraordinary courage of action, is of wide and profound historical significance. All those who believe in communism and support socialist ideas will be grateful to the CPC.

As for suggestions for China's future development, I can only speak from my own point of view. It is with a positive and friendly curiosity, as well as with my best wishes for deepening reform and other new things, that I would like to reiterate a few points here.

What I want to reiterate is that China's transformation and development achievements are unprecedentedly new to the world. In the near future, the world is bound to have various discussions, opinions and predictions about China, and there will certainly be many problems and misunderstandings. Don't wonder about it. These changes, as well as the vision expressed by President Xi Jinping to partners in bilateral and multilateral activities, will leave a good impression on people around the world. They are enlightening and will bring benefits to all mankind.

In the near future, there are bound to be many questions about China in the world: What changes will China's overall national strength and international influence bring to its political system? What will happen to China's foreign policy? How will China increase its involvement in international affairs? President Xi Jinping indicated at the 19th National Congress of the CPC that, for some time to come, China is expected to become a major socialist country with a modern national defense force, which will bring the country closer to the status of a leading player in global governance.

A variety of opinions and predictions also exist. It is widely hoped that China will continue to stick to its stated principles and objectives and develop in a way as it has done in the past. No matter how others question China's international status or create fear by spreading the "China threat" theory, China has repeatedly reiterated its vision for future development and responded to those skeptics. But in the future, China has to face these voices.

With its status and achievements in development, China has become an important factor in international relations. This involvement is not only the need of China, but also the need of the world. The world needs China to maintain stability, to be involved in world development, global governance, and international affairs. China needs to actively promote world peace, promote peaceful settlement of disputes and conflicts, and launch initiatives in international relations and make contribution therein. Few countries today can play as big a role in shaping global relations as China. China's future is promising. China's sustained development is the best response to the challenges of the world.

With the successful implementation of reform, China has made important contributions to updating the concept and understanding of socialism for the new era. This has been a process. The world has high hopes for China's development. Whenever I recall my conversation with former Chinese leader Deng Xiaoping at the time when China has just started its reform process and, given President Xi Jinping's good reputation and leadership role in the world today, I have gotten an impression that the historical process of innovation and development has never stopped, because China has always been carrying out the Communist idea that "all things cannot be sacred if they do not give way to the more advanced, more liberal and humanized latecomers." I am confident that the CPC and the People's Republic of China will embark on this sacred journey in the future.

China's Experience from an International Perspective

– An Interview with Megyessy Peter, Former Hungarian Prime Minister

Interviewed by Tang Fangfang[1]

Translated by Xie Shengzhe

Finalized by Wang Qiuhai

Megyessy Peter

Megyessy Peter was born in a bourgeois family in Budapest, Hungary in 1942. He is an internationally-renowned leftist politician. Around the period in 1989 when Hungary underwent the transformation of political system and society, he worked on important positions in the Hungarian government.

Megyessy Peter studied political economy at the Budapest University of Technology and Economics from 1961 to 1966 where he obtained a PhD and then worked at the Ministry of Finance after graduation. In 1980 he was appointed head of the Hungarian Economy and Budget Department, Deputy Minister of Finance in 1982 and Minister of Finance in 1987. Then he joined the central committee of the Hungarian Socialist Workers' Party in the summer of the same year. He was a key economic expert in the late years of the János Kádár administration. From

---

1 Tang Fangfang, assistant research fellow of the Academy of Marxism, Chinese Academy of Social Sciences.

China's Experience from an International Perspective

1988 to 1990, he was deputy prime minister in charge of economic affairs. In the second half of the 1980s, as a senior official in three Hungarian administrations, the prime ministers of which were György Lázár, Károly Grósz and Miklós Németh, he witnessed the critical moment of system transformation in Central and Eastern Europe.

At the end of the 1980s, the 14th (unconventional) Congress of the Hungarian Socialist Workers' Party adopted a resolution to change its name to "Hungarian Socialist Party". However, a group of party members opposed the change of the name and the nature of the party, resulting in a split inside the party. From December 17 to 18, 1989, some members of the Hungarian Socialist Workers' Party, with Károly Grósz, former general secretary of the party, and János Berecz, former member of the political bureau and secretary of the party's central committee as the core, reconvened the 14th National Congress of the Hungarian Socialist Workers' Party. Nearly 800 deputies from all over the country attended the congress. The congress elected Thürmer Gyula, diplomatic adviser to Károly Grósz, former general secretary of the party, as the party's chairman. In addition, there were numerous parties such as the Social Democratic Party of Hungary, the Alliance of Free Democrats, and the Independent Smallholders' Party in the 1990s. But Megyessy Peter did not join any one. He chose to leave political circles and work in the financial field, successively serving as the president of BNP Paribas (Hungary) and Hungarian Investment and Development Bank.

In the mid-1990s, the left-wing parties armed with modern ideas emerged in some European countries and the Hungarian Socialist Party also underwent positive changes. In 1994, the Socialists won parliamentary elections. Invited to return to politics with the backing of the then Prime Minister Gyula János Horn, Megyessy served as finance minister in the Socialist-Free Democrats coalition government from 1996 to 1998. After leaving office, he served as chairman of the Board of Inter-Európa Bank. In a critical election in 2001, Megyessy Peter met the challenge of the parliamentary election with the invitation and support of the Socialist Party

83

China in the New Era

leaders. He was elected as the candidate of prime minister at the congress of the Socialist Party in June 2001 and participated in the Hungarian general election. Megyessy Peter set a precedent in Hungary by running for prime minister as a non-party candidate. As a left-wing senior statesman, he finally won Hungary's hotly contested general election after winning the trust of voters. On May 27, 2002, Megyessy Peter officially became prime minister of the Socialist-Free Democrats coalition government. After taking office, he carried out the "100-day Program" at home to raise wages and welfare and to attract foreign investments and expand employment. Thus, he put Hungary's consumption-centered economy on the growth track driven by exports and investment in export-related competitive fields and cut the national fiscal deficit by three percent within two years. The government promoted the construction of highways and other infrastructure to reduce the huge gaps between different regions in Hungary. Externally, he promoted European integration and improved the relations between Hungary and neighboring countries such as Romania and Slovakia. He also strengthened the cooperative relations between Hungary and surrounding countries, Asian countries such as China and Russia, and completed the negotiations on Hungary's accession to the European Union. He resigned as prime minister in September 2004 to maintain the unity of the Socialist Party and Free Democrats and the stability of the coalition government. From October 2004 to May 2008, Megyessy Peter served as ambassador-at-large extraordinary and plenipotentiary upon the invitation of the government, making positive contributions to international affairs.

In recent years, Megyessy Peter has remained enthusiastic in international affairs and actively promoted international exchanges on folk culture. He is a member of the presidency of the InterAction Council – a group of former state heads, a member of the Nizami Ganjavi International Center, and a member of Leaders for Peace-a non – governmental organization founded by former French Prime Minister Jean-Pierre Raffarin. Megyessy Peter has done a lot of useful work in maintaining multilateral cooperation. He has met repeatedly with Israeli Prime

Minister Benjamin Netanyahu in an effort to defuse the conflict in the Middle East. He has been to Beijing many times to attend and speak at international political forums related to the Belt and Road Initiative. He has also been involved in the preparation of global economic analysis, attended and spoke at the Global Forum on Education and Skills in Dubai, and attended the Baku Forum of the Nizami Ganjavi International Center. And he was a keynote speaker at conferences organized by the InterAction Council in Ireland, Beijing and etc. At present, he also runs a consulting firm and is a member of the supervisory board of the TVK, Hungary's largest petrochemical company, which is part of Hungarian energy giant MOL Group – a leader that integrates oil and gas companies in Central and Eastern Europe. He is also the founder of the Foundation for Traditional Chinese Medicine of European Public Health, making active contributions to the promotion of traditional Chinese medicine and Chinese culture.

Mr. Megyessy Peter has visited China many times and done much work for the healthy development of China-Hungary friendly relations. In 2003, Megyessy Peter, then prime minister of Hungary, visited China, which was the first visit to China by a Hungarian prime minister after 44 years. During his tenure as Hungarian prime minister, the bilateral relationship was upgraded to friendly and cooperative partnership. As early as the end of 1987, János Kádár, general secretary of the Hungarian Socialist Workers' Party led a high-level delegation to China. As a member of the delegation, Megyessy Peter, then Minister of Finance of Hungary and chairman on the Hungarian side of the Hungarian-Chinese Intergovernmental Mixed Committee, visited China for the first time and participated in the talk between Kádár and Deng Xiaoping. After returning to Hungary, he was appointed deputy prime minister at the end of the same year and retained the post of Hungarian chairman of the Hungarian-Chinese Intergovernmental Mixed Committee. He has the opportunity to visit China almost every year. In 1990, he left politics and no longer held political positions. He was invited by the Chinese People's Institute of Foreign Affairs to visit Beijing, Xi'an and other places. From 1996 to 1998, he served again as Hungary's finance minister and the Hungarian chairman of the Hungarian-Chinese Intergovernmental Mixed Committee. During that period he visited Shanghai, Hong Kong and other places in China. In 2003, Megyessy Peter visited China in his capacity as Hungarian prime minister, pushing bilateral relations to a high level. In recent years, he is still working hard on the "New Silk Road" between China and Europe. In 2019, he was invited to participate in the roundtable summit of the Belt and Road Forum for International Cooperation. Megyessy Peter, cherishing profound feelings for China, has always been following the development and changes of China and made positive contributions to the steady development of China-Hungary relations.

Interview Summary

Former Hungarian Prime Minister Megyessy Peter held important political positions before and after the transformation of Hungary's political system. He engaged in the formulation of various major national guidelines and policies and witnessed the social transformation of Hungary. He has visited China many times over the past 30-plus years and witnessed the great achievements of China's reform and opening-up and the friendly development of China-Hungary relations. He has unique insights into how to view the political system and development path of various countries in transition as well as China's experience and practices. He argues that the secret of China's success lies in stability, foresight and long-term planning and that China has chosen a political system that suits its own characteristics the best. The system chosen by each country will gain vitality only if it is rooted in its own historical and cultural traditions. The development of China-Hungary relations shows that mutual respect is the cornerstone for the steady development of bilateral relations. In the long run, cooperation in culture, education, science and technology is more important than trade to bilateral relations.

I. Great achievements and successful experience of China's reform and opening up

Q: Nice to meet you, Mr. Megyessy Peter, We are glad to have you with us in this interview. As an old friend of the Chinese people, you have visited China many times in the past 30 years. Thank you for your interest in China's development. How do you evaluate China's development over the past 70 years and view socialism with Chinese characteristics?

A: China has made great achievements. China is successful. It is not only outstanding in comparison with other socialist countries or some earlier socialist models but also not inferior to other non-socialist countries. Here is a typical example. From 2008 to 2009 when the financial crisis broke out, most countries could do nothing but felt helpless, but China's performance was excellent and impressive. The measures taken by China to respond to the crisis were effective and quick, not only making China successfully avoid the impact but also helping the world get out of the financial and economic crisis as quickly as possible.

Q: You think China is successful. Could you elaborate on the specific achievements of socialism with Chinese characteristics?

A: According to my personal experience, I think most people in China are satisfied with life. In recent years, I have often had the opportunity to visit China. The last time I visited Beijing was on October 1, 2018. I saw the natural smile on people's faces in the street, so I felt that people's life was happy and they were relaxed and joyful.

Generally speaking, China's achievements over the past four decades of reform and opening up have been obvious to all: rapid economic growth, impressive progress in infrastructure construction, significant improvement in people's lives, and effective efforts to crack down on corruption. It is particularly worth pointing out that China's poverty alleviation has been very effective and set a good example for the rest of the world. China has changed the situation of poverty and backwardness in a short period of time, which is unprecedented in human society. Obama had a campaign slogan: "Yes, we can." I want to say: "Yes, China has done it."

Q: Your feelings and understanding are very inspiring to us. How do the Hungarian people view socialism and China's development?

A: China and the Chinese people are highly respected in Hungary not only because of China's splendid ancient culture and brilliant achievements but also because China has remarkable performance in the field of social equality. China has explored a model that is often referred to as the "Chinese Dream", which means that China is seen as a country of great opportunities.

Q: Thank you for your comments. In your opinion, what are the key reasons for the success of socialism with Chinese characteristics?

A: The secret of the China model is stability, foresight and long-term planning. I am convinced that China has chosen the system that suits its characteristics the best.

I promoted the economic reforms of the Republic of Hungary and I was very interested in China's reform and opening up during the same period. Back in 1987, I met Deng Xiaoping on my first visit to China as part of a high-level Hungarian delegation led by János Kádár. I think China's reform and opening up is mainly associated with the name and policies of Deng Xiaoping, I admire his wisdom and vision very much.

Since then, I have been to China many times over the past 30 years. I have been to Shanghai, Guangdong, Xi'an and other places, where I witnessed the development of Chinese cities at close quarters and experienced the rapid development of China. On my many trips to China, I have noticed that the Chinese people have a sense of long-term development. And they are persistent in implementing long-term plans and blueprints. Their vision and ability to execute are impressive. I saw preparations for the Beijing Olympic Games, the Shanghai World Expo and other major events on the spot. I learned that these big cities are capable of making detailed development plans for the next decade or even decades and are capable of realizing their grand plans and dreams. But in the western countries, planning with foreseeable result is often only limited to five to seven years or even shorter. I think the government should have a long-term plan and provide people with solutions to meet people's needs for security and stability. How to reconcile people's demand for democracy with their demand for security and stability is a global challenge.

China's foresight is also reflected on the layout of industrial upgrading. China provides financial and infrastructure support for the application of knowledge for modernization and increasingly focuses on training, education, research and development. It encourages returning overseas talents to set up small high technology enterprises. The old idea that China only produces cheap goods is no longer true.

II. The global significance of Xi Jinping Thought on Socialism with Chinese Characteristics for a New Era

Q: How do you view the global significance and influence of Xi Jinping Thought on Socialism with Chinese Characteristics for a New Era?

A: President Xi Jinping and other Chinese leaders often stress that political systems cannot be simply copied, exported or imported and differences in development paths of different countries should be respected. I appreciate that very much. Copying development models has always ended up in failure in the world, and the Arab Spring is such a lesson. No culture is more superior than others. It is necessary for countries to respect each other's culture, history and traditions. Each country's system should be based on its own history and traditional culture. And it should find the right way to achieve development and prosperity through inheritance and innovation. The innovation process needs to draw on the beneficial achievements of other countries.

China has opened up a new trail of success, showing the world that it can eradicate poverty and support the underdeveloped regions to make progress. China is showing a positive example to other countries and the world. Although China does not force other countries to adopt China's way of development, each country can benefit a lot from this way of development and progress and its unique features.

Over the past five years, China's remarkable achievements in poverty alleviation and reduction have attracted the attention of the world. The impressive achievements in rural poverty alleviation and revitalization in China gave people hope that it is possible to make significant progress in eradicating poverty and supporting relatively underdeveloped areas.

I have always been very concerned about helping backward countries and solving the problem of poverty. I think the solution to poverty is not only for social harmony, but also for social justice. While advocating the principle of free market competition, people should realize that competition should not be regarded as the only principle. We should attach importance to both market-based economy and solidarity and mutual assistance. A society without solidarity and mutual assistance will sooner or later fall into serious crisis. If such situation is not changed, it will bring serious social risks on the one hand and damage social justice on the other. The solution to poverty is to provide more training opportunities for poor people so that they can master their own destinies and do not need to be dependent on the state. People should provide poor children with learning opportunities and foster their abilities for the development and progress of society as a whole. China's outstanding achievements in poverty alleviation have proved that this is the right approach. China has made great progress in solving the problem of poverty, especially the problem of regional poverty, which has provided valuable experience for other countries to learn from.

Q: Thank you for your distinctive insight. As China's overall national strength and international status is rapidly rising, it is also facing external pressure and strong criticism from some western politicians and media. In your opinion, what causes such prejudice?

A: China's development has aroused suspicion, fear and envy of some hegemonic countries and their leaders. These suspicions have little basis. Some media outlets are also reluctant to accept the fact that there is more than one model for development in the world. Those who criticize China generally know little about China's history and way of thinking.

I visited Hong Kong just before its return to China. I highly appreciate the profound wisdom of the "one country, two systems" proposed by Chinese leaders. I understand the traditional wisdom, patience, way of thinking and culture of the Chinese people that contributed a lot to the handover issue. I am very interested in the thousands of years of Chinese history and, from the history of the First Emperor of the Qin dynasty who unified China, I also understand why the one-China principle is so important for China's diplomacy.

III. China's rise and the change of the world's landscape

Q: Back in the 1980s, you asserted that China was one of the world's powers that would play decisive roles and that China's influence would keep growing in the coming decades. In the preface to the Chinese version of your autobiography published in 2009, you indicated that a new world economic order without China is hard to imagine and that China has become an increasingly important factor in world politics. Now, how do you see the contribution of socialism with Chinese characteristics in a new era to the world?

A: China's influence on the international order is very important. Its influence on international affairs keeps rising. As a result, the world landscape has undergone profound changes, breaking the "unipolar world" pattern dominated by the US. In a short period of time in history, China has developed into one of the world's leading powers. It is now the second largest power after the US, and according to the analysis, China will soon be number one. When I visited China in 2003 as the prime minister of Hungary, I confirmed my view that the center of world political power may be in the United States and will remain there for a long time, but China will be the determining factor in the world economy in the next 20 years. At the same time, China's rising status implies growing responsibilities. The Chinese government still needs to do a lot of work in this area.

Q: In your view, what impact has China's rise had on the international order? Can you share your views on the trade war between China and the United States?

A: China has always been adhering to the principles of multilateralism, free competition and free market and China's performance in free competition is getting better and better. But as the world's leading power, the United States seems to have abandoned these principles. I do not think it is advisable to follow principles when they are good for you and to ignore them when they are less acceptable to you. Since the United States supports the principle of free competition, it should stick to it. It should not abandon this principle for fear that its world status will be threatened, let alone believe that the United States should decide everything in the world.

The underlying cause of the current problems in China-US relations lies in the change to the balance of power between the two countries. Some people attribute the trade war between China and the US to Trump alone. For example, Trump often changes his mind in a flash, goes back on his word, follows no common rules and so on. But these are only superficial reasons. Although the personality of the US president resulted in the difficulties in China-US relations to a certain extent and Trump's policies have their own weakness, in fact, no matter who becomes the US president, China-US relations will face such problems because the world landscape has changed. The rise of China has disrupted the "unipolar world" created and dominated by the US, the world's dominant superpower over the past three decades. China has become a strong competitor of the United States, which arouses the concern and fear of the American political elites and capitalists. The leadership of the United States is afraid of China. Whoever becomes president of the United

States will be afraid of China, but perhaps not as much as President Trump. The US fears the disruption of the "unipolar world". It fears that such disruption will affect its international standing and that it will lose its influence to decide everything in the world. Under such general circumstances, the United States feels threatened by the principle of free competition, so it stops adhering to it. Since the United States enshrines free competition as a common principle, it should uphold it.

I think that it will take time to solve the problems between China and the US and it will be difficult to solve them quickly. In addition, Trump's fickleness will make China-US negotiations more difficult. In the 2020 US election, Americans may elect Trump again, and there will still be difficulties in China-US relations.

Q: What is the impact of China-US relations on China-EU and China-Hungary relations? How can we solve the problems in China-US relations?

As the world is closely connected today, if problems in China-US relations are not resolved, both China-EU and China-Hungary trades will be affected and there will even be serious consequences. I hope that the impact of China-US relations on China-EU relations will be reduced to the minimum extent. For example, most of the Audi engines are produced in Hungary. If tariffs are imposed on Audi engines, this is equivalent to increasing tariffs on Hungarian products. I really hope that the tariff issue between China and the United States can be properly resolved.

I appreciate China's foreign policy of peaceful diplomacy and its stance for peaceful settlement of disputes through negotiations. I think the problem should be solved through negotiation instead of resorting to a trade war. A small number of thoughtful people in the United States also recognize this point of view. The issue of intellectual property protection can be solved through negotiation. Today, countries in the world can learn from each other in science and technology. Even if there are loopholes in intellectual property protection, they should not lead to a trade war. We can sit down and negotiate. China has the courage to face the challenges of political and economic competition, and tries to give a strong response, which is a good example for other countries.

IV. Hungary's social transformation and choice of development path

Q: As a national leader who witnessed the transformation of the Hungarian political system and as a promoter of Hungary's economic "reform", how do you see the development and change in Hungary in the past 30 years since the dramatic change?

A: As someone who has lived under both systems, I see the future of my country in a positive light. I think the change in the Hungarian political system is generally good. This shift has led to an overall improvement in the lives of Hungarians but it has also brought some problems. Some people are unhappy because of the impact on their property, income or social status. But in general, Hungarians have a better standard of living than they used to. Expectations were high then, such as catching up with Austria, but the goal didn't materialize. Achieving goals takes time, but people are impatient.

Q: How do you see the transformation of Hungary's political system and the choice of development path?

A: Western democracy has its advantages, but elections every four years do not guarantee policy stability. Europe, the United States and Asia have chosen different paths, each with its own advantages and disadvantages. Each country should choose a political system and path conforming to its traditional culture, it also needs to learn from the experience of others with an open mind.

On one hand, Hungary can learn from Asia's forward-looking experience and provide long-term solutions. It can make long-term plans and implement them. And it can continue to execute plans even if different people are in power. Plans should not depend on short-term political interests and the personnel composition of the institutions, but should be tailored to long-term goals and interests, such as the development of residential areas, road networks, drainage systems and water networks. On the other hand, a certain way of thinking can be learned from the United States, such as thinking thoroughly when looking for solutions, never giving up even if there is failure, and daring to start over again. But the development of Hungary and Europe should not copy the American model, nor the Asian model. On one hand, the traditional welfare model has drawbacks, because it limits people's ability to adapt and makes people lazy. On the other hand, it is not acceptable to think that no model is important except competition and achievement, and it is not feasible to solve all problems only by the market. The European continent, including Hungary, should achieve a more flexible, open and transformative way of social development than today, carrying forward and protecting traditional European values while adapting to the development of the modern world.

Q: During your tenure as Hungarian prime minister, you promoted European integration and the development of friendly and cooperative relations between Hungary and Asian countries. Why are diplomatic relations so important?

A: The process of globalization has highlighted the importance of diplomacy and international relations. It is not only big countries that should think about world political issues. Small countries should also incorporate themselves into the framework of world politics. Since I entered politics, I have been very interested in the development of neighboring countries, Europe, the United States, Asia and even the whole world. My experience in politics has prompted me to think about what is manipulating the world, how importance of oil, water and nature is, and why some countries play important roles. In my opinion, it is very important to have a view of the world. The world today is like a fast-flowing river. Only by having a clear view of the flow and its velocity can we control the development direction of our country, cross the most dangerous sections of the river, and avoid the suffering of collision, rupture and turbulence.

Hungary adopts a pragmatic policy in foreign affairs. On one hand, the first Hungarian government after the change of its political system was committed to joining the EU. After more than ten years of negotiations, Hungary became a member of the EU in the fourth Hungarian government, which was under my administration. Hungary joined NATO in the late 1990s. On the other hand, the

China in the New Era

fourth Hungarian administration refocused its attention on Asia. It recognized the importance of China and further developed good relations with China.

V. The sound foundation of China-Hungary relations and the attempt for further cooperation

Q: Hungary established diplomatic relations with the People's Republic of China in early October 1949. You visited China in 2003 as the prime minister of Hungary, marking the first visit to China by a Hungarian prime minister in 44 years. Thank you for your contributions to the friendly relations between China and Hungary. During our academic visit to Hungary, we also keenly felt the friendliness and enthusiasm of the Hungarian people. How do you view the relationship between China and Hungary?

A: China and Hungary enjoy traditional friendship and our bilateral relations have a sound foundation. Over the past 30 years, China and Hungary have followed different development paths. But the two countries have maintained steady development of bilateral relations on the basis of mutual respect. The friendly cooperation between China and Hungary can serve as a paradigm for state-to-state relations. Mutual understanding and trust between China and Hungary are the basis for maintaining friendly and stable China-Hungary relations.

During my tenure as Hungarian prime minister, I elevated China-Hungary relations to a friendly and cooperative partnership. And the friendly policies toward China I promoted during my term of office have continued to this day. When I became Hungary's prime minister in 2002, I drafted a new Asia policy that strengthened Hungary's traditionally good relations with Asia and placed relations with China at the top of its Asia strategy. What are the considerations behind this strategy? Seventy-five percent of Hungary's trade at the time came from contacts with member countries of the European Union, which meant over-dependence. Hungary's economic development required fast-developing markets and vitality which can be found in Asia. China's achievements, in particular, are impressive. China is committed to long-term development, with increasing emphasis on training, education, scientific research and product research and development. Chinese economy has made great progress in both scale and quality. Therefore, I have formed a basic view that Hungary should speed up its relations with Asia, especially with China, while maintaining and developing its relations with the EU.

The steady development of China-Hungary relations is based on mutual understanding and respect between the two countries and their leaders share the desire to continue to maintain sound relations. During my visit to China in 2003 as Hungary's prime minister, I proposed the idea that Hungary could become a bridgehead for China-EU cooperation. Hungary's EU membership would provide an initial advantage and a good opportunity for China-EU cooperation. Today, the areas of cooperation between China and Hungary are constantly expanding. Hungary continues to make unique contributions to the sustained and steady development of the comprehensive strategic partnership between China and Eastern Europe.

Q: What are your suggestions for the further development of China-Hungary relations?

A: At present, China-Hungary relations are at a high level. Not only do the good relations between the statesmen of the two countries serve as a link, but cultural exchanges and trade cooperation provide nutrients for the tree of cooperation between the two countries to blossom and bear fruit. China and Hungary have carried out sound cooperation in trade, and the ways and areas of long-term cooperation between the two countries will be further expanded in the future.

First, infrastructure development is a good area for long-term cooperation. The building of railway is a good cooperative project. Although there is some opposition in Hungary that the time for Hungary to repay the loans is too long, which will take 50 years or even longer, I think this view is wrong and short-sighted. The payback period of railway construction anywhere in the world is generally very long. People should not only focus on the payback time. Rather they should look at the benefits of the project in a long term. The idea of developing rural infrastructure came to me in 2002 when I was on a campaign tour in Hungary. What impressed me most was the lack of jobs in the Hungarian countryside. This is one of the biggest problems in the rural areas. Since there are no roads, railways, nor infrastructure of any kind, no one would think of investing in these hard-to-reach places. I am keenly aware that the construction of roads and infrastructure in the Hungarian countryside cannot be delayed any longer.

Second, China and Hungary should strengthen cooperation in academic research, science and technology, education, culture and other fields, which are conducive to maintaining and developing long-term relations between the two countries. China-Hungary cooperation in these areas has a sound foundation. In terms of cultural exchanges, I am very proud because, when I was the prime minister of Hungary, China listed Hungary as a tourist destination country. During a visit to China in 2003, I went to the Lu Xun Museum to unveil a statue of Sandor Petofi with Sun Jiazheng, the then Minister of Culture. I was deeply moved that Sandor Petofi's poem, *Freedom, Love*, is so well-known in China that almost every primary school student can recite it. In terms of scientific and technological cooperation, Chinese high technology enterprises have invested in Hungary. For example, Hungary has become Huawei's second largest logistics center in the world. In terms of education, I encourage Chinese students to study in Hungary and Hungarian students to study in China. In contrast to trade cooperation, which is vulnerable, cooperation in infrastructure, academic research, science and technology, education and cultural development has long-term prospect, which is more important to the development of bilateral relations. At present, the leaders of the two countries are aware of these issues and need to make great efforts to further long-term cooperation.

Finally, people-to-people exchanges between China and Hungary are also very important. In 1990 when I left the politics, the Chinese ambassador to Hungary at that time delivered to me an invitation from the Chinese People's Institute of Foreign Affairs, inviting me to China for academic and cultural exchanges. I was deeply touched. The Chinese government built a bridge for people-to-people exchanges between China and Hungary. I once traveled to Xi'an and visited Shaanxi History Museum. The historical evidence there shows the possible close relationship and common cultural history between Hungarians and Chinese people in ancient times, which made me have a very cordial feeling towards China.

The Hungarian government has also facilitated non-governmental exchanges between China and Hungary. As the only full-time Chinese public school in Central and Eastern Europe, the Budapest Hungarian-Chinese Public Bilingual School enjoys great popularity and reputation. It has not only solved the problem of teaching Chinese for the children of overseas Chinese in Hungary but also attracted friendly Hungarians. It is an epitome of the long-term and stable development of China-Hungary relations. This school was founded in 2004, which I initiated and helped set up when I was the prime minister. At that time, I decided that Hungary would pay for the construction and maintenance of the school. After 15 years of development, this school has developed from one mainly for Chinese students to one mainly for Hungarian students. Its educational system has also extended from 8 years to 12 years and I am very proud of this. When I visit this school, I can feel the friendship between the children and peoples of both countries.

Q: Thank you for doing so much work for the friendly exchanges and cooperation between the Chinese and Hungarian peoples. Looking into the future, would you please give us any suggestions as an old friend of the Chinese people?

A: Based on the principle I mentioned above, i.e., each country should choose its path which suits it, it is difficult to make recommendations. China's development model suits its own characteristics and provides valuable experience for other countries. It is important to learn from China's development experience and understand the key to its success. Different countries need to recognize their own characteristics. In the course of reform and opening up, China has been constantly readjusting itself, correcting some practices and moving forward. For example, in the past, corruption was a serious phenomenon in China. Since the anti-corruption campaign was launched, remarkable results have been achieved in effectively curbing corruption. Corruption is not just a personal problem, it also has objective reasons. China has solved this problem well in its development.

However, if I can put forward some pertinent suggestions, I would like to stress the importance of modernization and technological development. I suggest an in-depth research on the impact of artificial intelligence, robotics and biotechnology on the public. The advances of these technologies are overwhelming. But our understanding of them is very limited and we are not clear about their impact on human and individual lives. I would also like to stress the importance of eradicating poverty and narrowing regional gaps, an issue that we often do not emphasize enough.

Unsurmountable Significance of China's Reform Experience for the World

– An Interview with Leonid Danylovych Kuchma, Former Ukrainian President

Interviewed by Li Xiaohua[1]
Translated by Xie Shengzhe
Finalized by Wang Qiuhai

Leonid Danylovych Kuchma

Leonid Danylovych Kuchma was president of Ukraine for the decade from 1994 to 2004. He was the second president of the country after the disintegration of the Soviet Union.

Kuchma is a former professor at Dnipropetrovsk University, member of the International Academy of Astronautics (IAA), and founder of "Ukraine" – a presidential foundation and charitable organization. Both his wife and daughter are social activists. Kuchma Ludmila Mukolaivna is honorary president of the National Fund of Protection of Mothers and Children – "Ukraine for Children". His daughter Yelena Pinchuk is the founder of the Elena Pinchuk Foundation and head of the board of supervisors of Star Light Media, the Ukraine's largest media company. Kuchma was born on August 9, 1938 to a peasant family in Chaykino village in the

---

1　Li Xiaohua, assistant research fellow of the Academy of Marxism, Chinese Academy of Social Sciences.

North Novgorod region, Chernihiv State, Ukraine. Growing up in poverty, Kuchma worked his way up from a peasant boy to scientist and finally became head of state with his untiring efforts. After the outbreak of the Soviet-German War, Kuchma's family lost contact with his father. His mother raised her three children alone, so Kuchma tasted all kinds of hardships in life from his childhood. When Kuchma grew up, he learned that his father had died in the Soviet-German War.

In 1960, Kuchma graduated from the Faculty of Technical Physics of the Dnipropetrovsk University, majoring in mechanical engineering in the field of rocket technology, and later received a degree of associate doctor in technology. From 1960 to 1986, he worked in the Southern Design Bureau at Dnipropetrovsk in Ukraine, serving successively as engineer, senior engineer, designer director, chief designer assistant, first deputy chief designer, and so on. At the age of 28, he became the leader of experimental technology at the Baikonur Cosmodrome. He was praised as "the youngest leader of experimental technology in the history of the former Soviet rocket industry". From 1975 to 1982, Kuchma served as secretary of the Party Group of the Southern Design Bureau. In 1986, he was appointed the general manager of the Southern Machinery Manufacturing Co., Ltd., the largest carrier rocket and intercontinental missile manufacturer in the Soviet Union. He was awarded the Order of the Red Banner of Labor of the USSR for the development of the rocket-spacecraft system in 1976. He also received the Lenin Prize in 1981 and the state prize of Ukraine in the field of science and technology in 1993. In 1990, Kuchma became representative to supreme council of the Verkhovna Rada of the Ukrainian Soviet Socialist Republic. In October 1992, Kuchma was ratified by parliament as the second prime minister of Ukraine. During his tenure as prime minister, he failed to implement his proposed reforms and resigned twice over disagreements with the president. He formally resigned as prime minister in September 1993. Then, he began to prepare for the presidential campaign. In December 1993, Kuchma became president of the Union of Ukrainian Industrialists and Entrepreneurs. In the parliamentary elections held in March 1994, Kuchma was easily elected with the largest number of votes. In July the same year, he was elected as the second president of Ukraine after independence in the second round of Ukraine's presidential election and was re-elected in 1999.

When Kuchma took office as Ukraine's president in 1994, he faced a series of difficult problems. First, Ukraine's domestic economy was in depression. One-third of factories had closed or switched to other production. In agriculture, harvests had failed. And 90 percent of the population lived below the poverty line. Second, the political situation was unstable. Ukraine's president, prime minister and parliament had different political views and the conflict between the eastern and western regions existed for a long time. Third, the international environment was very unfavorable, and it was not an easy task to handle the relations with Russia and the West. Ukraine was heavily dependent on Russia economically. But at the time, the two countries had large disputes over the Black Sea Fleet, Crimea and nuclear weapons. After Kuchma came to power, he made a series of adjustments and reforms to the original internal and external policies. He emphasized that Ukraine's internal and external policies should start from the actual status and conditions of Ukraine, give priority to national interests, and deal with various matters in a flexible and pragmatic way. In order to stabilize the situation in Ukraine, he quickly brought matters under control and realized the direct management of the country by strengthening the president's power, constantly adjusting the members of the state authority, and enhancing legal construction. Facing the severe economic situation at home, he carried out economic reforms in a progressive manner. In his first term, Kuchma overcame the domestic crisis through effective reforms. He adopted the Constitution of Ukraine, introduced the national currency – the hryvna, established the Constitutional Court, the Court of Auditors and other important institutions, and passed many important laws related to the transition of a market economy, social democratization, civil society protection and Ukraine's integration into the system of international relations. During Kuchma's second term as president, Ukraine made great economic progress. The average annual growth rate of GDP was 8.4 percent and the average annual growth rate of household income was 12.1 percent. This was the highest level of economic development recorded in the former socialist countries under the Soviet Union at that time. And the achievement laid a foundation for the development of Ukraine's market economy, social and legal system and the establishment of a democratic social management system. In terms of foreign relations, Kuchma advocated all-round diplomacy and focused on targeted areas. He stressed the development of relations with Russia, China, the United States and other western countries and strengthened the ties with other countries of the Commonwealth of Independent States. Kuchma has tried to balance relations with Russia and the West: With Russia, he safeguarded the interests of Russian-speakers in Ukraine and pledged to make Russian the country's official language. With the United States, he expressed interest in joining NATO and the European Union and maintained a cautious anti-Russian tone in public. And his flexible foreign policy has created favorable external conditions for Ukraine's domestic development. Since the independence of Ukraine, domestic political, economic and social crises have occurred frequently. During Kuchma's presidency, the political and economic development of Ukraine was in the most stable period and the economy recovered from decline.

After the presidency ended in 2005, Kuchma focused on the foundation's work and writing. With the outbreak of Ukraine crisis in 2014, Kuchma became active in Ukrainian politics once again. In March 2014, the domestic political crisis in Ukraine evolved into a serious geopolitical disaster and the West and Russia launched a direct confrontation. Influenced by the annexation of Crimea to Russia, the separatist trend in eastern Ukraine constantly intensified. Donetsk and Luhansk regions have declared their independence successively. The government forces and militant groups in eastern Ukraine kept fighting fiercely with each other. In the same year, Kuchma joined the trilateral contact group of Ukraine, Russia and the European Union, serving as the Ukraine's representative to resolve the violent conflict in eastern Ukraine through peaceful means. In early July 2017,

Kuchma, acting as Ukraine's representative, held talks with Kurt D. Volker, the US government's special envoy for Ukraine, on the resolution of the conflict in Donbas, and again agreed on the principle of prioritization of the Minsk Ceasefire Agreement. In 2018, Kuchma in his 80s, withdrew from the trilateral contact group on the ground of his advanced age. Appointed by President Zelensky in 2019, he returned to the trilateral contact group and became the only person who signed the Minsk Agreement and has been involved in the negotiation process ever since. During his work in the trilateral contact group, Kuchma tried to mitigate the conflict so as to prevent the Ukrainian government forces and the militia side from engaging in large-scale military confrontation. Kuchma helped the release of more than 3,000 captured Ukrainian soldiers from the two "republics" of Donetsk and Luhansk. Thus, he was positively commented by the Ukrainian public for his role as a diplomat and mediator.

In addition to his political activities, Kuchma has published many books. His main works include *Ukraine Is Not Russia* (2003), *After Majdana* (2007), and *The Ruined Decade* (2010), etc. These writings fully reflect his worries about the future and destiny of the country and his reconsideration of the development path of the country since its independence. After years of political practice and deep thinking, Kuchma recognized and revealed the hypocrisy of the West and proposed that Ukraine should embark on a journey of independent development. On June 22, 2017, Kuchma delivered an enlightening speech at the opening ceremony of the international economic forum "Dawn of Europe: Historical Law of Civilization Progress" in Kiev. He criticized the hypocrisy of the United States and the greed of the European Union, pointing out that Ukraine is not a state in the full sense. Europe is turning Ukraine into a client state of raw materials by destroying its aircraft manufacturing, metallurgy and science through its quota system. Ukraine's leaders should protect domestic producers rather than piling up debts that no one will be able to repay in the future. The people of Ukraine should stop yearning for Europe because Europeans don't really care about Ukraine. They don't need poor people.

Ukrainians can only create a state of dignity with their own hands.

Interview Summary

Kuchma believes that the road of socialism with Chinese characteristics is the product of abandoning dogmatism. And China's reform experience is of world significance that cannot be surpassed. He spoke highly of China's great achievements and summed up China's successful experience by saying that, although China's international strength is growing, it will not follow the path of expansionism and colonialism. Kuchma also criticized and refuted the political prejudice of the Western media and politicians against China's system and the China road.

Kuchma is a witness and participant in the tortuous development of Ukraine since its independence. His understanding of the socialism of new era with Chinese characteristics and other issues deserves our attention and consideration. At the end of 2019, Kuchma sat down with us in an interview to elaborate his views on the thought on socialism with Chinese characteristics, China road, and China's role on the international stage.

I. The development of Ukraine after the disintegration of the Soviet Union

Q: Nice to meet you, Mr. Kuchma. I am very glad that you can accept my invitation for the interview. After the collapse of the Soviet Union, Ukraine became an independent country. How do you evaluate the development and changes of Ukraine since its independence?

A: Ukraine became an independent country in 1991, which was the first time in Ukrainian history. There is no doubt that the achievement of independence is a very important milestone in the history of the Ukrainian nation. The process of establishing state institutions is continuing and it is not going on in an easy way. Ukraine has gone through several different phases in the nearly 30 years since its independence.

First of all, the establishment of national institutional system is very important. Because of the political pluralism in Ukrainian society, such work was not easy. The president, the congress and the administration took this issue very seriously. However, the economic and social fields of the country were not given due attention. As a result, in the first half of the 1990s, Ukraine suffered a severe transition crisis with great economic losses and marked decline in people's living standards. The crisis came in 1994 when Ukraine lost almost 23 percent of its gross domestic product. The efficiency of the regime was not high, and people's trust in the regime was low. As a result, the country held early parliamentary and presidential elections. I was elected president of Ukraine at the moment and my top priority was to overcome the crisis through effective reforms. In the following five years from 1995 to 1999, we did it.

We took a series of measures to consolidate the state system. In 1996, the Constitution of Ukraine was adopted, which established Ukraine as a social, legal, democratic and market state. And this was recognized by the Venice Commission of the Council of Europe. A national currency, the hryvna, was also introduced. The Constitutional Court, the Court of Auditors and other important institutions were established. A number of very important laws were adopted, relating to the transition to a market economy, social democratization, civil society protection and Ukraine's integration into the international system.

During the five years of my second term as president from 2000 to 2004, Ukraine made great progress in its development. The average annual growth rate of GDP was 8.4 percent and the average annual growth rate of household income was 12.1 percent. This was the highest recorded level of economic development among post-socialist countries at that time. Ukraine's economic development index even surpassed that of China twice, with an annual GDP growth rate of 9.2

percent in 2001 and 12.1 percent in 2004. These achievements laid a foundation for the development of a market economy, a legal society and a democratic social management system in Ukraine.

But the global economic crisis of 2009 brought a severe test to Ukraine. Ukraine's economy became stagnant for a long time since the crisis. Ukraine has huge potential, so the average annual economic growth of 2-4 percent is not satisfactory.

Ukraine suffered heavy losses from the outbreak of the crisis in 2014, which added up to more than US100 billion according to an estimate by American economist Mancur Oslon. Ukraine today is actually in a state of war. In this complex situation, international support, especially from powerful countries in the world like China, is very important for Ukraine.

II. Xi Jinping develops the theory of Socialism with Chinese Characteristics

Q: You have been following China's development closely. Would you please talk about your understanding of socialism with Chinese characteristics?

A: With the founding of the People's Republic of China, China's socialist development immediately took on "Chinese characteristics". There is no simple application of Marxist-Leninist model in the programmatic documents of the Communist Party of China and the state. As time went by, China stopped focusing on class struggle and put its efforts mainly on economic development. China laid the foundation for a market economy, not through the "shock therapy" but in a progressive manner.

Deng Xiaoping put forward the goal of achieving a moderately prosperous society. It aims not only to eradicate poverty but also to establish a unique model of demand. This is a strategy of China's "Xiao Kang", which means "being not rich but well-off". Deng Xiaoping believed that the development of socialism in China could and needed to employ a market mechanism, which could last 50 to 100 years.

The task of this stage is "to basically achieve a moderately prosperous or well-off society before developing into a moderately prosperous society in all respects".

China's leaders boldly rejected the dogmatic understanding of socialism, which, I believe, is a step that determines the fate of the Chinese people. Socialist countries in Europe also tried this way. Some of such efforts were not permitted as they were more radical, such as the cases in Hungary in 1956 and in Czechoslovakia in 1968. But some of the more moderate measures succeeded, making it easier for them to adapt to market relations than the former Soviet republics. In my view, China's incorporation of the elements of market into its economic management practices is an innovative feature of socialism with Chinese characteristics, which has provided China with great potential for successful development for more than 40 years. This is a unique world experience that can be learned from.

Q: Xi Jinping Thought on Socialism with Chinese Characteristics for a New Era has drawn wide attention around the world. Could you share with us your views on it?

A: At this stage, Chinese leader Xi Jinping creatively developed the strategy of building a moderately prosperous society. He put forward the concept of the "Chinese Dream", which means a strong and prosperous country, the rejuvenation of the Chinese nation, and the welfare for the people. He specified three basic conditions for realizing the "Chinese Dream": following the China road, carrying forward the national spirit, or patriotism, and the spirit of the times, namely reform and innovation, and achieving national unity.

Xi Jinping developed the theory of socialism with Chinese characteristics and identified 14 fundamental policies and strategies with the main task of building a moderately prosperous society in all respects. The strategy means that, in the first two decades of the 21st century, China will build a moderately prosperous society, characterized by greater economic development, more progress in science and education, more flourishing culture, a more harmonious society, better living standard for the people, and improved democracy. In the long run, China will basically achieve modernization by the middle of the 21st century and become a great modernized socialist country that is prosperous, strong, democratic, culturally advanced, harmonious, and beautiful.

I think that the three basic conditions for the realization of the Chinese dream are also very important for Ukraine and for the consolidation of Ukraine's national institutions.

Q: Some people say that world socialism is undergoing a renaissance. Do you agree with that? If so, what is the basis for the revival of world socialism?

A: Yes. I think that there are at least two reasons for the revival of world socialism. The first has something to do with the situation in the capitalist camp. The weakening of capitalism in the last two decades has spurred efforts to revive socialism. The second reason can be attributed to China. The success of socialism in China has become a stronger argument for advocating socialism.

III. China's reform experience is of unique significance for the world

Q: China has made unprecedented achievements by sticking to the socialist road. What do you think is the decisive factor in China's success?

A: Within the period of one generation, China's economy has reached the leading level of the world. Over the past 40 years from 1978 to 2018, China's GDP has grown at an average annual rate of 9.5 percent and its resident income has grown at an average annual rate of 7.9 percent. The level and duration of such growth are unique in the world history and the factors that ensured these achievements are equally unique.

First, China chooses its own development path independently. China's leaders recognize that neither the Soviet model nor the western model of democracy is appropriate as a means of modernizing the country.

Second, state policies are for the well-being of the people. Using ancient Chinese governance principles, the country's leaders have declared poverty eradication a core human rights.

Third, China affirmed that the state is a necessary safeguard. On the basis of an analysis of its history in the past several centuries, China realizes that affluent times are often accompanied by powerful states and enlightened and effective regimes. Thus, the effectiveness of power should be assessed on the basis of achievements in development.

Fourth, China implements a social and ecologically-oriented policy on officials. Effectiveness in eradicating poverty and protecting the environment has become a key factor in officials' promotion. China attaches great importance to its ability to learn from others and adapt quickly to new challenges, and this is proofed by the fact that it has rapidly entered the new high-tech field and occupied the leading position in the world.

Fifth, China advocates harmony in diversity. Chinese leaders revived Confucianism in response to a large and complex society. The regime rejected the policy of confrontation and tried to emphasize the common ground of different interest groups, mitigate social conflicts caused by rapid changes, and establish a social security system for all.

These are the basics, and the most important ones. Besides, they are effective for other market economies. These factors should be taken into account in Ukraine.

Q: In addition to the above basic factors, what other factors do you think are conducive to China's development?

A: In fact, all these reflect the characteristics of China's development. Abandoning the dogmatic view of socialism and incorporating market elements into the economic system are the innovative features of the path of socialism with Chinese characteristics. I remember from my political economy course in college that the main principle of socialism is "from each according to his ability, to each according to his work". But in the Soviet Union and some other countries, socialism was distorted, sometimes to absurdness: excessive nationalization of economic relations, even prohibition of small-scale private ownership of means of production and fruits of labor, prohibition of market regulation of prices and competition, and so on. As time passed, these doctrines came to be criticized in the Soviet Union as well. But the process of abandoning them was very slow. These dogmatic rules completely hindered the full realization of the socialist principle of "from each according to his ability, to each according to his work".

China's leaders have been bold enough to reject these dogmatic rules and to stick to their guideline consistently. Because of this, China's economic and social development has recorded unprecedented achievements. There are many reasons for China's success. And its many initiatives have given it great potential to stimulate development and improve economic efficiency. For example, China has encouraged the development of private economy and opened up market relations. It has promoted the establishment and development of the enterprise system and implemented free pricing and competition. It has taken the appropriate measures to encourage efficient production. It has improved the governance of the state and coordinated the interests of the entrepreneur, company and the state. It has developed local autonomy, and so on. These policies and measures all proved effective in practice.

For me, China's rich experience with reform has always been the main argument for the need of reform in Ukraine. During my tenure as prime minister and president, I took China as an example several times when arguing with opponents of reform, especially with Ukrainian communists and socialists. I believe that China's reform experience is unique in the world and that it is a world heritage with the equally important value as Confucianism.

IV. An increasingly powerful China will not follow the path of expansionism and colonialism

Q: Never before has China been so close to the center of the world stage and attracted so much attention. Almost all the western powers in the history followed the non-peaceful path of colonial expansion to struggle for hegemony during their rise. Therefore, some people assert that China will also take the road of colonial expansion. How do you see China's future development?

A: China has never been an aggressor in history. The theory of China's peaceful rise or development fully manifests the overall strategy of China's diplomacy in today's world. The strategy began to take shape and was put into practice in the mid-1990s. This theory is based on the principle of peaceful development and aims to maintain world peace. Therefore, Xi Jinping stressed in one of his speeches that China is not only committed to its own development but also responsible for and contributes to the development of the whole world. China will bring benefits to both the Chinese people and the peoples of the world. The thought of "a community with a shared future for mankind" is the concept of a new world order in contemporary China. Chinese leaders have assured the international community that "China will never seek hegemony, expansion or spheres of influence."

Q: How do you view the Western prejudice against China's system and the China road?

A: I think I should refer to an old Chinese saying that real knowledge comes from practice. That, by the way, was Deng's creed. He believed that the ultimate test of truth was practice, not ideological dogma. I would like to answer the question according to this idea.

Frankly, I do not agree with those prejudices about China's system and the China road. The reason is simple: There is no basis for saying so. First of all, the system of contemporary China has come from its historical heritage. It is also the choice of the Chinese people after they have stood great tests. By the way, this institutional choice has indeed been influenced by external forces. Secondly, for the happiness of the Chinese people and the honor of the political elites, they have managed to find a path that can guarantee the successful development of their own country. The China road can even serve as a model for other countries and the people. Finally, results are a verdict on all prejudices. China's long-term great achievements in all fields of social development are a response to any prejudice.

I have read a lot about China and have been following its development. I have also read more than once that China has serious problems, development risks and the potential of crises. But I ask a question for those authors: In which country are there no such problems? No one can answer my question. The world has changed and will keep changing. It is full of instability and contradiction. But these changes may also spawn development from a philosophical point of view.

At the same time, it cannot be denied that there are obvious reasons for these prejudices. The West used to believe that cooperation with China was necessary to solve the common problems facing the mankind, especially the maintenance of peace. But those who see China as a threat to the West have strengthened their positions as China's economy and military technology have grown rapidly. As a result, western policy towards China shows a trend of alienation, isolation and competition. The West sees China's growing status as an "authoritarian state" that poses a serious threat to democracy. Xi Jinping's speech at the 19th National Congress of the Communist Party of China was interpreted in the West as saying that China has become arrogant and is ready to export its development model to other developing countries. This interpretation is no longer a secret.

Chinese leaders have declared a new type of relationship with the West aiming at "avoiding conflicts, achieving mutual respect and win-win cooperation". Such a policy is in the interests of China and the Chinese people because all countries in the world need a stable geopolitical situation. But in any case, it is clear that China will not copy the western model of development and will not develop in the way as the West expects. China will solve its problems in a way different from that of western countries, depending on the country's specific conditions.

Q: Thank you for your recognition of the China road. How do you predict China's future development?

A: Today, China has become the world's second largest economy. According to various estimates, it could become the world's largest economy in the first half of the 21st century. China is already the world's largest exporter of digital technology products, ahead of Japan, the European Union and the United States. There is no doubt that, in the past 40 years or so, China has risen from a regional power to one of the world leaders. Today, no major global issue can be resolved without China. China is playing an increasingly dominant role in many areas of civilization development. At the same time, China also faces more and more opportunities. If we say that China's development in the past was mainly dependent on labor, its development now increasingly depends on materials and technologies as well as the wisdom of people. China has successfully reached the world level in terms of intellectual development, quantity of intellectual property rights, new technologies as well as scientific and technological development. China has successfully exploited space, the world's oceans and the country's mineral resources. In particular, it is commendable that China has put priorities on intellectual development, human capital and knowledge economy.

At present, China is faced with a major choice due to serious problems brought about by its unprecedented growth and unpredictable consequences. Some complex problems remain to be solved, such as economic overheating, ecological pollution, and the income inequality between different classes, regions and urban and rural residents. I believe China's leaders insight these problems and are mobilizing the whole society to address them.

V. China-Ukraine relations and the vision for China's future development

Q: According to your knowledge, how do the Ukrainian people view China's political system and development path?

A: In different periods, different political factions in Ukraine had different opinions on China's political system and development path. During the Soviet era and after its collapse, it was often heard in Ukraine that the Soviet Union should take the road of China. In today's Ukraine, some people think that China, unlike the

Soviet Union, is confidently demonstrating the success of its socialist development. However, many people do not realize that China's socialism is no longer that of the Soviet Union in the 1960s and 1970s.

Q: You have visited China many times. How do you view the relations between China and Ukraine?

A: China recognized the independence of Ukraine on December 27, 1991. It was one of the first countries to recognize Ukraine's independence, ahead of Japan, the UK, France and other Western European countries. China and Ukraine have signed more than 80 bilateral agreements. Altogether 300 documents signed have laid the legal foundation for bilateral negotiations between China and Ukraine.

I am pleased to find that the relationship between our two countries was the most positive during my presidency. In 28 years, Chinese leaders visited Ukraine three times, two of which were during my presidency. The presidents of Ukraine have visited China five times, among which I have visited China three times. My three meetings with Jiang Zemin in 1994, 1995 and 2001 and my two meetings with Hu Jintao in 2002 and 2003 are my most beautiful memories.

The most important thing is that the relationship between our two countries has developed effectively. During my second term as president from 2000 to 2004, trade doubled between our two countries. During my terms, my negotiations with Chinese leaders have set the course for our cooperation, which is particularly important to both countries. Our views were very close and agreed on cooperation in the fields of space and military technology. Most of over 70 projects agreed upon and jointly implemented were related to space rocket technology, control systems and modern materials for use in space.

Ukraine today is actually in a state of war. In this situation, we need China's support very much. We thank China for its neutrality in many decisions of the United Nations Security Council on Ukraine. And China can do more for Ukraine.

Q: As a senior statesman, what are your suggestions for the future development of China?

A: China has contributed Confucianism to the world. It is no exaggeration to say that Confucianism has been applied all over the world, so it is very difficult for me to give advice to such a great country and people. Still, I have a few visions.

First, china is a country with prestige. As the world's second largest economy, a member of the international community and an engine of international development, China held the celebration its 70th anniversary. Now that China is becoming an increasingly dominant global power, it has recognized its important status in the world economy. This has fundamentally changed the logic and structure of China's relations with its neighbors.

At the same time, Chinese leaders have positioned their country as "the largest developing country in the world", emphasizing the importance of further development and the arduous task of building a moderately prosperous society in China. This is an extension of the legacy of Deng Xiaoping, who noted that China should "bide its time and hide its strength", "never take the lead" and "stand firm" in its diplomatic affairs. Following these principles, Chinese President Xi Jinping declared that "China's development poses no threat to any country. No matter how much China develops, it will never seek hegemony or expansion."

Given this, I think it is very important for China not to over-militarize itself. And this is in line with the spirit of the Chinese people: China has never been an aggressor. I know that China was once the target of invasion and occupation because of its weakness. But the final result of the militarism policy of the aggressor state (Japan) backfired, it surrendered.

Second, it is very important to strengthen China's peacekeeping policy and expand its influence on the international stage. After all, China is the most populous country and cares more about the peace of over a billion people than any other country in the world. It should, therefore, be a leader in peacemaking.

In the first half of the 20th century, more than a dozen empires fell apart. And altogether, a total of more than 30 empires emerged in the history of human civilization. Empire is an outdated way of civilization that is not worth pursuing now. Empires are no longer liked, they are even hated, while successful countries are respected around the world. In the last 40 years, China has adhered to the policy of successful development. As the country grows stronger, it is important that China will continue to pursue such development policies in the future.

Third, it is very important to adopt active environmental protection policies and actions to tackle climate change on a global scale, so China should take the lead in dealing with environmental pollution.

The Road Taken by China Bears on the Destiny of Socialism in the World

– An Interview with Adrian Nastase, Former Prime Minister of Romania

Interviewed by Liu Xinxin[1]

Translated by Xie Shengzhe

Finalized by Wang Qiuhai

Adrian Nastase

Adrian Nastase was born on June 22, 1950 in Bucharest, Romania.

In 1973, Nastase graduated from the Department of Law, University of Bucharest in Romania and obtained a master's degree. In the same year, he was employed in the Ministry of Foreign Affairs of Romania. Later, he returned to the Department of History and Philosophy of his alma mater to study for a doctoral degree in sociology and received a doctorate in law. From June 1990 to October 1992, he served as minister of the foreign affairs of Romania as an independent candidate. In December 2000, he took the office of the prime minister of Romania and then left the post. In June 2001, the Romanian Democratic Party merged with the Romanian Social Democratic Party and became the Social Democratic Party

---

1 Liu Xinxin, assistant research fellow of the Research Center for Xi Jinping Thought on Socialism with Chinese Characteristics for a New Era, Chinese Academy of Social Sciences.

with Nastase as the chairman. In December 2004, Nastase was elected as the speaker of the House of Representatives of Romania. In April 2005, he was elected as the executive chairman of the Social Democratic Party at the special representative assembly of the Romanian Social Democratic Party. In 2006, he resigned from the two aforementioned posts.

Nastase visited China for many times. On May 14, 2003, at the invitation of Wen Jiabao, the then Chinese premier, Nastase paid a formal visit to China as the prime minister of Romania.

Interview Summary

On the historical junction where the socialism with Chinese characteristics has entered into a new era and the world is full of complicated changes and contradictions, Nastase made his prudent analysis and prediction about the state of development of Romania and China, Romania-China relationship as well as the situation of the world and the prospect of world socialism. He believes that the development of the contemporary socialism with Chinese characteristics is of great significance in the world socialist movement and that Xi Jinping Thought on Socialism with Chinese Characteristics for a New Era provides an important key for us to understand today's China. In particular, Nastase aired his opinion on the issue of Hong Kong, emphasizing that the Hong Kong issue is China's internal affairs, which allow no interference from any other country. After drastic changes in Eastern Europe, the socialist parties in Eastern Europe and even the whole European region at large experienced transformations. At present, the socialist force is still weak and it is necessary to carry out inter-party cooperation with the Communist Party of China if it intends a further development. The deep-seated reason for the eye-catching trade war between China and the US in 2019 is that the rise of China has threatened the position of the US as "the single super power in the world". Trade protectionism runs counter to the historical trend, which will not work at present or in the future.

Nastase is a famous expert at international law in Romania and concurrently serves as a research fellow in many renowned international academic institutions. On August 26, 2019 Romanian time, an academic delegation from the Chinese Academy of Social Sciences, led by Gong Yun, vice director of the Research Center for Xi Jinping Thought on Socialism with Chinese Characteristics for a New Era under Chinese Academy of Social Sciences, visited Romania and exchanged views with Nastase, former prime minister of Romania and chairman of the European Foundation. The two sides communicated on issues of common concern to academic circles and the peoples of the two countries such as the trade war between China and the US, the China-US relationship and matters related to Hong Kong of China. During the exchange, Nastase expounded his personal observation and thinking on China in a new era, Xi Jinping Thought on Socialism with Chinese Characteristics for a New Era and the prospect of socialism. His views are worthy our study.

I. Xi Jinping Thought on Socialism with Chinese Characteristics for a New Era is a medium and long-term strategic thought for a country's development

Q: Mr. Nastase, thank you for your warm reception and accepting our interview. It is well-known that after the 19th National Congress of the Communist Party of China (CPC), the world has been paying more attention to China. As an academic institution and think tank, we'd like to know your opinions on the socialism with Chinese characteristics that has entered into a new era, including your viewpoint on China's international strategy against the background of the drastic changes that have taken place in the world and the future direction of the development of China-Romania relationship and China-European Union relationship and so on. And how do the academic institutions in Romania look on Xi Jinping Thought on Socialism with Chinese Characteristics for a New Era?

A: These years, I have received many Chinese delegations, including delegates from educational and business circles. I have got to know about the new changes in China through them. In recent years, the most typical change is that the socialism with Chinese characteristics has entered into a new era. For the purpose of understanding China in a new era and Xi Jinping Thought on Socialism with Chinese Characteristics for a New Era including his working style, in my opinion, his report delivered at the 19th National Congress of the CPC is very important because it is the key for one to study and understand Xi Jinping Thought on Socialism with Chinese Characteristics for a New Era. The report reflects the core theory of General Secretary Xi Jinping and China's medium and long-term strategic thinking as well as the relationship between China and other countries. One should have a deep understanding of the spirit of the speeches delivered by General Secretary Xi Jinping through careful reading.

The road taken by China bears on the destiny of the world socialism. Whether after 1989 when drastic changes occurred in the Eastern Europe and the Soviet Union collapsed, resulting in a low tide of world socialism or after 2008 when socialism had new opportunities, the enormous achievements made by China in its construction and the development of socialism are of great significance to the whole world. We believe that this is an important achievement in China's exploration of a development road with Chinese characteristics.

Q: How do the Romanian people regard China at present?

A: China is a No.1 socialist country in the world. Even after 1989, the feeling of the Romanian people toward the Chinese has not changed and the two countries are still good partners. The tradition of a friendly relationship between Romania and China enjoys a long history and has been maintained up to now. As far as the people of Romania are concerned, they feel that China is very mysterious. The Romanian people are both amazed at and very curious about how a socialist country has become a world power. In addition, when the force of communism and socialism in

Romania basically disappeared, China has made such a remarkable achievement and development, its experience attracts the attention of not only the Romanian people but also the former socialist countries and their peoples in the Eastern Europe.

Q: In 2019, the issue of China's Hong Kong kept on escalating. What's your opinion about it?

A: First, what I want to emphasize is that Hong Kong belongs to China and the issue of Hong Kong is the internal affairs of China. How China deals with it is in the sphere of China's internal affairs, which allows no interference from any other country. In this point, I believe that China's leaders have time and ability to handle this issue in an appropriate way. But anyway, I hope that it can be solved in a peaceful manner through negotiation.

II. The socialist forces in Europe are still weak

Q: Thank you very much for your analysis and judgment of the matters above. Would you make an analysis of the Social Democratic Party of Romania and the socialist forces in Europe?

A: The reasons for the drastic changes in the Eastern Europe 30 years ago were rather complicated, which involved many aspects such as economic pressures, the development of various parties and political forces and the realization of social democracy.

After drastic changes in Eastern Europe, as "a successor party of communism", the Social Democratic Party of Romania has been making self-adjustments in transforming into a social democratic party in these years. In this process, we have always adhered to the reform of socialist market economy and objected to capitalism. The Social Democratic Party has always attached great importance to self-construction, strengthening inner-party supervision and democracy.

In my view, in the contemporary world, the Social Democratic Party of Romania and even new social parties in the whole European region should pay attention to the inter-party cooperation with the Communist Party of China. Economically and politically, after economic transition was realized in various countries, the US and other western powers tried their best to strengthen the influence of capitalism on Europe. At the same time, democratic socialism is supported by the broad masses of people, this is related to the history and basis of socialism in these countries. The real value of socialism does not disappear, instead, it is deeply rooted in the people's minds.

At present, the economy of European countries, especially Eastern European countries, is very weak. Therefore, the governments of these countries should give priority to tackling unemployment and controlling inflation. To reach this goal, not only should the countries in Europe make great efforts but also the European Union should play its role in integration and coordination.

III. The trade war between China and the US is the manifestation and tool of the US to prevent China's development

Q: It can be said that the trade war between China and the US in 2019 affected the whole world. What do you think of the vehement trade war between China and the US at present?

A: For nearly 30 years, the world can be called a unipolar world dominated by the US. The US has always maintained its absolute dominant position as the "only super power" in the world. However, in recent years, China's rise has broken this structure and China has become a powerful contender of the US. This is a question that the political elites and capitalists in the US are very worried about. In particular, at present, the leadership of the US is afraid of China very much, regardless of who is the president. Whoever is the president of the US will be fearful of China. Perhaps Donald Trump is nothing but behaves more extremely.

Americans are always the loyal advocates of free competition and free trade. However, once they cannot profit from free competition, they would not support it any longer. Now, China's performance in economy is getting better and better. In this context, some American politicians think that China has threatened the position of the US as "the only super power". Therefore, it is apparent that the China-US trade war provoked by the US is a means adopted by the US to contain China's development.

In my opinion, since the US claims to go by the principles of free trade, it should first of all adhere to and follow them by itself. However, being afraid that its unipolar role is likely to be broken, the US is accustomed to thinking that all should be determined by it. Therefore, the conflict between China and the US cannot be solved soon. Caprices are only a superficial phenomenon. The latent factors are difficult to deal with. The balance of power between China and the US is a headache for the US and their frequent conflicts make the negotiation very hard to proceed.

For 30 years since the drastic changes in Eastern Europe, China has won a great victory in its reform and opening up, leading to its rapid rise in economy. China is not a poor and weak country as it used to be. Behind the US's attempt to block China's development is the trial of strength between the two countries. It cannot be denied that this situation per se is also a test for China. China should endeavor to maintain its own international status.

According to my observation, the leaders of China look to the world to have a good understanding of the global situation. At the same time, they attach importance to fundamental fields such as education and research in the country and are dedicated to self-development, which I think is very important.

Q: In your opinion, can the China-Romania relationship and even China-Europe relationship be influenced by the China-US trade war?

In my opinion, as far as the China-Romania relationship is concerned, the China-US trade war cannot produce a serious influence on inter-governmental exchanges. However, it will trigger a certain negative influence on economy and trade because the tense relation between China and the US has also influenced the normal operation of some projects in Romania. The current prime minister of Romania pays great attention to these projects, hoping to keep promoting the implementation of large-scale projects through the Belt and Road Initiative. For Romania, the economic and cultural exchanges between China and Romania are very important. Therefore, I also hope that the Chinese friends in Romania can play an important part in consolidating and strengthening the exchanges between the two countries.

Q: In your opinion, what principles should be followed in the state-to-state exchanges in the future?

A: In my opinion, the emphases placed on developing inter-state relations should not be based on ideology, nor should friends are made by relying on ideology.

It is well-known that after the drastic changes in Eastern Europe, Romania always supported the European integration. In the 1990s, Romania's work on international exchanges was mainly focused on the relations between Romania and the western European countries. Romania became an associate member of the European Union in 1993 and a full member of the organization in 1995. In addition, Romania participated in the Peace Partnership Plan initiated by the North Atlantic Treaty Organization (NATO) before becoming a full member of the organization.

At present, every country has its own development model. Especially in the past 30 years, in Romania, the distinction between the leftists and the rightists has almost not been emphasized. People see the society in a practical way. Few people talk about "ism" issue again and the same thing holds true in state-to-state relations. We emphasize the development of market economy and the enhancement of exchanges.

With a large population, China is certainly different from any other country in how the society is operated and organized. The same goes for the US. Therefore, the development of state-to-state relations should never be based on ideology. The experience of China' development is like an efficacious prescription made by a doctor. In spite of the differences in social systems, a medicine that can cure the illness should be regarded as effective no matter who prescribes it.

Q: What is your expectation for the China-Romania relation in the future?

A: I think that the cooperation in the fields of science, education and culture between China and Romania should be strengthened because these are the fields that can make the two countries maintain a long-term relationship. If trade is a short-term behavior, then cultural and academic exchanges and infrastructure construction constitute a fundamental task crucial for generations to come. For example, the Romanian students with poor family conditions may not have the opportunity to study abroad. However, China could provide subsidies and academic degrees for them as an important part of the exchanges between the two countries. These measures are very important, which can continue our traditional friendship. Now, young Romanians have a limited knowledge of the communist party and the tradition. They have no personal experience in this regard. The tradition should be continued and worth promoting and carrying forward.

At present, the leaders of both China and Romania attach great importance to the issues above. In order to achieve a long-term cooperation and put various exchanges between the two countries into practice, we feel it necessary for the two sides to make joint efforts. The world is closely connected. Since both China and the US are major countries, the trend of the relation between the two countries will surely affect the China-Europe relation, which will have an influence on the trade between China and Europe and that between China and Romania. We hope that China and the US will settle conflicts through negotiations instead of launching a trade war.

The relationship between China and Romania is based on mutual understanding. In 2003, I paid a visit to China and got to know a lot about the customs in China from local people. For many years, a large number of projects have been completed through the cooperation between China and Romania. Bilateral relations and multilateral relations between different regions of the two countries enjoy a very good development momentum. And I have close exchanges with the Chinese embassy in Romania. I hope such exchanges will be maintained so as to promote and motivate the two countries to develop various kinds of cooperation including economic and trade cooperation and continuously explore the new areas and ways of cooperation. While expanding the bilateral trade, Romania is willing to strengthen the cooperation with China in fields such as investment, finance, highway construction, hydropower and telecommunication.

A Prosperous World Requires a Prosperous China
– An Interview with Anatoly Tozik, Former Vice Premier of Belarus

Interviewed by Kang Yanru[1]
Translated by Xie Shengzhe
Finalized by Wang Qiuhai

Anatoly Tozik

Anatoly Tozik was born in 1949 in Homyely, Soviet Union (now Belarus).

In 1971 Tozik graduated from the Belarusian State University. Then in 1974, he completed a postgraduate program at the university and became a Candidate of Science in History and a professor.

Tozik began serving as the secretary of the committee of the Communist Youth League of Belarusian State University in 1974 while working as a lecturer and associate professor there. From 1979 to 1994, he assumed posts at national security organization of the Republic of Belarus during the period of the Soviet Union and after the Republic of Belarus became independent from the Soviet Union. From 2000 to 2006, Tozik was the president of the State Supervisory Committee of the Republic of Belarus.

From 2006 to 2010, Tozik served as the ambassador of the Republic of Belarus

---

1 Kang Yanru, assistant research fellow of the Academy of Marxism, Chinese Academy of Social Sciences.

China in the New Era

to the People's Republic of China. From 2010 to 2014, he was the vice premier of the Republic of Belarus. He has been serving as the president of Confucius Institute at Belarusian State University since 2014. Below is an article carefully written by Tozik during a correspondence interview.

Interview Summary

Tozik believes that China's national and social development system has more superiority in the 21st century. In the future, only China has the possibility of balancing national, social and individual interests and integrating social justice with economic efficiency in a most effective and dialectical way. One of the characteristics of this era is that the prosperity of the world cannot be achieved without the prosperity of China. For the first time in history, the strategic interests and goals of a major country are in consistent with those of the mankind. The more powerful China is, the more it can exert impact on the formation of a new international order. At this period when mutual trust and mutual understanding between China and the rest parts of the world are required more than ever, Confucius Institute can make more contributions in this respect. The thoughts of "a community with a shared future for mankind" and the Belt and Road Initiative represent the new pattern of international cooperation and global governance that can replace the present global economic relationship system which exhibits a negative trend.

I. China's state system will represent the most superior social development pattern in the 21st century

Q: Dear Mr. Anatoly Tozik, you served as the ambassador of Belarus to the People's Republic of China from 2006 to 2010. What do you think about the changes of China over these years?

130

A: While I served as the ambassador of Belarus to the People's Republic of China, I was honored to attend the grand ceremony of celebrating the 60th anniversary of the founding of the People's Republic of China. I witnessed how the Chinese society was brimmed with fervent patriotic enthusiasm at that time. Until today the spectacular scenes of the Tian'anmen Square on October 1, 2009 still leave deep impression on me. Ten years later, the grand ceremony of celebrating the 70th anniversary of the founding of the People's Republic of China was held on a large scale and in a jubilant atmosphere. Although I was in Belarus at that time, I watched on television screen the beaming happiness on people's faces. People were as happy as they were 10 years ago. Then what is the source of happiness of the Chinese people? In my opinion, happiness stems from the fact that people's expectations are not failed, and that the motherland is powerful and stable with its development meeting people's hope. I am convinced that such a commemorative ceremony will have profound impact upon China which is one of the most prosperous countries in the world, the Chinese society and the unity of the Chinese people. The ceremony of commemorating the 70th anniversary of the founding of the People's Republic of China will become an important milestone in fulfilling the Chinese Dream of rejuvenating the Chinese nation – the most important dream for the Chinese people.

Q: Thanks you for recognizing the achievements of China's development. I can feel that you have deep affection towards China and the Chinese people. Next, would you please make comments on socialism with Chinese characteristics?

A: The Chinese nation went through chaos caused by wars and turbulences for more than a century in modern history, when people shed tears and blood and were exhausted. As was pointed out by president Xi Jinping, the Chinese nation endured numerous sadness and miseries in modern history. Construction conditions were harsh in the early days of the People's Republic of China after it was founded in 1949. However, China has scored unique achievements in social-economic development in the world over the past 40-plus years since the implementation of opening-up and reform policies. In a short span of 40 years, China has developed from a populous country with a vast territory into a powerful country in the world, which is the only one in world history.

Based on tough and repeated experiments and studies from the end of the 1970s to the early 1980s, China concluded that imitating the development patterns of other countries or subjectively accelerating the national development did not conform to the realities of China. In his speech at the opening ceremony of the 12th National Congress of the Communist Party of China in 1982, Deng Xiaoping, the great leader of the Chinese people, mentioned for the first time the concept of "socialism with Chinese characteristics". Only does China embark on the road of building "socialism with Chinese characteristics" can it achieve national modernization. I believe the two essential principles of socialism with Chinese characteristics constitute the basis of reform and opening-up policies and fundamentally guarantee their success: people's rights and interests and right guiding principles. Such a move of China triggers various reactions in the world at large: admiration, surprise and even doubt…

Q: What do you think the value of China's experience for other countries?

A: Having studied China's social-economic development in various sectors, I believe that China Experience is of practical significance for China's own future development as well as many other countries in Asia and the rest parts of the world. Probably people will conclude before long that the national social development system that is formed in China will be more superior in the 21st century. I do not idealize the social conditions in China. Instead, it is necessary to understand that China is still at the stage of development and will resolve internal and external problems and contradictions step by step. It is more and more reasonable to believe that China will be the only country that can balance the national, social and individual interests in a most effective way and integrate social justice with economic efficiency in a dialectical way. Of course, those in defense of Western-style democracy would by no means acknowledge the existence of any other social development pattern that is more effective than Western-style democracy.

The understanding of the role played by the Communist Party of China is indispensable to the understanding of "China Phenomenon". The collapse of the Communist Party of the Soviet Union is a tragedy that weighs extremely heavy on my mind, since I am a member of the Communist Party of the Soviet Union with more than 20 years of party membership. The tragedy of the Communist Party of the Soviet Union lies in that it failed to make progress and lost the capability of making scientific and critical analysis of domestic and international events. Nor could it define its corresponding action strategy either. In addition, with a dogmatic attitude towards Marxism, the Communist Party of the Soviet Union made Marxism a kind of directive that leaves no room for accommodation. It is without doubt that Marxism is of strongly practical relevance even in the 21st century and is a methodology that can be used to analyze, judge or predict social development. As was pointed out by Xi Jinping at the Seminar on Philosophy and Social Sciences held on May 17, 2016, "Marxism does not put a lid on truth but opens a path to truth."[1] The development of China over the past 40 years proves that the CPC and state leaders have developed the strategic potentials of knowledge and talents, can set realistic goals for China and the Chinese people; and equally important, they can encourage and lead people to see to it that they fulfill these goals. The Communist Party of China rallies people around to build the country not only by seeking truth based on Marxism but also by leveraging national governance experience accumulated over thousands of years and traditional philosophical experience. Only through unity can China attain future development in a conspicuous way.

II. A Prosperous world requires a prosperous China

Q: In your eyes, what influences China's development will have on the order of the world? While the comprehensive national strength of China is enhanced, some

---

1 "Speech Made by Xi Jinping at the Seminar on Philosophy and Social Sciences," *People's Daily,* May 19, 2016.

Western media constantly criticize, reproach or even discredit China, thinking that the development of China poses a threat to other countries. What do you think about this question?

A: China is more and more important to the development of the contemporary world in terms of its influences and contributions. People were full of joy and hope upon the end of the cold war. However, the joy and the hope soon subsided, because the world did not turn for the better, the problems arose one after another, and it became more difficult to predict the future of the world. All these could be attributed to the collapse of the international system of checks and balances established following the Second World War, a system that used to provide relative stability and predictability. The contemporary world is in urgent need of a new system of checks and balance. To be more exact, it is in need of a new international order reflecting the reality of the 21st century. In such a new order, elements of politics, economy and virtues will play due roles while military affairs would never gain a foothold as they did in the 20th century. And there is no other choice. The roles and the influences of China can never be underestimated.

Will the development of China pose a threat to other countries? This is an unavoidable question. It is known to all that some countries worry that they may be under the threat of China as China is showing rapidly growing potentials in economy and politics. China is keenly aware that it cannot realize the great rejuvenation of the Chinese nation in an unbalanced and unsafe world where it cannot win trust or is treated with extreme attitude. China cannot achieve development if it is isolated from the rest parts of the world. The same is true of the rest parts of the world, which also require China to achieve common prosperity. Therefore, to create more prosperity, China will help other countries and people achieve common prosperity. One of the characteristics of the modern era is that the world will never achieve prosperity without a prosperous China. For the first time in history, the strategic interests and goals of a major country are in consistent with those of the mankind. China is growing stronger in the fields of economy, science and technology, and such growth promotes China to become a powerful political country. The more powerful China becomes, the more it will influence the formation of a new international order. The new order will not only make it possible for mankind to continue to survive, but also enable everyone to live in a sound and rich environment. This accounts for why the development and emergence of China will bring opportunities instead of posing a threat to the world.

III. Expanding the role of Confucius Institute to promote the mutual understanding between China and the international community

Q: In your eyes, what main problems that China is faced with in the international community? Do you have any advice in this respect?

A: One of the problems that the contemporary China is in urgent need of addressing is to enhance the international understanding of China in such respects as China's development process, the contents and goals of China's policies on domestic and international affairs, China's objective interests in economic development and the benefits of such development for other countries. In this era when mutual trust and mutual understanding between China and the rest parts of the world are required more than ever, as the president of Confucius Institute at Belarusian State University, I believe Confucius Institute can make more contributions in this respect. As of date, 536 Confucius Institutes and 1,128 Confucius Classrooms have been established in 157 countries. Fifteen years have passed since the founding of the first Confucius Institute. Over these years, Confucius Institute has done a lot of works and obtained considerable achievements. Most Confucius Institutes still specialize in the fields of culture and education, and play important roles in helping the people of the countries where they are located become familiar with Chinese culture, traditions and language. At the same time, China is entering a new era of development, and is actively integrating itself with the development process of the world as a powerful country. It is therefore necessary to change Confucius

Institutes into research centers on Sinology and information analysis centers on the communication and cooperation between China and the countries where Confucius Institutes are located (At least Belarus has needs in this respect).

Q: You have been serving as the president of the Confucius Institute at Belarusian State University. Would you please talk about the conditions of Confucius Institute in Belarus?

A: At present, there are four Confucius Institutes and two Confucius Classrooms in Belarus. The Confucius Institutes and one Confucius Classroom are established at Belarusian State University, and the other Confucius Classroom is set up in a general secondary school. All of them are branches of corresponding education organizations. In other words, all Confucius Institutes and Confucius Classrooms are Belarusian cultural and education organizations operating within the framework of Belarus, with their behaviors fully in compliance with the national interests of Belarus. The same is true of Confucius Institutes and Confucius Classrooms in other countries. However, some politicians intend to misguide the general public of other countries and attempt to regard Confucius Institute as a tool that is used by China to exert its external influences. All Confucius Institutes and Confucius Classrooms in Belarus are set up at the request of Belarus. In addition, with the support of the Ministry of Education of China, the Ministry of Education of Belarus and Belarusian State University have set up dozens of research centers on Belarus and Belarusian language and culture centers in the universities in China. On October 16, 2019, Gansu Institute of Belarus Research was founded at Lanzhou University of Finance and Economics. Isn't it an example of mutual trust between countries and peoples?

IV. The Concept of "a Community with a Shared Future for Mankind" and the Belt and Road Initiative promote the formation of a new pattern of international cooperation and global governance

Q: The concept of building "a community with a shared future for mankind" and the initiative of co-building the "Belt and Road" put forward by China have important immediate significance for the entire mankind. What's your comment on them?

A: It is based on the profound understanding of the condition and law of human civilization development in the 21st century that China puts forward a number of initiatives closely related to the destiny of mankind, such as "a community with a shared future for mankind" and the Belt and Road Initiative. These are all sincere voices from a great country appealing to all other countries to be aware of the crisis and give mutual help and join hands to build a beautiful homeland. China not only gives publicity on these initiatives but also puts them into practice.

China was one of the first countries that proclaimed to recognize the Republic of Belarus. On December 27, 1991, the Chinese government made a corresponding declaration, and both countries signed an agreement on establishing diplomatic relationships on January 20, 1992. Both countries have undergone the processes of engaging in early official contact, achieving mutual understanding, establishing a comprehensive strategic partnership and developing cooperation for mutual benefits. In 2016, Alexander Lukashenko, president of Belarus and Xi Jinping, president of the People's Republic of China proclaimed that both countries would devote to establishing "a comprehensive strategic partnership featuring mutual trust, cooperation and win-win results". Belarus and China launch cooperative development in all fields. Such cooperative development is fully in the strategic interests of Belarusians. This is understood not only by state leaders of Belarus, but also by ordinary Belarusians. China and Belarus have established an effective bilateral cooperation & coordination mechanism. Such a function is performed by the China-Belarus intergovernmental committees on cooperation. The committees total five, including committee on economic and trade cooperation, committee on science and technology, committee on education, committee on culture and committee on security. Since 2010 the cooperation between two countries has been promoted within the framework of the Shanghai Cooperation Organization.

With the support of China, Belarus obtained the status of dialogue partner in the Shanghai Cooperation Organization on September 28, 2010, and formally became an observer country on July 10, 2015. I am convinced that in the near future Belarus would become a full member of the Shanghai Cooperation Organization which is an authoritative international organization.

Q: Finally, would you please talk about in what fields does the Belt and Road Initiative exert influences in Belarus? In your eyes, what are the main differences between the Belt and Road Initiative and other patterns of international cooperation?

A: Participating in the Belt and Road Initiative put forward by China has provided Belarus with great opportunities. Belarus is geographically located on the economic belt of the Silk Road, which is favorable for bringing the potentials of Belarus into play in fields of economy and trade, science and technology, humanities and traffic. Participating in the Belt and Road Initiative has initiated the comprehensive modernization of the traffic system composed of railways and highways in Belarus. Since the launching of the Initiative, the container service volume of the railways in Belarus has increased by 30 times. More than 90 percent of the containers bound for Europe via Belarus come from China, which benefit the economy of Belarus. In addition, funded by Bank of China, more than 30 large projects in the fields of traffic, energy, industry, building industry and forestry resource processing have been completed or are under construction. The largest bilateral cooperation project is "Kitajska-Bielaruski Park", the China-Belarus Industrial Park. Occupying an area of 112.5 km^2, the industrial park is 25 km away from Minsk, capital city of Belarus, and is conveniently located close to an international airport, railways and cross-country highways. There are industrial zone and residential zone, office buildings, commercial buildings, financial centers, research and exhibition centers in the industrial park. In fact, the industrial park is being built into an international modernized ecologically-friendly city featuring high export potentials, high technologies and innovative industries. It is called a "pearl on the economic belt of the Silk Road".

138

An important characteristic of the Belt and Road Initiative is that China attaches neither conditions nor requirements when inviting other countries to participate in this initiative. Each country has the right to decide the form of participating in the Belt and Road Initiative. China proposes projects of connectivity to the countries participating in the Belt and Road Initiative, help these countries adjust their development strategies, explore the potentials in regional cooperation, strengthen investment and consumption, expand demands, create jobs, enhance the communication between governments and people-to-people and cultural exchanges. Belarus regards the Belt and Road Initiative as a new pattern of international cooperation and global governance that can replace the modern global economic relationship system that exhibits a negative trend.

Belarus is consistent with China in setting goals for social-economic development. The experience of China's reform and opening-up policies has been of important significance to Belarus which enters a stage of modernizing economic system in recent years. As learning, drawing lessons from and using such experience is a gigantic and complicated task, the Belarusians hope that they can obtain help and advice from their Chinese colleagues. The help will also become a response to the advice of "supporting international academic circles and funds to conduct research on topics on China" put forward by president Xi Jinping in 2016.

Adhering to the Socialist Road in the Process of Reform and Opening up Is China's Key to Success
– An Interview with Gennady Zyuganov, Chairman of the Central Committee of the Communist Party of the Russian Federation

Interviewed by Chen Airu[1]
Translated by Xie Shengzhe
Finalized by Wang Qiuhai

Gennady Andreyevich Zyuganov

Gennady Andreyevich Zyuganov was born on June 26, 1944. He witnessed and personally experienced the disintegration of the Soviet Union. He was instructor and section head of the Propaganda Department of the Central Committee of the Communist Party of the Soviet Union from 1983 and deputy head of its Ideology Department from 1989.

In June 1990, at the founding conference of the Communist Party of the Russian Soviet Federation Socialist Republic, Zyuganov was elected as a member of the Central Committee, member of the Political Bureau and secretary of the

---

1 Chen Airu, associate research fellow of the Academy of Marxism, Chinese Academy of Social Sciences.

Communist Party of the Russian Federation (CPRF). From November 1990, he also served as chairman of Humanity and Ideology Commission of the Central Committee of the CPRF.

In February 1992, Zyuganov became the chairman of "Motherland" of Patriotic Forces Coordination Committee. In October of the same year, he worked as one of the chairmen of an opposition group called "National Salvation Front". In February 1993, he was elected chairman of the Central Executive Committee of the CPRF. On January 25, 1995, he was elected chairman of the Central Committee of the CPRF and the chairman of the Coordination Committee of the Russian People's Patriotic Alliance on August 7 of the same year. Before and after the disintegration of the Soviet Union, behind the seemingly simple resume of Zyuganov is his little-known arduous struggle for the socialist ideal and belief.

In the mid-1980s, the Communist Party of the Soviet Union (CPSU) was a big party with 19 million members. However, during the short span of a few years when Gorbachev carried out the so-called reform of "humane and democratic socialism", the CPSU began to fall apart. In 1990, before and after the convening of the 28th Congress of the CPSU, in the intense debate centering on "reform", many factions such as "the Faction of the Creed of the CPSU", "the Faction of the Creed of Marxism", "the Movement Faction of the Initiative of Communism" and "Faction of Democratic Creed" took shape in the CPSU. In addition, as a branch of the CPSU in the Russian Soviet Federation Socialist Republic, the Communist Party of the Russian Soviet Federation Socialist Republic was founded during the period from June to September in 1990. Even in this regional organization, there were different factions. Therefore, the important task for Zyuganov was to try his best to unite the thought of the whole party. In the 1990s, in spite of the different thoughts in the communist movement of Russia, thanks to the efforts made by Zyuganov, the communist forces, with the CPRF as the mainstay, experienced the development process from reconstruction to prosperity. In terms of the organizational size and public support, the communist forces took up more than one third of the political

China in the New Era

arena in Russia. [1]

After the disintegration of the Soviet Union, Zyuganov devoted himself to the struggle for the re-establishment of the Communist Party and the unity of the Left Front. After the "August 19 Incident" in 1991, the Communist Party was forbidden to conduct activities for a time. Led by Zyuganov, the CPRF united other leftist forces and, through struggle in court, rebuilt the Communist Party of the Russian Soviet Federal Socialist Republic into the CPRF in February 1993.[2] In 1996 when Zyuganov ran for presidency against Boris Yeltsin, the CPRF boasted 500,000 members and was the first party in Russia and the first political group in the Duma. As the opposition faction of the ruling party, the CPRF once played an important role.

Zyuganov actively promoted the establishment of an alliance among the communist parties in the former Soviet Union, and with the purpose of restoring and rebuilding the Communist Party of the Soviet Union, he established a transnational communist union – "the Communist Union-the Communist Party of the Soviet Union" in the territory of the former Soviet Union. Since its establishment in March 1993, this organization has been always dedicated to uniting communist parties across the former Soviet Union. [3]

In addition, Zyuganov is a famous political activist and doctor of philosophy in Russia. He has written many monographs, books and political articles about his thinking on the current socialist movements in Russia and the world. To date, he has published more than 80 books and monographs, such as *A Drama Staged by the Authorities, A Major Power, October and the Contemporary Age, The Basis of Geopolitics, Globalization and Human Destiny, At the Turn of the Century, The*

---

1 Liu Shuchun et al., *Theory and Practice of the Communist Parties in Commonwealth of Independent States*, China Social Sciences Press, Beijing, 2016.
2 Liu Shuchun et al., *Theory and Practice of the Communist Parties in Commonwealth of Independent States*, China Social Sciences Press, Beijing, 2016.
3 Liu Shuchun et al., *Theory and Practice of the Communist Parties in Commonwealth of Independent States*, China Social Sciences Press, Beijing, 2016.

Adhering to the Socialist Road in the Process of Reform and Opening up Is China's Key to Success

Builders of a Great Power, *On Russia and the Russians*, *Loyalty*, *Move Forward*, *Stalin and Modernity*, *On the Eve of Daybreak* and *Russia at Gunpoint from Globalism*.

Interview Summary

Zyuganov thinks highly of China's development path and Xi Jinping Thought on Socialism with Chinese Characteristics for a New Era. He pointed out that the reform and opening up blazed by the Chinese Communist Party and the whole Chinese people guided by Deng Xiaoping, designer of "Chinese Miracles", has made China No.1 industrial power in the world and that the adherence to the path of socialism is China's key to success. Since Xi Jinping was elected general secretary of the Central Committee of the Communist Party of China (CPC) and president of China, he has continued to lead the CPC and the whole Chinese people to march on the development and construction path under the guidance of Xi Jinping Thought on Socialism with Chinese Characteristics for a New Era. China's national strength keeps on increasing day by day and China is playing an increasingly important role on the international arena. China's development and construction experience is worth studying and learning by Russia and the CPRF.

As chairman of the Central Committee of the CPRF, today's biggest communist organization in the region of the former Soviet Union as well as the leader representing the CPRF in the Russian Duma and the leader of "the Communist Union - the Communist Party of the Soviet Union", a communist union in the region of the former Soviet Union, Gennady Zyuganov enjoys wide influence among the communist and left-wing parties in the region of the former Soviet Union. Having witnessed the disintegration of the Soviet Union, he has a representative understanding and view of socialism. At the same time, Zyuganov is also a doctor of philosophy, so his insight and evaluation of China's road and China's new era has theoretical depth, representing the views of quite a few people, thus being worthy of our understanding. We had an interview with Chairman Zyuganov on these issues. The main contents of the interview are as follows:

I. Deng Xiaoping initiated China's reform and opening up with great foresight

Q: Nice to meet you, Chairman Zyuganov. Thank you for accepting my interview. In recent years, China has maintained a high-speed development and is attracting more and more attention on the international stage. How do you think of the achievements made by China?

A: In my opinion, the first reason for great achievements made by China is its adherence to socialist system. Instead of a utopia, as what opponents around the world instilled to the people, socialism is a reality with a huge potential. In the past 30 years, China has been a convincing example characterized by taking advantage of the opportunities offered by socialism.

As everyone knows, in the last 25 years of the 20th century, China began to rise again and has made real breakthroughs in science and technology and industry. Its potent economic growth and achievements in various fields have surprised the whole world. Not long ago, China was treated by imperialist powers in an insolent way. Today, it has already maintained its position commensurate to its great history. What is the reason behind the historic leap? To answer this question, in addition to our recognition of the capability and diligence in the blood of the Chinese people, we have to pay our respects to a man. He is qualified to be considered as the general designer of "Chinese miracles" by the entire world. His name is Deng Xiaoping. His life was closely related to the most important milestone that indicated the development of China in the 20th century. Deng put forth an unheard-of proposition: to learn from the whole world and draw on the experience of other countries in economic development. The Chinese understood his idea, though they did not understand it immediately. In the western world and even in Russia, people cannot understand Deng at all. Deng was described to be a "market-oriented reformer". However, the key issue is that Deng is different from Mikhail Gorbachev who advocated the transition from socialism to capitalism and was deeply trapped in his own experiment before setting about destroying socialism to cover up his crime.

Q: Just now, you've mentioned the historic leap realized by China, which is related not only to the capability and diligence in the blood of the Chinese people but also to the contribution made by Deng Xiaoping to promoting China's reform and opening up. Please talk about your understanding on Deng Xiaoping and China's policy of reform and opening up.

A: Ok. The policy of reform and opening up initiated by Deng is of direct significance in providing the necessary material and technological basis for socialism in China. Just as Xi Jinping emphasized not long ago, "We communists have a clear direction, stance and principle in our struggle – the general direction is to uphold CPC leadership and the socialist system." [1] Only under such circumstances can China cope with all dangers and challenges it faces.

Deng's statement of learning from the West is far from learning the early capitalist movement as Gorbachev did after the failure of his "reform". On the contrary, in 1979, Deng timely put forward such a viewpoint that the realization of the four modernizations must be firmly based on the adherence to the Four Cardinal Principles-adherence to the socialist road, to Communist Party of China's leadership, to the people's democratic dictatorship[2] and to Marxism-Leninism and Mao Zedong Thought. Even today, these principles are still followed by the CPC and have been written into the Constitution of the People's Republic of China.

---

1 *People's Daily*, September 4, 2019.

2 On March 30, 1979, Deng Xiaoping delivered an important speech entitled "Upholding the Four Cardinal Principles" at the Party's Theoretical Work Meeting, which was "adherence to the dictatorship of the proletariat" and changed into "adherence to the people's democratic dictatorship" in the 1982 Constitution.

In other words, there is no such thing as knuckling under to capitalism. Deng Xiaoping, "father of China's reform", firmly believed that only socialism can lift China out of poverty. "We should combine the Marxism's universal truth with our specific situation, going on our own way and building up the socialism with Chinese characteristics. This is the remark made by Deng in his speech delivered at the 12th National Congress of the CPC held in September 1982 which turned on a new page in the history of the development of the CPC. In fact, the country is in the primary stage of the development of socialism. In order to ensure a transition to the next stage, it is necessary for the country to develop its productive force and improve the people's material life.

Another major concept of Deng Xiaoping that helped to reform China is that personal interests constitute the most important engine of the progress of the whole country. He pointed out that in socialist conditions, personal interests are consistent with collective interests in nature with the former subject to the latter. Partial interests should be subordinated to overall interests and temporary interests should comply with long-term interests. In other words, local situations should be subject to overall situation and minor principles should be subordinated to major ones. Under the socialist system, in the final analysis, personal interests and collective interests are united and it is necessary to adjust the mutual relations between various interests in accordance with the principle of overall consideration. All these are only a brief introduction to the most important concepts proposed by Deng Xiaoping. It is these concepts that have motivated China to take such a massive leap forward.

II. China in the new era keeps on creating "Chinese miracles"

Q: Would you like to talk about your opinions and reflections on the socialism with Chinese characteristics entering into a new era?

A: Ok. I'd like to give my descriptions by using the word "increasingly" for three times.

Firstly, China's international influence is becoming increasingly prominent. Forty years ago, China's GDP ranked the 11th in the world and now it is the second largest economy. Just as western experts said, in the foreseeable future, China will elbow aside the US – the number one in the current world. In 2018, China celebrated its 40th anniversary of reform and opening up which has created "Chinese Miracle". The sphere of this miracle is much bigger than the so-called "German Miracle" or "Japanese Miracle". It is just because of this that China today has replaced the previous leaders of the world economy.

Secondly, China's circle of international friends is growing. Under the guidance of Xi Jinping Thought on Socialism with Chinese Characteristics for a New Era, China keeps on extending the cooperation with the countries in the world. For example, in 2018, the value of trade between China and Russia reached US$108.3 billion. In the first seven months of 2019, it increased by 5 percent. In this way, the goal set by the leaders of the two countries – to increase the value of trade between the two countries to US$200 billion in five years – is expected to be fulfilled ahead of schedule. The further development of China's Belt and Road Initiative has helped more people. Several dozen countries have participated in the initiative. China endeavors to promote the construction of "a community of shared future for mankind" on the world stage. It is constructed on the basis of solving newly-emerging threats in a fair, righteous and coordinated way. Its aim is to construct a common prosperous and secure future. In line with this idea, the countries on earth will unite to give the best and most powerful response to the actions of hegemonists. Like the majority of the countries in the world, Russia is dedicated to the construction of equitable global trade rules, insisting on the termination of the steps that undermine the exchanges between various countries on an equal footing. The CPRF holds that on the international stage, there will be more and more supporters of the rule of good faith which means that China will surely find more new supporters and allies.

Thirdly, the leading force of China in science and technology is becoming increasingly powerful. China has not only turned into a top industrial power in the world, it has also joined the ranks of the leaders of science and technology and innovation in the world. For instance, China boasts the densest high-speed railway network and its total number of super computers stands first in the world. Washington is so frightened by the achievements made by Beijing that it bluntly says that it is uneasy about China turning into a space power, because Beijing has planned to build its own orbital space station in recent years. The remarkable development achievements were fully displayed in the 70th anniversary of the founding of the People's Republic. China is entitled to celebrate this great day through a grand military parade, spectacular fireworks and celebrations all over the country.

Q: What do you think of today's China from the perspective of the world communist movement?

A: China is becoming an important center for the world communist movement. The extraordinary achievements made by the CPC are not only the precious treasures of the Chinese people but also have set a good example for the whole mankind. "Practice is the sole criterion for testing truth." This point has been profoundly proved by the achievements of reform made by China in the past 40 years. China is becoming a world power. China's development has successfully smashed the rumor that "the thoughts of Marx, Engels and Lenin have completely lost reality". On the contrary, as an example, the People's Republic of China has demonstrated the vitality of socialist thoughts and creatively treated the effectiveness of the basic principle of Marxism and Leninism. Judging from this angle, China is becoming an important center for the world communist movement.

III. It is extremely important that the Chinese leadership follows a series of important principles

Q: In your opinion, what are the important principles for China to make great achievements?

A: The extraordinary achievements made under the leadership of the Communist Party of China are not only the precious treasures of the Chinese people but also an excellent example for the whole mankind. Since the economic reform was launched, the leadership of China always has been following a series of important principles.

Firstly, the "shock therapy" was not allowed, nor was China allowed to fall into "wild capitalism". All reforms were prudently considered and carried out in a gradual way. Every success and failure was analyzed in an earnest way before learning experience and lessons which were drawn on for further reforms. The state has not let go of its economic leadership, which was manifested in retaining planned economic system, and some strategic sectors and enterprises are still owned by the state. Although adopting the market approach, China's economy still adheres to serving the whole society. For example, today the expansion of retirement security system has covered residents at all levels.

Secondly, China did not destroy state apparatus, which, instead, has been in continuous improvement. The Communist Party has become the protector of social and political stability and the major driving force of modernization. Therefore, the issue of strengthening the Party's disciplines, the Party building and inner-Party supervision is always the focus of the leaders of the Party and the state.

Thirdly, China does not give up the objective of socialism development. The present stage is considered as a transitional stage for developing into a new society. All the protective measures are aimed at preventing the PRC from being trapped into dilemma and suffering the crushing blow Russia has experienced.

Q: Thank you, Mr. Chairman. Please give your comments on the effectiveness of the political system under the leadership of the CPC.

A: The Chinese Communists fully understand that in order to successfully build a socialist society, the most important thing is not to ignore the specific cultural and historical characteristics of the country, but to use these cultural and historical characteristics to move forward. The CPC always goes by communist ideology which does not allow the renouncement of Marxism-Leninism. This point was proved by the statement made by President Xi Jinping in 2016: We must unswervingly adhere to our ideology. "The reason why the Communist Party of China has been able to accomplish the arduous tasks over the past 95 years that all kinds of political forces couldn't accomplish since modern times is that it always takes the scientific theory of Marxism as its guide to action, and insists on constantly enriching and developing Marxism in practice," "Our Party has never wavered in its belief in Marxism either under favorable or unfavorable circumstances." [1] Marxism and its development have made enormous contribution to the development of China. However, instead of turning Marxism into a dogma, the Chinese communists regard it as their guide of action. If it is compared with military science, it is a strategic plan which can be adjusted in accordance with the conditions of specific battles. People should have understood that Western democracy is far from being a model. It has many shortcomings, although these shortcomings are covered up by western propaganda and are not known to the public. The Chinese people have chosen their development paradigm which is most suitable to fulfilling the most important task and satisfying the developmental demand of the state. The practice shows that this is a very successful choice. And the success achieved by China is also the best testament to the effectiveness of the political system under the leadership of the CPC.

All of these have become the prerequisite for the establishment of a very flexible management mechanism which can respond to the demand of the era in a timely and, most importantly, effective manner. This point can be clearly seen if we compare China with the most developed capitalist countries. The crisis that broke out in 2008 dealt a heavy blow to the society and economy of the most developed capitalist countries, triggering large-scale layoffs and the adoption of so-called

---

1 *Xi Jinping: The Governance of China*, Vol. II, Foreign Languages Press, Beijing, 2017, p. 33.

economic austerity measures. The authorities began to set about canceling various social security measures. At the same time, a few of major banks became winners in speculative activities and, supported by the authorities, estimated their respective profits. However, China managed to avoid such turmoil. The main reason is that the state retains the economic management leverage.

Q: What do you think of the poverty alleviation and the building of a moderately prosperous society led by the CPC, which has attracted world attention?

A: The leadership of China has officially announced its objective in the next few years that social difficulties such as poverty will be completely eradicated. Such an objective has never been set by any western country. In China, the health care service enjoyed by the public has been increasing year by year. The coverage of the aged people who receive pension has expanded consecutively. Every year, millions of new jobs are created. Many of the objectives proposed by Deng Xiaoping in the 1980s have been realized. China has developed into a strong industrial and military power. And the task of overcoming poverty has been accomplished. As the most populous country in the world, China once had 90 percent of the population living in poverty, and more than 80 percent of the population living in rural areas. Now, China has made a huge breakthrough toward the future. In the past 40 years, more than 750 million people have been lifted out of poverty. In 2021, the 100th anniversary of the CPC, no poverty-stricken people will be found in China. I sincerely recognize the great significance of China's efforts to achieve the goal of poverty alleviation.

IV. The CPRF actively studies and publicizes Xi Jinping Thought on Socialism with Chinese Characteristics for a New Era

Q: How does the CPRF under your leadership view Xi Jinping Thought on Socialism with Chinese Characteristics for a New Era?

A: The CPRF always pays close attention to China's development. The attention covers various aspects of China's social life including economy, society, internal affairs, diplomacy as well as culture with particular emphasis placed on the changes that have taken place in the field of China's ideology. The reason is that in history the Communist Party of the Soviet Union (CPSU) could not correctly evaluate the process of domestic development and was unable to make a correct summary and take necessary measures in a timely way according to its domestic development. Even worse, those who worked at leading positions conspired to ruin socialism. Taking advantage of the power in their hands, they undermined the foundation of the soviet society. When Gorbachev began his so-called "reform", what he relied on was the bureaucrats who betrayed the lofty ideal. At the same time, when they were destroying the cause of the Party and the state, thousands of the members of the CPSU failed to foresee the threat and take actions to get rid of it. On the contrary, the Chinese communists made an earnest summary of the lessons that had caused the failure of the CPSU and succeeded in avoiding the same old disastrous road. The detailed analysis of historical experience and lessons is an important part of historical summary which can ensure the CPC to recognize the task of national development in an accurate way.

From today's perspective, the CPC develops in a steady way and keeps on making self-improvement. This is a fundamental guarantee for the vitality of any organization. The Communist Party of China, which is the leader of a big country, has set a grand goal for itself.

Obviously, all the achievements made by China rely on the CPC that has firmly paved the way for leading the Chinese people to march toward the highly developed socialist society. The CPC is good at making prudent analysis of the current developmental process and drawing a conclusion that the society in China is in transition to a higher development stage. Particularly after the 18th National Congress of the CPC and Xi Jinping began to serve as the leader of the Party and state, great strides were made in this regard, and proposed "Xi Jinping Thought on Socialism with Chinese Characteristics for a New Era" in 2017. China has completed the task of realizing socialist modernization and national rejuvenation. In the middle of the 21st century, China will be developed into a great modern socialist country that is prosperous, strong, democratic, culturally advanced, harmonious and beautiful. "Xi Jinping Thought on Socialism with Chinese Characteristics for a New Era" and the magnificent and epic process of socialist development guided by the thought have provided a whole set of methodologies. It is not confined to a certain field but includes all aspects of social life including politics, economy, society, culture and ecology. In addition, it also includes the "Four-pronged Comprehensive Strategy" – completing a moderately prosperous society in all respects, deepening reform, advancing the rule of law and strengthening Party discipline. All these deserve serious study on the part of the CPRF.

Q: What world significance does Xi Jinping Thought on Socialism with Chinese Characteristics for a New Era have?

A: Xi Jinping Thought on Socialism with Chinese Characteristics for a New Era has opened the way to a better future for China and set a good example for the whole world at the same time. We can say it with confidence that the People's Republic of China is standing on the starting point of a great journey. China has drawn important lessons from gradual reformation and real modernization. Both the ground-breaking achievements made during the periods of Lenin and Stalin and the contemporary CPC indicate that after various grueling hardships, only socialism can ensure the rise of a country. I firmly believe that for countries with vast territories and unique features like China and Russia, only with socialism can we overcome poverty and backwardness. As far as the Russian people are concerned, capitalism is a road to failure and collapse.

Q: How does the CPRF pay attention to Xi Jinping Thought on Socialism with Chinese Characteristics for a New Era?

A: The CPRF, as a rule, discusses the issues related to Xi Jinping Thought on Socialism with Chinese Characteristics for a New Era and the development of China on a regular basis. In the learning system set by the CPRF, these issues are included in the CPRF's political education targeted at its members and supporters. Whenever the CPRF meets the delegation sent to Russia by the Central Committee of the CPC, Xi Jinping Thought on Socialism with Chinese Characteristics is almost one of the topics that are discussed.

While researching the CPC's ideology, the branches of the CPRF in various areas pay attention to almost all aspects of theoretical innovation of CPC. They pay particular attention to the contents related to Xi Jinping Thought on Socialism with Chinese Characteristics for a New Era, which are enshrined in the China's amended Constitution. It is our firm conviction that these amendments, which are embodied in the mechanism of national governance, will bring about a positive influence. They can guarantee the stability of national political system from the perspective of a long-term development vision.

In the documents of the congresses and plenary sessions of its central committee, the CPRF often analyzes the important issues concerning the ideological work of the CPC and national development prospect. According to the CPRF, the successful reform carried out by China by holding high the red flag has ensured China's realization of an unparalleled historic leap.

China's Xinhua News Agency and news organizations under the Central Committee of the CPC invite the leaders of the CPRF to make comments or conduct interviews with them at regular intervals on some major theoretical and practical problems so as to let the CPRF have a timely and accurate understanding of the changes that have taken place in China.

Media controlled by the CPRF systematically publicize and report the issues related to "Xi Jinping Thought on Socialism with Chinese Characteristics for a New Era" and China's development. These tasks are mainly undertaken and completed by Pravda, Sovetskaya Rossiya, "Red Line" Television Channel, the website of the Central Committee of the CPRF as well as all the party's local mass media system. President Xi Jinping's report of "Secure a Decisive Victory in Building a Moderately Prosperous Society in All Respects and Strive for the Great Success of Socialism with Chinese Characteristics for a New Era" delivered at the 19th National Congress of the Communist Party of China was fully published in the 1st issue of *Political Education*, a periodical of the CPRF, in 2018. The main content of the report was published in the 125th issue of *Pravda* entitled "the Socialism with Chinese Characteristics has entered into a new era" from November 10 to 13, 2017.

The two volumes of the book *Xi Jinping: the Governance of China* by Xi Jinping have aroused a strong interest of Russian experts. The issuance of the Russian edition of the book is of extreme importance because it is used whenever the CPRF's "Red Line" Television Channel is planning the program related to contemporary China.

V. The basic analysis and judgment of China-US trade war

Q: Not long ago, the Information Office of the State Council of China released a white paper titled "The Facts and China's Position on China-US Trade Friction", to which you gave a completely clear interpretation, namely, the bilateral economic relation between China and the US should follow the principle of mutual benefit and win-win cooperation. How do you view the issue of China-US trade war?

A: In the China-US trade war, China enjoys more support than US does and the final winner will be China.

Since the establishment of China-US diplomatic relations, such basic principles as mutual benefit and win-win cooperation have been observed. It simply cannot avoid for China and the US, the two largest economies in the world, to experience some economic and trade frictions. What truly matters is to find solutions through dialogue and consultation. Only in this way can the relationship between the two countries become more mature. For many years, China has been an important trade partner of the US and vice versa. However, after Donald Trump was elected the US president, the White House began to revise "the rules of the game". The unilateralism of the US has posed a serious challenge to the world economy. The

US groundlessly accused China of "stealing technology and intellectual property." In these fields, all the achievements made by the PRC are the results of long-term, arduous and creative efforts.

China has been forced to respond to attacks on itself, citing trade data from China and the US to refute the accusation. However, China has always insisted on settling disputes through negotiations. Therefore, China conducted trade consultations with the US, striving for finding a mechanism which can be accepted by both sides. However, Washington has broken its promise on more than one occasion and furtively disrupted the dialogue. In addition, it has constantly put forth new demands and restrictive measures. Therefore, the US should bear the sole and entire responsibility for the failure of negotiations.

Beijing always expresses its wish to cooperate with Washington and realize bilateral mutual benefit and win-win cooperation. However, what the comrades in China follow is the "red line", which is a matter of principle. Therefore, although China does not want to be engaged in a trade war, its proposal won't be accepted by Washington. I believe that the PRC has enough strength to win the fight imposed on it from outside and is prepared to safeguard its national interest under any circumstances.

Will China's success damage the interest of the US? Is the China-US trade relation is based on mutual benefit or on the profit on one side and loss on the other? In my view, the economic trade relation between China and the whole world is characterized by following strict rules. It operates not only in the framework of bilateral agreements but also in accordance with the norms of the World Trade Organization. For example, in its cooperation with Russia, Beijing adheres to its stand of partnership which is responsible and capable of carrying out relevant agreements. China expresses its attitude regularly that it is going to settle disputes through consultation and negotiations instead of advocating the use of unilateral pressure measures. Likewise, China's economy and trade relations with the US are established on the same basis. It is even hard to imagine that the US, the largest economic entity in the world, can allow China to adopt any discriminatory and dishonest trade principle. Therefore, it is ridiculous for the US State Department to accuse China of trade imbalance with the US. The US is a capitalist country. It is well-known that capitalists give priority to profits when they do business. Washington's expansion of the economic connection with China and other countries with trade deficits can only be in the interest of American corporations. Nobody has forced them to take such actions and no one has delivered an ultimatum to them. From beginning to end, all the decisions have been made by themselves.

Trump uses the slogan "America first" and defending the interests of American producers to attract public attention, manipulate social consciousness and establish an image of China as the enemy of the US. However, in the final analysis, the action taken by the US against China will harm the interest of the American people. For example, the trade war with Beijing has led to the bankruptcy of some farmers. In this regard, the US authorities are acting recklessly.

Q: Mr. Chairman, what do you think of "America First" proposed by the US president Trump?

A: Speaking of the standpoint of "America First", I think the first thing is to look at Trump himself and whose interest the Trump Administration represents. All this is intended to maintain and consolidate its global leadership and obtain maximum profit. It is just because of this that they are eager to maintain the US superiority in the world and weaken China, Russia and Europe, dreaming of making Latin America dependent on the American regime. However, Washington will never admit its real purpose, but only continue to strengthen the propaganda of the so-called democratic and human rights values. At the same time, American imperialists continue to strive for the consolidation of its world leadership, firmly carrying out the policy of imposing sanctions against Russia and shamelessly suppressing rapid development of China. When they are shouting "America First", they mean nothing but worm their way into the support of the laboring people in their country. The source of the instability and conflicts in the world resides in the policy implemented by the US authorities which is completely inconsistent with the interest of the average citizens in the country. The policy is beneficial to the most aggressive imperialist groups. All the communists in the world should expose the essence of the policy and fight against it.

Q: What do you think is the relationship between China's reform and opening up and the process of world economic globalization?

A: China's integration into the world economy has accelerated the process of globalization. Following the path of reform, China keeps on strengthening bilateral and multilateral economic relations by establishing connections with big corporations. China has become a formal participant in global economic relation after her accession to the WTO.

The PRC today is a major driver of global economic growth. China has contributed over 30 percent to global growth. In global imports, China is the second (accounting for almost 11 percent of the world's imports), slightly lower than the US. China's market is a major force for maintaining the growth of global consumption. According to statistical data, from 2013 to 2016, China's average rate of contribution to world consumption growth was 23.4 percent, surpassing all other countries including the US and euro-zone countries.

With the continuous growth of its proportion in world economy, China feels it increasingly necessary to formulate fair rules for global economy. The Belt and Road Initiative is a convincing and fair model of economic cooperation, which is based on the concept of "a community with a share future for mankind" proposed by Beijing. Various countries in various continents in the world are more and more interested in this initiative.

VI. The responsibilities and obligations of contemporary communists

Q: How do you view the responsibilities and obligations of contemporary communists?

Adhering to the Socialist Road in the Process of Reform and Opening up Is China's
Key to Success

A: Like their predecessors, contemporary communists should do everything possible to make socialism in the world to achieve new success and victories. The most important condition for this goal is the ability of analyzing contemporary issues. Experts from Chinese Academy of Social Sciences have put forward an important initiative to publish a series of collected essays and translations on world Marxism and leftism. I'm grateful to them for this initiative because my book, *Russia at Gunpoint from Globalism*, is the first volume of the series. The book has been translated into Chinese.

While looking forward to the future, waging political struggles and completing the pioneering work, communists must defend socialist thought and its historical achievements and fight against anti-communist forces. At present, the most important ideological work of the CPRF is the preparation for the 150th anniversary of the birth of Lenin, the 140th anniversary of the birth of Stalin and the 75th anniversary of the victory of the Soviets in the Great Patriotic War. Now, one of the most important activities that is being prepared is the visit to "Victory Park, Memorial Park and Life Park". During the period of fighting against German fascists and Japanese imperialists, the Russian and Chinese people lost thousands of lives. The meritorious service of these people will be remembered by us forever.

Q: The last question. What expectations do you have with regard to the China-Russia relationship and the exchanges between the CPC and the CPRF? Thank you!

A: Two more famous 70th anniversaries were celebrated along with the 70th anniversary of the founding of the PRC. On October 1, 1949, Mao Zedong proclaimed the founding of the PRC. On the following day, the PRC and the USSR established formal diplomatic relations. Four days later, on October 5, the Association for Friendship between China and Russia (its predecessor was the Association for Friendship between China and the Soviet Union) was established, which laid a foundation for the great brotherhood between the two countries and had a great influence on the development of the world history. Today, to the new generation of Chinese and Russian communists, it is necessary to consolidate the ties between the two great nations. Not long ago, Ivan Melnikov, first vice-chairman of the Central Committee of the CPRF, was elected president of the Association for Friendship between Russia and China. The CPRF will do everything it can to promote the cooperation between China and Russia.

Since the mid-1990s, the CPC and the CPRF carried out cooperation according to regular agreements. This year, a memorandum of interaction between the two parties for the next three years was signed. Thanks to the concerted efforts, more than 100 young members of the CPRF have been to the PRC for academic visits to study the experience of reform in China. While preparing for the 100th anniversary of the great October Revolution, the CPRF not only organized important festivities but also completed many important and interesting plans. One of them is a book titled *Wind in October* about the life and activities of Lenin. The book was published in both Chinese and Russian.

Socialism with Chinese Characteristics for a New Era Has Blazed a Trail for the Rejuvenation of World Socialism
– An Interview with Thürmer Gyula, Chairman of Hungarian Workers' Party

Interviewed by Yu Haiqing[1]
Translated by Xie Shengzhe
Finalized by Wang Qiuhai

Thürmer Gyula

Thürmer Gyula is a famous Hungarian politician, diplomat and expert on international relations and also the most important leader of the Communist Party after the transformation of Hungary.

Gyula was born in Budapest, capital of Hungary on April 14, 1953. His father was one of the founders of military economics in Hungary. When Gyula was young, he studied at the famous Fazekas High School. From 1971 to 1976, he went to Moscow State Institute of International Relations to study international relations. From 1976 to 1980, he returned to Hungary and worked at the Ministry of Foreign Affairs of the People's Republic of Hungary, successively working at the Department of Far East Affairs and the Department of the Soviet Affairs. From

---

1   Yu Haiqing, research fellow of the Academy of Marxism, Chinese Academy of Social Sciences.

China in the New Era

1980 to 1982, he held the post of first secretary with the Hungarian Embassy in Moscow. From 1982 to 1985, he was in charge of the Department of Soviet Union under the International Bureau of the Hungarian Socialist Workers Party. From 1985 to 1989, he was an advisor of Károly Grósz, general secretary of Socialist Workers Party in foreign policy and security issues. In this capacity, he attended many international summit meetings of the former socialist countries in Eastern Europe. Gyula witnessed the drastic changes in Hungary. After the Hungarian Socialist Workers Party was reorganized into the Social Democratic Party, he began to rebuild the Communist Party of Hungary. Later, due to the prohibition of using the name and symbol of "Communism" according to related laws, the Communist Party of Hungary was renamed as the Hungarian Workers' Party. Since December 1989, Gyula served as chairman of the party.

At present, boasting several thousand registered members, the Hungarian Workers Party led by Chairman Gyula is the second-largest Communist Party in the former Eastern Europe. The party has its relatively perfect grass-roots organizations and fixed offices. However, influenced by international and regional situations as well as domestic and international factors, the Hungarian Workers Party has encountered difficulties in its development for a long period of time. Since its founding, the party has not entered into the parliament of the country. The national election in 1998 saw its highest approval rating, which was only 4 percent. Even in such an unfavorable situation, Chairman Gyula persistently adhered to the ideal of communism, held high the banner of Marxism, defended the interests of the laboring people and promoted the development of Hungarian socialist movement, thus earning a high reputation among the leftists and socialists in the West.

One of Chairman Gyula's hobbies is to learn languages. He can fluently speak Russian, English, German, Spanish, Serbian and Italian. He can also proficiently read Chinese and Japanese. Gyula has read a lot of books related to classical Chinese literature, the history of the CPC and politics in contemporary China. In August 2019, the delegation from the Research Center for Xi Jinping Thought on

Socialism with Chinese Characteristics for a New Era under Chinese Academy of Social Sciences paid a visit to the headquarters of the Hungarian Workers Party. We found important works such as *Xi Jinping: The Governance of China* and *Ninety Years of the Communist Party of China* on his desk. After the 1990s, Gyula visited China for many times and met Party and state leaders of China such as Jiang Zemin and Hu Jintao. He takes a great interest in China's development and attaches particular importance to the latest advancement of the theory and practice of socialism with Chinese characteristics. He has great interest in China's development, especially the latest progress in the theory and practice of socialism with Chinese characteristics. Through http://www.xinhuanet.com/ and http://www.people.com.cn/, he learns about the new measures of China's reform and opening up, and witnesses the development and historical leap of Chinese society.

Interview Summary

Thürmer Gyula, chairman of Hungarian Workers' Party, sang high praise for the six historical achievements made by the socialism with Chinese characteristics. Through the comparison with the socialism in Eastern Europe, he revealed the four critical factors about the success of Xi Jinping Thought on Socialism with Chinese Characteristics for a New Era, expounded the six aspects of international significance of Xi Jinping Thought on Socialism with Chinese Characteristics for a New Era, threw light on the reasons of the external difficulties facing China's rise, analyzed the history and status quo of the socialism in Hungary and discussed the interaction and prospect of China-Hungary relationship, emphasizing that the socialism with Chinese characteristics will inevitably become the mainstay of the rejuvenation of world socialism.

I. History of socialism in Hungary and 30 years of transition

Q: Nice to meet you, Chairman Gyula! We are glad that you agree to have an interview with us. Thirty years have elapsed since the profound changes in Eastern Europe. No matter how they have been interpreted by the people, they are all significant events in the history of the development of international socialism. As a witness to the socialist practice in Hungary for more than 40 years, how do you understand and evaluate the socialist period in Hungary?

A: From 1948 to 1990, Hungary was in its socialist period and made enormous achievements in various fields such as economy, society and politics. Although Hungary suffered great losses in the Second World War (1939-1945) including the damage of 40 percent of buildings and the complete destruction of Danube Bridge, Hungary reconstructed cities such as Budapest in the first several decades in its socialist period. During this period, the national industry entered into a new stage featuring rapid development. Some brands of national industrial products such as IKARUS buses, MÁVAG trains and MEDICOR in pharmaceutical industry were well-known around the world.

During that period, the agriculture in Hungary was among the best in Europe. Through the effective combination of cooperative and private ownership, the agriculture in Hungary succeeded in meeting the internal consumption of the people with high-quality foods and made contribution to agricultural export of the country. The socialism in Hungary provided the people with good living standard and Hungarians lived a better life than peoples in other socialist countries in Eastern and Central Europe. In spite of the fact that the people's living standard did not keep up with that of many capitalist countries in Western Europe, the gap was bridged by free medical care and free education. Besides, socialism granted full pension to all citizens including farmers. In the socialist period of more than 40 years, the people of Hungary lived in peace without being involved into any war. Hungarian soldiers took part in only one overseas military operation during Czechoslovakia Incident in

1968.

Q: As a witness to drastic changes in Hungary and the subsequent social transition in the country, what do you think of the development and changes in Hungary in the past 30 years after the drastic changes?

A: In the late 1980s and the early 1990s, with drastic changes in Eastern Europe and the disintegration of the Soviet Union, socialism around the world was faced with serious difficulty. In 1990, Hungary became a capitalist country. Hungary's transition to capitalism is a serious and controversial process. Famous national industries such as bus manufacturing, pharmacy and sugar were sold to foreign corporations. Agricultural products including wheat and meat were reduced and food trade was controlled by foreign companies. The emergence of capitalism has led to great differentiation in people's clothing, mood, wealth and way of life. The direct consequence of the transition to capitalism was that unemployment and poverty became new social problems. One and a half million people were unemployed. GDP decreased by 20 percent. Domestic market was completely opened to Western commodities and capital. As a result, industrial and agricultural structure was destroyed. The loss of national wealth was even higher than that in the Second World War. The dependence on foreign investment became increasingly serious.

After entering the threshold of the 21st century, the Hungarian government has to choose between liberal and conservative economic policies. Since the administrations of both the Liberal Party and the Social Democratic Party approved the liberal policy, they refused to allow the state to play an active role. According to these administrations, the state has only one task: to ensure free competition in the market. They placed hopes on the market, thinking that it can solve all problems. Important sectors, including energy production and supply, were privatized. The privatization of health care and education was also put on the agenda. The world economic crisis in 2008 led to further deterioration of Hungary's economic and social situation. Unemployment rate rose to 12 percent in 2010 and social spending

China in the New Era

was cut down. From the end of 2008 to the beginning of 2009, the Hungarian forint (HUF) fell 15 percent against the Swiss franc (CHF) and 17 percent against the euro (EUR), which led to bankruptcies and a credit crunch and an increase in households' foreign-currency debts (Swiss francs and Euros). In order to offset the destructive influence of liberalization and privatization of economy, in 2008, Hungary became the first EU member state to seek financial support from the International Monetary Fund. The policy triggered massive protests in Hungary. It was clear that the liberal policy had broken down. The government could not guarantee internal stability without the use of force.

Hungary's changes in economic situation began in 2010 when conservatives came to power. The Conservative government introduced the policy of state capitalism. As a result, energy supply, national defense industry and some banks were nationalized once more. Now more than 50 percent of the banking system is state-owned, and more than 50 percent of the Hungarian media are in the hands of the state. The capitalist state interferes in the market process, leading to the control of education and health care by the state. The conservative government has imposed a special tax on banks, big foreign companies, energy, retail trade and telecoms, and VAT reached 27 percent, the highest in the European Union. The conservative government returned some of the excess profits to the state, provided new social subsidies for almost all social groups, and began to establish multi-layered foreign trade and international cooperation. As a result of these measures, Hungary's direct foreign investment increased by EUR1,646.15 million in the first quarter of 2019. From 1995 to 2019, Hungary's direct foreign investment averaged EUR732.18 million. In the fourth quarter of 2013, it reached an all-time high of EUR4,221.4 million. In the fourth quarter of 2015, it reached an all-time low of EUR-15,097.1 million. The domestic political situation tended to be stable once more. While some social problems, such as the wealth gap and the poor public health-care system, have not disappeared, people are now becoming more and more tolerant.

Q: What changes have taken place with regard to Hungary's attitude to socialism in the past 30 years?

A: Over the past 30 years, Hungarian socialist history has been demonized and Hungarian socialism has been regarded as the "evil past". Hungarian law also forbids "the use of symbols of fascist and communist dictatorships in public occasions". According to the law, statements related to socialist history, such as communism and liberation, cannot be used in the names of political parties, organizations or even streets and other public places. As a result, one cannot find the Liberation Square in Hungary, as it will remind people of the role played by Soviet troops in the liberation of Hungary in 1945. In addition, all monuments constructed in the socialist period have been demolished. When there are still a number of statues of Marx in Germany, including a new statue of Marx presented by China to Trier, the hometown of Marx, no memento of Marx can be found in Hungary.

Although there exists a great deal of anti-communist propaganda and a new generation of people knows little about the history of socialism, we should also note that socialism still lives in the memory of the old. Kádár János (1912-1989), who is still one of the most popular historical figures, was the leader of Hungary's Socialist Workers' Party from 1956 to 1988. When capitalism displays its negative side, as when people are paying for private hospitals, they would miss the free health-care system provided by socialism. When people lose their jobs, they would cherish the memory of socialism because it secured everyone a job and income.

The problems facing Europe and even the world are enormous. The EU cannot solve the problems of modernization and internal innovation as well as millions of migrants coming to Europe from Africa and the Middle East. The European Union has imposed sanctions on Russia. The NATO and the United States are sending more and more troops to the border between Europe and Russia. Europe is becoming increasingly hostile to Russia, and so on. This means that Europe, including Hungary, still has a lot of problems to solve. It is becoming increasingly clear that the capitalist system is far from what the people really need. Things are changing so fast, so we can re-examine the socialist value. The history of socialism

China in the New Era

in Europe is far from over.

II. The great achievements made by socialism with Chinese characteristic have drawn the attention of the world

Q: Thanks a lot. Your feelings and understanding are fairly inspiring to us. Now please share with us your views on socialism with Chinese characteristics.

A: Thirty years ago, the cause of world socialism encountered a serious setback due to the drastic changes in Eastern Europe and the disintegration of the Soviet Union. While some socialist countries collapsed under the international and domestic pressure, China's socialism developed vigorously and made great achievements in the economic, scientific and military fields. In my opinion, the successful development of socialism with Chinese characteristics is an important mark of the formation of new and modern ideas. It has inspired the people of the world to struggle for social justice, thus opening up new horizons for the development of socialism in the world.

Q: Socialism with Chinese characteristics has proved to be successful. So, in your opinion, what is the key to the success of socialism with Chinese characteristics as compared with socialism in Eastern Europe?

A: The successful development of socialism with Chinese characteristics is the result of the role of both political and economic factors. It seems to me that these factors are particularly important if they are compared with the lessons of socialism in Eastern Europe.

Three decades ago, the socialist countries in Eastern Europe underwent a transition to capitalism. They came to a wrong conclusion that the internal resources of socialism were exhausted and that eastern European countries had to abandon socialism and introduce capitalism if they were to cope with the inevitable modernization. The wrong decision led to painful consequences. On the contrary, China decided to save socialism through reform and opening up, a far-sighted decision that can modernize the socialist society.

Thirty years ago, the communist countries in Eastern Europe abandoned the leadership of the Communist Party and decided to adopt the western multi-party system. However, China has never given up the leadership of the Communist Party, and all of China's achievements have been made under the leadership of the Communist Party of China. A Chinese revolutionary song goes like this, "Without the Communist Party, there would be no new China", which mentions that without the heroic struggle of the Communist Party of China, the new China would not have been established, and the same is true in this era. As General Secretary Xi Jinping has emphasized, "The leadership of the CPC constitutes the most essential attribute of socialism with Chinese characteristic. Without the Communist Party, there would be no new China, nor a prosperous and strong China either." [1]

It was also 30 years ago that the socialist countries in Eastern Europe decided to emulate the social development model of the capitalist countries. The first bills, including the electoral system and the constitutional court, were introduced from the capitalist countries in Western Europe that had developed under different historical conditions. After accession to the EU, the legal system of the new member states of the EU needed to be "coordinated" with the European Common Law, but this Law deviates from the basic fact that the individual laws of the European countries were generated and developed under different conditions. This practice infringed upon the fundamental national interests, because these countries brought in new systems and regulations that are not in line with their national conditions. However, what China has decided to build is socialism with Chinese characteristics. This means that China has not adopted the western model of social development that was formed and developed under different conditions. China has decided to follow a political system that embodies its national conditions, which is in full accord

---

1 Xi Jinping, "Speech at the Congress to Celebrate the 60th Anniversary of the Founding of the National People's Congress," People's Publishing House, Beijing, 2014, p. 6.

with the basic interests and aspirations of the Chinese people. I strongly agree with the following remark made by General Secretary Xi Jinping: "Blindly copying the political systems of other countries will never work in China. They will never adapt to our country. Such a course of action will 'turn the tiger you are trying to draw into a dog.' It could even spell an end to the independent destiny of our country. Only a system deeply-rooted and fully nourished in our own soil is reliable and will serve our purposes." [1] In particular, since the outbreak of COVID-19 this year, the Chinese government has taken the most comprehensive and strict prevention and control measures with a high sense of responsibility for the health of its people. Its efficiency is impressive and difficult to describe in words. No other country in the world is able to mobilize all its human and material resources in such a short period of time, which demonstrates the great strength of the socialist political system with Chinese characteristics.

During my first visit to China in 1990, General Secretary Jiang Zemin pointed out that history was indivisible. China has a history of more than 5,000 years, during which socialist stage is only a short period. In recent years, General Secretary Xi Jinping repeatedly talked about the close relationship between Chinese history and the socialist historical period, pointing out that the splendid Chinese civilization can date back to more than 5,000 years ago. Under the leadership of the Communist Party of China, the Chinese people have scored new success on the road of socialism, thus paving the way for further success. However, in eastern European countries including Hungary, this historical continuity is often broken. New political systems and new governments are often reluctant to mention the positive aspects of their predecessors, only emphasizing their own achievements and superiority. History is a process consisting of the right and the wrong as well as success and failure. China's recognition of the continuity of historical development has offered broad possibilities for drawing on the achievements and wisdom of historical

---

1 *Xi Jinping: The Governance of China*, Vol. II, Foreign Languages Press, Beijing, 2017, p. 286.

periods in the past.

Q: In your opinion, what specific achievements has socialism with Chinese characteristics made in the past 70 years?

A: In my opinion, the basic prerequisite for the success of socialism with Chinese characteristics is that China won the national independence and sovereignty. On October 1, 1949, the People's Republic of China was founded, and China became an independent and sovereign country. In spite of repeated external interference since then, China has been able to maintain and strengthen its national independence and sovereignty. Recently, China has faced some international challenges. In particular, the United States has taken large-scale actions against China, including launching a trade war against Chinese companies, interfering in the matters related to Hong Kong and trying to undermine the established system of socialism with Chinese characteristics so as to force China to succumb to the interests of the US. I believe that, based on the consistent policy of socialism with Chinese characteristics for a new era, the CPC can meet the challenges of the United States, safeguard China's national interests, national independence and sovereignty.

Economic take-off marks the most important achievement in the development of new China in the past 70 years. Since the founding of the People's Republic of China, especially since the reform and opening up in 1978, China has made great progress in agriculture, transportation, foreign trade, environmental protection and scientific research. China's economy overtook Germany's in 2007 and Japan's in 2010 and is expected to overtake that of the US in 2026. At present, China is the second largest economy after the United States, and both the speed and quality of its development are unmatched by any other country in the world.

Another important achievement of new China in its development in the past 70 years is the eradication of poverty. Over the past 70 years, China has succeeded in feeding nearly 1.4 billion people, enabling them to have a high standard of living and providing a secure future for later generations. For more than 40 years, China has lifted some 750 million people out of poverty. The life of the common people in China has improved a lot, from the lack of food and necessities in the past to abundant food and satisfying lifestyles at present. With the substantial increase of income, urban and rural residents have shifted from essential food consumption to recreational and personal development consumption. The living conditions of the people have improved significantly. More and more urban and rural families bade farewell to the dilapidated, poorly equipped bungalows and moved into spacious, bright, well-equipped buildings. No other country in the world has made such great achievements.

Over the past 70 years, China has made steady progress in building democratic politics. China has established a broad system of democratic institutions. Chinese people now enjoy more freedom of speech and access to information. China's legal system has gradually improved, and people feel safer and more secure. Openness and modernity can be seen on the streets of China's big cities.

China has also made much headway in science and education. In particular, since the beginning of the 21st century, China's investment in scientific experiments has increased substantially, up to RMB19.7 trillion in 2018 from RMB12.5 billion in 1990. A lot of major scientific and technological achievements have been made. The telecom industry is developing very fast, and many Chinese companies have launched 5G phones, attracting extensive attention worldwide.

In conclusion, I would like to emphasize an achievement of global significance, namely, China's contribution to promoting international exchanges and cooperation. It is fair to say that China has shouldered its responsibilities as a major country and has made its due contribution to geopolitics. Especially with the starting of the Belt and Road Initiative, China is committed to developing the infrastructure and connectivity among BRI countries. At present, more than 150 countries, regions and international organizations have participated in the Belt and Road, most of which are the beneficiaries. Through Hungary's participation in the Belt and Road, I have a strong feeling that the initiative focuses on economic development without pursuing political goals. On the basis of openness and cooperation, it transcends protectionism and is committed to mutual benefit and win-win result between countries instead of zero-sum game. At the same time, adhering to international rules, it is not intended to start a new model. The Belt and Road Initiative has passed on the message of peace, harmony and development, facilitated people-to-people contacts and mutual understanding and promoted trade and tourism. It will surely serve as a model for economic and trade development in the future. The practice of "the Belt and Road" shows that on the basis of mutual understanding, countries can establish interdependent relations, thus eliminating misunderstandings to a large extent.

III. The global significance of Xi Jinping Thought on Socialism with Chinese Characteristics for a New Era

Q: Since the 18th CPC National Congress, the CPC has made a lot of theoretical and practical achievements, the most important of which is Xi Jinping Thought on Socialism with Chinese Characteristics for a New Era, indicating that the great practice of Socialism with Chinese Characteristics for a New Era has demonstrated strong vitality. How do you see the global significance and impact of it?

A: I think that Xi Jinping Thought on Socialism with Chinese Characteristics for a New Era was put forward on the basis of an in-depth analysis of China's historical development and the general trend of its contemporary development. It is an extensive synthesis based on political reflections on theory, ideology, politics, economy, society and foreign relations and an outstanding theoretical achievement in the 21st century. Therefore, Xi Jinping Thought on Socialism with Chinese Characteristics for a New Era is of great world significance. Although it is impossible for us to predict all the effects it will produce in the future, it has begun to influence the international process at least in the following aspects.

First of all, the world has changed a lot in the last few decades. The mankind is facing new problems such as digitization, social media, 5G technology, large-scale migration, climate change and so on. New approaches are needed if the mankind is to survive and create a secure future for generations to come. China is now at the forefront of addressing the great challenges facing the world today. Although the developed capitalist countries including the European Union have implemented a large number of modernization programs, the reality is that no matter what kind of adjustment is made to capitalism, the basic contradiction will not change. That is to say, the profit-driven nature of capital will not change, nor will the western value of egoism, and the working class people are still in the state of being oppressed and exploited. Xi Jinping Thought on Socialism with Chinese Characteristics for a New Era serves the interests of the broad masses of the working people and the general public, meets the need of safeguarding social fairness, freedom and a good life, and is the most valuable theoretical concept and practical guidance to respond to these challenges.

Secondly, our planet is going through tremendous development, but it is also facing profound transformation and changes. The world is moving towards multi-polarization and economic globalization. In order to take advantage of the positive aspects of this process and prevent and reduce negative consequences, we need a comprehensive strategy. At the same time, innovation is the main driving force for economic growth and social development, but it should not be limited to economic field alone. Being faced with modern challenges, we need to seek innovation in many aspects including theory, science and technology, way of thinking, decision-making process. Xi Jinping Thought on Socialism with Chinese Characteristics for a New Era is the key to constructing a comprehensive strategy and understanding the necessity of multi-faceted innovation and its realization.

Thirdly, the people need a peaceful and secure environment if they are to realize their national dreams. At present, the world development is faced with many difficulties, such as increasing political competition and regional tensions, and the threat of a new round of global war is becoming more and more realistic. If we take a different attitude toward international relations, war and destruction are likely to be avoided. Xi Jinping Thought on Socialism with Chinese Characteristics for a New Era has provided a new way of thinking for building a new international relation. It should be noted that some people now accuse China of engaging in "superpower diplomacy", but this argument is wrong. Of course, China is one of the major powers in the world, but it does not have the ambition to become a superpower. The great power diplomacy with Chinese characteristics aims to foster new international relations, build a "community with a shared future for mankind", resolutely defend multilateralism and free trade, and move the global governance system toward a fairer and more equitable direction. I am confident that China will always stand firmly on the correct side of historical development and progress and will become an important source of stability in an unstable world.

Finally, all countries, nations and peoples in the world should regard respect for sovereignty as the most important criterion in handling state-to-state relations. Respect for sovereignty is the most important guarantee for the existence of nation states. According to Xi Jinping Thought on Socialism with Chinese Characteristics for a New Era, it is necessary to uphold sovereign equality and strive to ensure equal rights and opportunities for all countries. This is in fact to encourage people of various countries to fight for the existence of independent and sovereign states.

Moreover, the New China grew out of a semi-feudal and semi-colonial society. The socialist reform and opening-up policy has profoundly changed China, bringing about earth-shaking changes. In particular, China's recent successful development under the guidance of Xi Jinping Thought on Socialism with Chinese Characteristics for a New Era will surely be important in affecting global development. Some developing countries have similar experiences with China. Although they can't completely copy China's development path, the success of China's road has provided ideas and experience for them to get rid of backwardness, put an end to the colonial exploitation and cast off their dependence on western approaches. It has also provided an alternative choice for the countries that want to realize rapid development and maintain independence at the same time.

Q: In your opinion, what contributions has Xi Jinping Thought on Socialism with Chinese Characteristics for a New Era made to promoting the development and innovation of world socialist theory and practice?

A: In the contemporary context, only by insisting on the wide diversity of development and political practice can the world socialist movement highlight the characteristics of the Communist Party and serve the overall interests of the Communist movement. From this perspective, Xi Jinping Thought on Socialism with Chinese Characteristics for a New Era is undoubtedly of great significance in promoting the development and innovation of world socialist theory and practice.

Xi Jinping Thought on Socialism with Chinese Characteristics for a New Era is a theory based on Marxism because it adheres to the basic principles of Marxism. It is a theoretical and systematic form of the valuable experience gained from China's active exploration along the road of socialist modernization. At the same time, it is not only the program for China to build socialism, but also the program for solving the problems that have never been solved in the history of the development of Marxism. It is the creative development of Marxism because it contains many aspects of the development trend of the contemporary world, including the struggle of the working people against the unjust capitalist system and the construction of socialism. Therefore, it is of global significance to the development of the revolutionary theory of the working class.

I am particularly impressed by the tremendous achievements made by the socialism with Chinese characteristics in the new era, which has filled the Chinese people with hope for the future. The Chinese people can proudly say: we live better today than yesterday, and we believe we will live better tomorrow than today. Who else in the world dare make the same remark? It is these great achievements that have demonstrated the correctness of Xi Jinping Thought on Socialism with Chinese Characteristics for a New Era. It shows that socialism does not stand for the past, but represents the present and ushers in the future. Socialism never means backwardness and poverty. Socialism guarantees human development and the prospect of achieving common prosperity for all.

I personally witnessed the collapse of communist regimes in Eastern Europe and the dramatic changes that took place in socialist countries 30 years ago. One of the painful lessons I have learned is that these parties and states failed to find good solutions in line with their national traditions, habits and characteristics. We should realize that there are no common rules and standards for socialist development. The communist party and the workers' party have no common ideological and political program; instead, they are characterized by a wide range of ideological and political diversities. All countries and parties should decide their development paths and methods in light of their own national characteristics. Copying the model of other countries will lead nowhere. All countries should go their own way and find the best solution to national development. What Socialism with Chinese Characteristics for a New Era follows is just such a path of development.

The practice of Socialism with Chinese Characteristics for a New Era also indicates that socialist society should carry out continuous reform to improve and develop the socialist system and enhance the governance capability of the communist party. The communist party should become the leading force for promoting, changing and developing socialism. I have noted that the reform of the Party and state institutions started in China at the beginning of 2018. I believe this plan has achieved the desired results and paved the way for China's future reform and development. The reform has strengthened the leadership of the Communist Party of China. The central government agencies will assume more responsibility for management and coordination and play a leading role in all aspects of work. This is an important outcome of the development of socialism with Chinese characteristics in the new era.

Q: After the drastic changes in Eastern Europe and the disintegration of the Soviet Union, the world socialist movement was at its low ebb. Now, 30 years later, how do you evaluate the current development of the world socialist movement?

China in the New Era

What role does China play in promoting the development of world socialism in the new era?

A: Although the current world socialist movement has not yet bottomed out and is still faced with severe problems, it has not disappeared and people have not forgotten socialism. Capitalism is facing more and more problems. For example, Europe cannot solve the problem of mass migration, liberal forces want to replace developing countries with a global "melting pot", and climate change issue cannot be solved because of the obstruction from big capitalists and so on. The crisis of capitalism is far from over. The workers and other laboring masses began awakening. They want to have a voice in the future of Europe and the world. They have come to realize that today's capitalism seeks to maintain its rule regardless of any consequences. It is ready to destroy nations and human environment and to wage a devastating war. With more and more personal experience of modern capitalism, people are beginning to understand that they need another world in which there is more to people than just money. The next generation of people will see the revival of world socialism.

At the same time, China's development has clearly proved that socialism cannot succeed without sound planning and hard work. Xi Jinping Thought on Socialism with Chinese Characteristics for a New Era is a comprehensive plan, a strategy for building a modern society in an all-round way. Its realization needs constant study and arduous efforts. The achievements of socialism with Chinese characteristics in the new era have also proved that modern states will not disappear but will go through a process of national rejuvenation. This is both the goal of socialism with Chinese characteristics for a new era and the primary message it transmits to the people of the rest of the world. Socialism with Chinese characteristics inspires the working people around the world to continue to struggle for socialism. Socialism with Chinese characteristics for a new era has set an inspiring example for socialism in the 21st century.

The success and strong vitality of socialism with Chinese characteristics have shown to the world that capitalism is not the only choice for the future development of mankind. Socialism is not a dying theory, but a living reality. It is the only realistic concept that can overcome existing dangers and threats and open up a true vision of human life and progress. We should attach importance to the significance of China's great achievements to the former socialist countries in Eastern Europe, because large-scale anti-socialist propaganda is now prevalent in these countries. Every real, imagined or fabricated mistake of socialism in the past is regarded as a mistake of the system itself. It seems to some people that socialism is only a curse in the past that did not play a positive part but a historical cul-de-sac, and capitalism is the only social system that will work successfully. However, with the rapid development of socialism with Chinese characteristics in the new era, socialism is increasingly exerting great influence, which will surely bring profound changes to the positive dissemination of socialist ideas.

Happily, communism and workers' movement still exist. At present, in about 100 countries in the world, more than 130 political parties either use the name of the communist party or are Marxist political parties in nature, of which 80 to 100 participate in regular international conferences of communist parties and workers' parties. The CPC is a member of the working group of the international conference of communist parties and workers' parties. There are extensive debates in the international communist movement about the nature of socialism, the lessons of socialism in Eastern Europe and the ways to overcome capitalist exploitation. The current international movement is characterized by ideological and political diversity. It's no exaggeration to say that socialism with Chinese characteristics has restored confidence in socialism among the people of the world. Although there is much discussion about socialism with Chinese characteristics in the current international communist movement, no one can deny the real success of China. More and more political forces believe that China can become the mainstay of the world's socialist revival because of its experience.

IV. Reasons for the external difficulties which China faces during its rise

Q: Could you please share your views on the external environment facing the rise of China? For a long time, some politicians and media in the West have been fighting China head to head. Especially in recent years, with the rapid rise of China's comprehensive national strength and international status, various accusations, criticism and censure from the West have been constantly heard. In your opinion, what causes this situation?

A: In my opinion, the main reason why Western politicians and media criticize China is that socialism with Chinese characteristics has become a realistic alternative to the Western liberal model of social and political development. Western liberal model has eliminated the distinction between countries while socialism with Chinese characteristics has strengthened it. Western liberalism has destroyed classical and traditional morality and cultural values, opening the way for non-traditional forms of sex, drug abuse and fascist worship. On the contrary, socialism with Chinese characteristics has strengthened traditional values and is able to cope with the new challenges that are constantly emerging.

The Western world has always regarded China as one of its biggest challenges. China has developed into the world's second largest economy, which does not make the Western world feel surprised because it can foresee this. But what they have not anticipated is that China is able to surpass the West in the field of communication technology. Huawei's success, especially China's success in 5G technology, is considered by the West as a nightmare. At the same time, the Trump administration's policy toward China has clearly done nothing to deter China. China continues to defend its interests and rights in the South China Sea. It has not made any major concessions in the trade war started by the United States, and continues to promote the Belt and Road Initiative. The West simply cannot force China to accept the liberal model. China has successfully resisted all attacks on its policies concerning human rights, governance, Xinjiang and Tibet.

Moreover, the concept of socialism with Chinese characteristics has become a realistic alternative to the Western liberal model of social and political development, which is clearly seen by liberal forces around the world. Some time ago, George Soros repeated in the *New York Times* what he had said earlier in Davos, he thought China poses the most serious threat to the open community, "We hope that the Americans concerned will correct their attitude," he added. At the same time, Western politicians and media have actually noticed that the Chinese experience is an attractive option for many people. Direct confrontation with China is more detrimental to the West's competition with China, so they are changing their tactics. They have taken the measure of direct intervention in the issues related to Hong Kong which are China's internal affairs. It should be noted that the Western media now talk less about the danger of China than about the ability of the US to defeat China. Their aim is to ensure that the United States can compete with China. As a result of China's proposed global role and Belt and Road Initiative, Western politicians and media have begun to seek co-operation with the countries that have accepted BRI so as to "strengthen their ability to negotiate favorable terms for investment in China". These media have great influence, especially among liberal intellectuals.

V. Interaction of Hungary-China Relations and the Further Strengthening of Relations between the Two Parties

Q: On October 6, 1949, shortly after the founding of the People's Republic of China, Hungary established diplomatic relations with China. According to what you know, how do the Hungarian people view China's development? How do you look at Hungary's relations with China?

A: Hungary is one of the first countries that established diplomatic relations with new China in 1949. However, Hungarians, like many Europeans, know little about China.

In the more than 70 years of exchanges between Hungary and China, there have always been exchanges between the two countries in socialism. History shows that positive exchanges are beneficial to the development of socialism. However, when that interaction was interrupted by external factors or erroneous decisions, people in both countries were denied the opportunity to take advantage of each other's experience.

During the first decade in the development of socialism, Hungary and China began exchanging delegations. Statesmen, economists and intellectuals were all likely to witness the development of China and Chinese socialism with their own eyes. In 1953, the first Chinese Film Festival was held in Hungary. In 1956, Zhu De, vice president of the People's Republic of China, visited Hungary. From 1956 to 1958, China played an important role in defending Hungary's socialist cause. Zhou Enlai's visit to Hungary was a great event in the development of Hungary-China relations. Unfortunately, due to the pressure imposed by Soviet leaders, the development of Hungary-China relations came to a sudden halt in the 1960s. Like most socialist countries in Europe, Hungary followed the decision of the 20th Congress of the Communist Party of the Soviet Union (CPSU). History proved that the line of the 20th Congress of the CPSU was wrong which resulted in more mistakes.

Since then, Hungary-China relationship has been frozen for almost 20 years. During this period, Hungary was completely cut off from China, and no books, films or newspapers were introduced from China. Mao Zedong's works were last published in Hungary in 1956, and only a few leaders had access to materials from the congresses of the Communist Party of China or to the works of Chinese leaders. But even during this period, interest of experts and the general public in China did not disappear. The Hungarian people always appreciate the learning and working capabilities of the Chinese people. When it comes to Chinese people, it always brings to mind innovation, diligence, hard work and self-discipline.

In 1968, the New Economic Mechanism (NEM) was launched in Hungary, which had some similarities with China's reform and opening up policy initiated in 1978. This provided new opportunities for the interaction between the intellectual communities of the two countries. In spite of this, since the Hungarian Socialist Workers' Party followed the line of the CPSU in all matters concerning China, it was unlikely for the two parties to have close contact in the realm of ideology.

After the 1970s, Hungary-China relation was full of twists and turns. At first, the relation between the two countries showed a good momentum of development, with more and more delegations exchanging visits. János Kádár (1912-1989), leader of the Hungarian Socialist Workers' Party, visited China and met Deng Xiaoping in 1987. This was a historic meeting, during which, Kádár stressed that China was more than an economic superpower and that socialism with Chinese characteristics had the potential to contribute to the rejuvenation of world socialism. At that time, European socialism was in the last years of its history. Kádár hoped to draw on the experience of Chinese socialism to provide important arguments for those who want to defend Hungarian socialism. However, Kádár was replaced in 1988. The new leadership announced that socialist reform was out of the question, and the party leadership began to move toward the path of the transition to capitalism. In 1989, the Hungarian government's political line towards China suddenly changed and Hungary joined the anti-China camp dominated by the West. Before long, however, the situation was reversed. In 1990, Hungary-China relationship was normalized and economic ties were quickly established. After 2010, the two countries began a new era of cooperation, with Viktor Orban's government announcing a policy of "opening up to the East". This new political line blazed a path not only for economic relations, but also for cultural, scientific and human relations. Hungary's ruling Fidesz Party has also established official ties with the CPC.

Hungary is the first European country to sign the "Belt and Road" cooperation agreement with China, which chimes in with Hungary's policy of "opening up to the East" and is in accord with the general trend of China-EU cooperation and conducive to promoting the connectivity between Europe and Asia. Hungary is willing to maintain closer high-level exchanges with China, expand cooperation in the fields of trade, investment, finance and education, keep close coordination and cooperation in multilateral affairs and promote a new development in bilateral relations.

In my opinion, all these changes have helped Hungarians to better understand China. Now, the public in Hungary, including the younger generation, has begun to focus on China with great interest. For example, the Hungarian-Chinese bilingual primary school was established in Budapest in 2004 and has become so popular in Hungary that it now has more Hungarian students than Chinese students. Business and cultural ties between the two countries are an important reason why the school becomes increasingly popular. More and more Hungarians have decided to learn Chinese. Now, the number of the Chinese in Hungary is between 100,000 and 200,000. Since 2012, Orban's government has been selling government bonds worth about 250,000 euros (now about 300,000 euros), which, in effect, provided residence permits for Chinese investors. So far, about 2,000 Chinese citizens have bought the bonds.

Q: Against the backdrop of the new development in China-Hungary relations, how does the Hungarian Workers' Party understand its relations with the CPC?

A: The Hungarian workers' Party has a good desire to carry out in-depth cooperation with the Communist Party of China and Chinese scientific research institutions and publicize Socialism with Chinese Characteristics for a New Era in Hungary, which has provided new impetus for the new development of bilateral relations in the contemporary context. The Hungarian Workers' Party attaches great importance to the study of socialism with Chinese characteristics. In the history of the Hungarian workers' movement, it is the first time that the works of Mao Zedong and Deng Xiaoping have been translated and edited as part of the political education of the Workers' Party. It is also the first time that some of Deng Xiaoping's articles have been translated and published in Hungarian by the Workers' Party. The

Hungarian workers' Party has been deeply analyzing and timely informing its members of the theory and practice of socialism with Chinese characteristics. It has carried out a large number of activities such as commemorating the 100th birthday of Deng Xiaoping, the 120th birthday of Mao Zedong and the 40th anniversary of the reform and opening up. Now, let me call on communists around the world to firmly stand on the side with the CPC in the struggle against endangering the socialist system, undermining China's sovereignty and security, and hindering the realization of the two centenary goals and the Chinese dream of great rejuvenation of the Chinese nation.

China Is a Successful Socialist Country in the World
– An Interview with Toma Ioan, Secretary of the Central Committee of the Former Romanian Communist Youth League

Interviewed by Lei Xiaohuan[1]
Translated by Xie Shengzhe
Finalized by Wang Qiuhai

Toma Ioan

Toma Ioan was born in January, 1954 in Victoria, Lasi in Romania.

On the eve of the drastic changes in the Socialist Republic of Romania, Toma Loan was a senior leader in the Communist Party of Romania. He served as a member of the Central Committee of the Communist Party of Romania, an alternate member of the Central Political Executive Committee, first secretary of the Central Committee of the Communist Youth League and director of the Department of Youth Affairs under the Youth League.

When Toma was young, he studied at the Department of Law of the University of Iasi in Romania and got his degree in 1981. He pursued advanced studies

---

1   Lei Xiaohuan, assistant research fellow of the Academy of Marxism, Chinese Academy of Social Sciences.

and graduated from the Department of Political Economy at the University of Bucharest, Romania, in 1986. As a college student, he threw himself into the socialist development in Romania. From 1972 to 1979, Toma worked at a synthetic fiber plant in Iasi. From 1979 to 1985, he worked in Iasi County Committee of the Romanian Communist Youth League, successively serving as director of Publicity Department, secretary and first secretary of County Committee of the Romanian Youth League. From 1985 to 1987, Toma served as secretary of Central Committee of the Romanian Youth League. From 1987 to 1989, he assumed posts such as member of the Central Committee of the Communist Party of Romania and alternate member of the Central Political Executive Committee, first secretary of the Central Committee of the Communist Youth League and director of Department of Youth Affairs of the Youth League. From 1985 to 1989, Toma was elected member of the Grand National Assembly.

But Toma's career did not go on without a hitch. In December 1989, dramatic changes took place in Romania when the National Liberation Front was reorganized into the Interim Governing Council, and the country was simply renamed "Romania". At the same time, Romania's political system also underwent fundamental changes, namely, from the former one-party system to a multi-party system. Thoma's work and life experienced radical changes due to the drastic changes. Many senior Communist Party officials were arrested, brought to trial and sentenced. Toma was not spared either. He was sentenced to 14 years in prison. After serving three years in jail, he was released ahead of time. Then Toma was engaged in the liquidation of insolvent enterprises and worked as a legal adviser. From 1994 to 1998, Toma served as a legal advisor and director of the Legal Division of the Institute of Aeronautical Materials in Bucharest. From 1998 to 2007 he held the post of secretary of the Board of Directors of the Business Company under Romanian Aeronautical Institute. Since 2007, Toma has been the legal adviser and director of the Legal Division of the Romanian Institute of Aerospace Research and Development. In 2008, he obtained a master's degree in business law from the

China in the New Era

University of Titulescu in Bucharest, Romania. Since 2010, Toma has served as member of the Executive Board of Chamber of Commerce and Industry of Romania (CCIR). As a senior leader of the Communist Party and state during the Socialist Republic of Romania, Toma experienced the coup in Romania and the upheaval in Eastern Europe. From a politician to an ordinary citizen, this change of status made Toma have a deep understanding and reflection of the history and socialism. He also has his own understanding of the development of socialism in China.

Interview Summary

According to Ioan Toma, Romania learned a painful lesson from the drastic changes in Eastern Europe and the disintegration of the Soviet Union. After these changes, Romania suffered great losses in terms of economy and human resources, as well as fundamental changes in social life accompanied by pains and division. And the resultant destruction was no less than experiencing a war. Toma praised China as a successful socialist country in the world. China's economic, political, cultural and social practices have proved that China has made great achievements in socialist development. Nowadays, only China is entitled to talk about the future of socialism. China is and will be a major power in the world. The achievements and development of socialism with Chinese characteristics have an important impact on the international social order. The practice of socialism with Chinese characteristics has enriched the experience of world socialism and made significant contributions to the development of world socialism. As far as the world is concerned, socialism with Chinese characteristics has a brought good remedy to it, and China can serve as a model for other countries to learn from.

As a senior leader of the party and state during the period of the Romanian Socialist Republic, Toma witnessed the dramatic changes in Eastern Europe. He has done in-depth thinking on the socialism with Chinese characteristics and the world socialism from a unique perspective, which deserves our attention. Scholars from the Academy of Marxism under Chinese Academy of Social Sciences interviewed Toma on August 25, 2019, and asked him to share his views and feelings on the history of the dramatic changes in Romania and his understanding of Socialism with Chinese Characteristics for a New Era.

I. The development of Romania before and after the drastic changes in Eastern Europe

Q: Nice to meet you, Mr. Toma! I am very glad that you can accept my interview. 2019 marks the 30th anniversary of the profound changes in Eastern Europe, which is an important event in the history of the development of socialism. As a senior official of the Socialist Republic of Romania, how do you evaluate the development and changes in Romania in the past 30 years since the drastic changes?

A: Glad to meet you. In 1989, drastic social changes took place in Romania, and in the political system in Romania. The sudden upheaval has brought great changes to personal lives and the whole society.

Before the drastic social changes in Romania in 1989, Romanian socialism had been developing continuously and made some achievements in socialist development under the guidance of Marxist theory. Especially in the 1970s and 1980s, Romania received high praise for its development. Known as the "granary of Europe", Romania made tremendous achievements in national industrialization, agricultural modernization, educational development, health care, scientific and technological research and culture. In international relations, Romania always pursued an independent policy. At that time, we carried out a creative and forward-looking foreign policy, and Romanian diplomats were highly professional and experts in dialogues and negotiations on many sensitive issues in the contemporary world, such as the eradication of poverty and illiteracy, total disarmament, establishment of a new international economic order, peaceful settlement of tensions and conflicts through negotiations, normalization of relations between the world powers, and support for the developing countries which are called the "third world". The friendship as well as the lasting cooperation with China in various fields is the top priority of all Romania's international activities. By the end of March 1989, our country had paid off all its international debts which were mainly used to realize the broad development of the national economy, especially in industry, transport, scientific research, education and health service.

The drastic social change that Romania experienced in 1989 led to the social division that has not yet been repaired. It was a tragic upheaval that took a heavy toll on the economy and human resources. The destruction it caused was no less than experiencing a war. After the drastic change in Romania, fundamental changes took place in the country's economic, political and social life accompanied by pain and disruption. Firstly, people lived in extreme poverty. For some Romanians, the door to get rich quickly has been opened by crazy economic plunder. However, due to the continuous increase of living cost caused by the high price of basic products (mainly food, social services and public facilities), many families had to withstand harsh living predicament. As a result, poverty was aggravated with each passing day. Secondly, the Romanian economy was severely damaged by the massive loss of state assets. In a short period of time, more than 1, 000 state-owned enterprises in Romania disappeared because they were sold off at cheap prices. Consequently, the number of jobs across the country has been greatly reduced. Thirdly, there was a serious brain drain in Romania, which caused many social problems. After the social upheaval, Romania's domestic economy was relatively in depression. The transition period resulted in the collapse of most industrial and agricultural enterprises, leading to a surge in unemployment, particularly among the youth. Unable to earn money at home, many people chose to work abroad. As a result, a large number of laboring people flew abroad. According to data, Romania has about 4 million people working abroad, second only to Syria. At present, Romania is one of the countries with the largest numbers of people working in other countries. With the loss of labor force, countless families have disintegrated, and there are a large number of left behind children. At the same time, problems of organized crimes, corruption and environmental pollution have also emerged one after another. Fourthly, the Romanian people were deeply traumatized. They rejected and refused socialism. Material poverty exerted a further negative impact on the mentality of the Romanians. They are suffering psychologically. On the one hand, the social values and norms in the past have not been eliminated. On the other hand, new excessively high expectations and unattainable assumptions have emerged. This situation has intensified the tense situation within society. The mass uprising in December 1989 led to radical changes in the political system and left many unanswered questions. Until now, the criminal investigation files about the events of December 1989 and June 1990 have not been fully declassified, nor have we clarified how to restore the normal state of society, or uncovered the mystery of those tragic days that enveloped the whole country from the perspective of collective psychology. As a result, people refused to talk about socialism for a long time after the social upheaval. Many even believe that Romania's tragedy was caused by socialism and that there would not have been such problems if Romania had adopted a different social system.

After the drastic changes, many theorists and thinkers in the former Party found it difficult to accept Romania's retreat from socialism to capitalism. There is a view that Romania's current capitalism is primitive and barbaric. Although we have joined the EU and NATO, our sovereignty and interests are limited and our capitalist development is dictated by the European Parliament, the European Commission and the US.

II. Reasons for drastic social changes in Romania

Q: Thank you very much! Your feelings and views on Romania before and after the social upheaval are very helpful to us. So, in your opinion, what are the reasons for the drastic changes in Romanian society?

A: In my opinion, the reasons for the social upheaval in Romania are complex with various factors intertwined, which can be summarized as follows. First, foreign intervention was the external cause of the drastic change in Romania. The dramatic change in Romania was premeditated. Instead of happening overnight, it occurred under the instigation of outside forces and the influence of powerful forces. Before the upheaval in Romania, the whole Europe was in the economic crisis of the 1980s which was also keenly felt by socialist countries. Against the background of the economic crisis, the Communist Party of Soviet Union changed its leadership and proposed to carry out the socialist reform, which had an important impact on Europe and the world at large. At that time, countries with close relations with the Soviet Union also followed suit. As for Romania, after the 9th Congress of the Romanian Communist Party, especially after Nicolae Ceausescu (1918-1989) assumed the supreme leadership, it pursued an independent policy which led to strained relations between Romania and the Soviet Union, both overtly and covertly. In addition, the West also participated in fermenting the upheaval. The West had always been plotting to overthrow the rule of Ceausescu. Just to take a simple example, in 1986 and 1987, Ceausescu intended to take measures to improve the life of farmers, such as building beautiful streets and buildings and re-planning the country's rural area. Therefore, he proposed a national rural construction program. Shortly after Ceausescu delivered the related speech, some European countries and the United States vilified Ceausescu, accusing him of destroying the Romanian countryside and traditions by restricting farmers' freedom and impeding their contact with the outside world.

Secondly, from a domestic perspective, Romania did not form a socialist development model suitable to its national conditions. After the World War II, the Soviet-style socialism was rapidly carried out in Romania. By the end of 1989, the situation in Romania had become very complicated. Some people wanted a rapid transition to the standard of western democracy. However, in the complicated process, people realized that there was a need to give a long-term and gradual guidance to the people who had lived for many years under the "proletarian dictatorship", which was originally marked by the Soviet model, and then by the worship of the country's leaders. The Soviet model did not fit in with the national conditions and reality of Romania at all. In such a rapid change, many problems were bound to arise, which affected the stability of the regime. Moreover, under the influence of the Soviet model, many measures adopted in Romania were detrimental to the country's long-term development. The military, political, economic, diplomatic and cultural measures decided and supported by the Soviet Union have caused serious damage to Romanian people's lives, which they have not recovered so far. I can think of, for example, the unjustified nationalization of all means of production, which simply stressed the nationalization of everything without considering differences. In those days, the important intellectual class and political elites in Romania were eliminated. The agriculture was excessively collectivized. In other words, Romanians were forced to separate themselves from their faith, property and tradition.

Thirdly, for the purpose of coping with the economic crisis, the life of the Romanian people was sacrificed and their interests were neglected. In the 1970s and 1980s, Romania applied for loans from the International Monetary Fund (IMF) and the World Bank (WB) to develop its industrialization, but later, the country had trouble repaying her debts. The IMF and the WB began to intervene in the internal affairs of Romania, forcing the country to revise its economic decisions according to their suggestions in an attempt to change the indicators and data of Romania's economic development, which was hard for Ceausescu to accept. Because the policy of Ceausescu and the Central Committee of the Communist Party of Romania was consistent, that is, completely using their own policies to guide the country's economic construction, and rejecting all foreign policies, negotiations between Romania and the IMF broke down. This prompted Ceausescu to take the sudden step of paying off the debts at short notice. However, after the debts were paid off, Ceausescu borrowed a large sum of foreign debts from international organizations, which stood at US$10 billion to US$12 billion. He promised to pay back the debts within eight years. Ceausescu's decision took no account of the interests and life of the broad masses of the people. The measures such as maintaining a high level of development funds, limiting consumption funds, and paying off foreign debts in a short period of time triggered discontent from some people in Romania. In the eyes of the public, these measures ignored the minimum material conditions that were needed by individuals and families to achieve development. That is why after the uprising in December 1989, the leadership of the Communist Party of Romania was overthrown. Free elections were organized, resulting in the separation of legislative, executive and judicial powers. A new Romania constitution was drawn up. The principles and standards for the market economy were laid down. The agricultural structure was adjusted and support was provided to the small-scale peasant economy. The ideology and doctrines of the former regime were replaced by the values of Western society such as freedom of speech, freedom of association and freedom of immigration.

In addition, the Party's personality cult, which began in the 1970s, was also a big reason for the dramatic change. After 1974, Ceausescu's wife was elected into the Political Bureau of the Central Committee, and the Party's leadership became a "mom and pop shop" in effect. Another point is that the central leadership of the Party was unwilling to engage in dialogue with the people. The lack of dialogue inside and outside the party, cold weather, inadequate food supplies and a failure to listen to the voices of the people created widespread fear and discontent within the Party. At the same time, the general public also harbored doubts about socialism's ability to solve the difficulties of the common people. That was why people rose in revolt. In this way, they expressed their dissatisfaction first with Ceausescu, then with the Romanian Communist Party and its guiding ideology.

III. China is a successful socialist country in the world

Q: Thank you for your answer. Now, please talk about your views on China's socialist development.

A: Please allow me to answer your questions all at once. I have noticed many developmental tendencies in China, such as the remarkable growth of the economy (industry, agriculture, transport, energy, and tourism) and science and technology, making full use of the potential for creativity and innovation that dates back to several thousand years ago, advocating serious and effective work, strengthening the cultivation of the younger generation (education, health care and culture), taking an open-minded attitude to all new things on a global scale (high technology/Internet technology, medicine, ecology, outer space exploration, etc.), especially through being amazingly open to the world and Europe. Moreover, Hong Kong and Macao, after returning to China, gradually adapted to the motherland's social politics and way of thinking. Other changes are promoting sensible and realistic patriotism, a firm and transparent foreign policy aimed at facilitating peace and mutual understanding among peoples, and so on.

There is no doubt that in terms of what China has achieved today, the reality of China has been manifested by many practices in economic, social and political life.

I must say frankly that I am very much looking forward to visiting your beautiful country with my family soon. Before 1990, I had a chance to stop over in China for a few hours on my way to take part in some international youth activities.

Q: In your view, why has China made so many achievements?

A: In my view, institutionally, China attaches great importance to correcting past mistakes and long-standing inaction in some sectors, as well as to overall and long-term planning. China pays attention to a holistic and long-term planning and the formulation of an overall plan in economic, social, demographic, educational, cultural and spiritual fields, through which people can see what should be valued and clarified in the development of the country.

It is praiseworthy that the key to China's great achievements lies in the fact that the Chinese government and President Xi Jinping are most concerned about continuously improving the living standards of the people in the world's most populous country.

China has succeeded in combining a truly dynamic domestic policy with a pragmatic and proactive foreign policy. This diplomacy is characterized by the resumption of effective cooperation with traditional partners of the former socialist countries, while making new partners, including those from the Western countries and regions, and overcoming – often the Chinese side taking the initiative-the problems of inopportune constraints as well as the problems caused by political and ideological differences.

Today, we see many businessmen, bankers, investors, university teachers, researchers, experts of diplomacy and international relations, students and tourists from various provinces of China visiting Western, Central and Eastern Europe, the Middle East, Africa, North America (especially the United States and Canada), Latin America and other countries and regions.

In my view, many Western countries have responded in a broad and constructive way to the proposals and concrete activities for mutual exchanges in the aforementioned areas in a new language of dialogue, mutual respect and understanding. The Chinese are welcome. Personally, I am optimistic about this trend. I believe that, fundamentally, it helps to promote the normalization of relations between countries at all levels.

Q: According to your understanding, what impact will the achievements of China as a socialist country have on the international order?

A: In my opinion, China is and will be a major power in the world. As we all know, with a population of about 1.4 billion, China has a huge potential in population. That figure itself represents the basic requirement for human resources, which are needed in many sectors of social activity, above all in productive sectors such as industry, agriculture and energy. As I mentioned above, Chinese society as a whole has always attached great importance to cultivating the younger generation, and your young people studying in other economically developed countries are living proof of this.

China also has great potential for sustained growth in economy, finance, commerce and tourism. The results of scientific and technological research will benefit all sectors of China's economic and social activities. By the same token, no one can underestimate China's military potential, including military research and production of military equipment. Let's not forget the historical fact that gunpowder was first invented by the ancient Chinese and later widely spread and used all over the world. In this context, it is important to emphasize that China's new inventions and facilities in this field are solely for defensive purposes, because China hopes, at any time, to be able to protect her people, territory and all the great achievements made during the reform era.

At the same time, I would like to emphasize one thing that has a global significance: China has been a permanent member of the UN Security Council since its inception. In the end of World War II, as a victorious nation, China joined four other major powers – the United States, Britain, the Soviet Union and France – as a permanent veto-exercising member of the Security Council. On the strength of this position, China has the ability to influence or block any decision related to some of the major issues in the contemporary world.

IV. The significance of socialism with Chinese characteristics to the world socialism

Q: As you said just now, China has made great achievements in socialist development and is exerting a positive influence on the international social order. So, how do you view Xi Jinping Thought on Socialism with Chinese Characteristics for a New Era and its world significance and international influence?

A: China is building socialism in accordance with its own national characteristics, which is followed by the international community with interest. China sets objectives and tasks with precise timetables step by step, and attaches great importance to identifying ways and means of achieving each objective and task. While setting priority objectives, China does not neglect other objectives. These goals will depend on available resources and will be achieved gradually in the future.

Through his own practices and conviction, Xi Jinping has become a national leader respected by various countries around the world, which has greatly contributed to the continuous improvement of China's regional and global reputation. I would like to take this opportunity to pay my sincere tribute to Xi Jinping, leader of the Chinese people.

The intensive development of China's economy is impressive. As far as economic achievements are concerned, China has placed itself in the first echelon in the world. At the same time, China's investment at home and abroad attracts people's attention with its scale, quality and undisputed demand.

Many strong evidences indicate that the "Chinese miracle" is not just a sheer platitude or a polite metaphor. Its full meaning can be found in the dynamic reality, in many completed plans, and in the achievements that reflect China's widespread prosperity.

All of us have seen the occurrence of this miracle, and it is not just an imaginary one. Its source can be found anytime and anywhere in finance, commerce, culture, tourism, in modern infrastructure such as roads, railways, aviation, river transport and maritime transport, in health facilities, in education at all levels, in science and technology, in the creativity and innovation of the Chinese people and even in distant human civilization. It can be verified in daily achievements.

It can be said that the ingenuity of the Chinese people – reflected in the outstanding works of the great inventors, thinkers and writers in ancient times as well as in great projects like the Great Wall – has now been brought into full play, impressing the whole world with its vast scale of future-oriented openness and unique modernity. To all these domestic achievements should be added significant achievements in the field of Chinese foreign policy, which I will talk about later.

To be fair, the topic of the "Chinese Miracle" often appears in the study of forecasting the future and in the analysis and writings of experts in political philosophy, sociology, demography, economics, banking, national defense strategy, and so on. At the same time, important issues related to China often appear in various important activities in academia, universities, cultural circles and political organizations on all continents in the world.

Q: What do you think it means for China to hold high the banner of socialism in the world? What role will China play in the world socialist movement?

A: I think that China's widespread prosperity, which is reflected in its achievements in various fields such as economy, society and political life, will become a very attractive and inspiring example to some regions in the world.

In my view, some regions outside China can draw on the reality and development prospects of China as their action guidelines. These regions see and believe that the construction of socialism with Chinese characteristics is a process characterized by continuous progress.

Of course, this is not a question of the relation with some theoretical assessments or evaluations, but a question of the relation with the practical and credible reality based on concrete facts and the unique Chinese way of work and life. No one can deny that some principles accumulated in consistent experience can provide justification for subsequent viewpoints of principled and absolute value. Some countries in Asia or other continents that are interested in this can apply them creatively according to their own specific circumstances.

Q: So, in your opinion, 30 years after the drastic changes in Eastern Europe, has world socialism come out of recession?

A: Based on persuasive logic and factual arguments, I don't think anyone today, except China, can talk about socialism coming out of recession. What really reminds us of the "miracle" is the fact that while the political systems of the socialist countries in Eastern Europe and the Soviet Union collapsed, China's socialism developed by leaps and bounds and, with its amazing strength, raised itself to a height that shocked the whole world.

V. How to view China-Romania relations and China's international image

Q: The year 2019 marks the 70th anniversary of the founding of the People's Republic of China and the establishment of diplomatic ties between China and Romania. How do the Romanian people see China's development? How do you view the relationship between China and Romania?

A: As you may know, just 30 years after the overthrow of the former regime, the influence of the socialist movement in Romania, especially among the younger generation, has obviously regressed in concept and attitude. Now young people are even ignorant of the Communist Party and socialism. At the same time, it should be pointed out that the socialist movement in the past 30 years is completely different from any old socialist dogma that existed in the past two centuries but declined in the 1990s.

The great interest of the Romanian people in learning about the current changes in China embodies the normal continuation of the time-honored tradition of friendship and bilateral cooperation. Romanian people's feelings towards China have not changed since 1989, and the two countries remain friends all the same. The relationship between the two countries has not turned into a hostile one, and the former friendly relationship has remained. In my opinion, the relations between countries in the future should not be established through political doctrines and theories, or based on ideology, but should be mutually beneficial. Only in this way can the relations be developed better. Like a doctor, China offers prescriptions of the governance for other countries. No matter where the medicine comes from, it works if it can solve the problem. Therefore, it is not necessary to use social system to determine whether a relationship is friendly or not. The future development of relations between Romania and China should be based on mutual cooperation and mutual benefit.

In my capacity as first secretary of the Communist Youth League and director of Division of Youth Affairs, I always devoted myself to promoting exchanges among young people, students and children in the last few years of the 1980s. At the same time, over the years, bilateral cooperation has developed well in the international organizations joined by our two countries.

In terms of cooperation, China and Romania have carried out a large number of activities in governmental affairs, academic exchanges, tourism, art, literature, military, science, diplomacy and journalism. Contacts and exchanges between delegations at the local level, including town halls, rural administrative departments, district and municipal councils, secondary schools, colleges, museums, cultural centers, folk troupes, symphony orchestras, publishing companies, libraries, news organizations and so forth, have also been developed. More and more Romanians have started to learn Chinese as a way to know the life of the great Chinese people. I am absolutely confident that the relationship between our two countries and peoples will become even stronger and new effective and interesting ways of dialogue and interaction will be put forward.

Q: For a long time, the Western media have been used to viewing China with colored glasses. In your opinion, why do the Western media have preconceived notions about socialism in China?

A: In my opinion, the viewpoint of socialism in China, which is widely disseminated by the Western mass media, is an obviously universal preconception which is based on the assumption that after the drastic changes in Eastern Europe and the collapse of the Soviet Union, the world socialist movement has fallen into a low ebb. In the eyes of the overwhelming majority of such mass media, China's socialist path is a dead end.

Undoubtedly, in my opinion, any preconceptions can be dispelled by presenting specific facts about China to people in various countries. I believe the Chinese media has the ability to dispel these preconceptions, as I have seen in other parts of the world I have visited in recent years.

Q: 2019 marks the 70th anniversary of the founding of the People's Republic of China. What are your suggestions for China's future development?

A: It seems to me that instead of offering a proposal that could provide predictions and an action plan for Chinese politics, I have a friendly wish: May the great Chinese people make more and more achievements, enjoy prosperity and live in happiness.

I would like to assure you that we Romanians congratulate from the bottom of our hearts the 70th anniversary of the founding of the People's Republic of China and wish our two countries to maintain long-term friendly relations and cooperation.

The celebration of China's National Day is not only an opportunity to publicize heroic deeds and evaluate great achievements, but also an opportunity to design an ambitious road for the progress of the country and the future happiness of the people. It is also an opportunity to turn dreams and ideas into reality through dedicated work.

Thank you very much for giving me this opportunity to express my views and feelings in this interview.

Ukraine and Other Countries Should Learn from China's Experience
– An Interview with Petro Symonenko, First Secretary of the Central Committee of the Communist Party of Ukraine

Interviewed by Kang Yanru[1]

Translated by Xie Shengzhe

Finalized by Wang Qiuhai

Petro Symonenko

Petro Symonenko was born in 1952 in Donetsk, Soviet Union (now Ukraine). In 1974, Symonenko graduated from the Donetsk Polytechnic Institute and got a degree in electrical engineering. After that, he worked as a designer at the Donetsk Design Institute for a year. From 1975, Symonenko worked at the Donetsk Municipal Committee of the Komsomol of Ukraine (Leninist Communist League of Youth of Ukraine) as instructor, director and second secretary. In 1978, he joined the Communist Party of Ukraine and started to work at the Secretariat of the Donetsk Municipal Committee of the Komsomol in 1980. In 1982, he was elected the secretary of the Donetsk Central Committee of the Komsomol.

Since 1988, Symonenko's career has been linked with the work of the

---

1   Kang Yanru, assistant research fellow of the Academy of Marxism, Chinese Academy of Social Sciences.

Party more than once. He successively served as secretary of the Mariupol Municipal Committee of the Communist Party of Ukraine, secretary in charge of ideological work of Donetsk Prefectural Committee of the Communist Party of Ukraine and second secretary of the prefectural Party committee. In 1991, Symonenko completed his studies at Kiev Institute of Political Science and Social Administration by correspondence, obtaining a degree in political science. After 1991 when the Communist Party of Ukraine was banned, Symonenko worked as an vice manager at Ukruglemash (Укруглемаш) company. Following the failure of the action taken by the National Emergency Council in the Verkhovna Rada of Ukraine (the national parliament), the Verkhovna Rada adopted a resolution to depoliticize state institutions on August 4, 1991. The next day, the Presidium of the Verkhovna Rada passed a resolution to nationalize the property of the Communist Party of the Soviet Union and the Communist Party of Ukraine. A day later, the activities of the Communist Party of Ukraine were suspended. Four days later, such activities were completely banned.

From October 1992 onward, Symonenko was at the helm of an informal initiative group – the Preparatory Committee for the All – Ukraine Communist Party-for the revival of the Ukrainian Communist Party. In 1993, local Party organizations were re-established. Symonenko headed the Party organization of the state of Donetsk. In June 1993, the congress of the All-Ukraine Communist Party was held in Donetsk, which marked the re-establishment of the Ukrainian Communist Party. More than 500 Communist Party representatives from all over the country attended the conference, and Symonenko was elected first secretary of the Communist Party of Ukraine.

In the spring of 1994, as first secretary of the Central Committee of the Communist Party of Ukraine, Symonenko was elected to the Verkhovna Rada via Krasnodar constituency (Donetsk), and 84 parliamentary representatives formed the group of the Communist Party. In the parliamentary election in 1998, Symonenko was elected to the Verkhovna Rada for the second time. The Party won nearly a quarter of the votes, thus having a chance to become the largest parliamentary faction. In 1999, Symonenko was nominated as the Party's presidential candidate and stood second in the first round of the election with about 23 percent of the votes, but lost to Kuchma in the second round. In early 2000, all parliamentary leadership positions were transferred from the group of the Communist Party to the hands of the center-right coalition. In each of the subsequent parliamentary elections, Symonenko was unexceptionally elected to the Verkhovna Rada, but the Communists won fewer and fewer seats. In 2014, the activities of the Communist Party were banned by the authorities. Since then, Symonenko has been devoted to restoring the legitimate rights and position of the Communist Party.

Interview Summary

Symonenko believes that after the collapse of the Soviet Union, Ukraine has been reduced from the second most developed Republic of the Soviet Union to the poorest and backward country in Europe, and the 30 years since the restoration of capitalism in Ukraine is a period of decline and retrogression. The Communist Party of Ukraine speaks highly of socialism with Chinese characteristics and believes that China's success has shown to the world that socialism is not only possible, but also the fairest and most effective social system. In spite of its advanced productive forces and traditional advantages, capitalism cannot solve the acute problems facing contemporary society. The value and significance of Xi Jinping Thought on Socialism with Chinese Characteristics for a New Era not only lie in the fact that it has not only armed the whole Party and the Chinese people with a concrete and scientifically proven program of action, but also opened up broad prospects for the world socialist movement. The vitality of Xi jinping Thought on Socialism with Chinese Characteristics for a New Era has been testified by the Chinese socialist development, and has shown to the world that socialism is not dead and that only by replacing the capitalist system which has run out of its positive potential with socialist society can the acute problems facing the humanity in the new era be solved.

The Ukrainian Communist Party did not cease its activities after the collapse of the Soviet Union. After being banned for a brief period of time, it was re-established in June 1993 with Petro Symonenko as first secretary of the Communist Party of Ukraine. Before 2014, the Communist Party of Ukraine was the only left-wing party to enter the national parliament through the general election in Ukraine, and won a certain number of seats from the second to the seventh national parliament elections. But in the national parliamentary election which was held ahead of time in 2014, the party failed to get 5 percent of the votes to enter the parliament. In 2015, the Verkhovna Rada of Ukraine passed a draft to ban the use of the symbols of Ukrainian communism and Nazism, followed by the passing of three "de-communized" laws, which dealt a heavy blow to Ukrainian communist organizations and political parties. At present, the Communist Party of Ukraine is almost unable to carry out activities in Ukraine. However, under the leadership of Symonenko, the party has never given up its struggle for restoring its legitimate rights and status.

I. The 30 years since the restoration of capitalism have been a time of decline and regression for Ukraine

Q: Glad to meet you, Mr. Petro Symonenko! Nearly 30 years have elapsed since the collapse of the Soviet Union. What do you think of the development of Ukraine after the disintegration of the Soviet Union?

A: In the past nearly three decades after the anti-socialist coup in the 1980s and 1990s, Ukraine has witnessed the tragic consequences of the return of capitalism. Ukraine was once the second most developed republic after the Russian Federation in the Soviet Union, maintaining a leading position in important economic and social indicators. After the collapse of the Soviet Union, Ukraine's gross domestic product failed to exceed the level in 1990 for 25 years and more than half of the population fell into poverty. Workers lost most of the social benefits they had enjoyed in the Soviet era, including job security, free health care and education, old-age security, a happy childhood and a stable life. Today, Ukraine has degenerated into the poorest and most backward country in Europe. Now the country is characterized by low industrialization and rampant corruption. In effect, the country has lost the independence it claimed when it became independent in 1991, and its domestic and foreign policies and even official appointments are dictated by the United States, Europe, the International Monetary Fund and NATO. The "charm" of capitalism has all come back to Ukrainian society in a sickening way – a serious division of wealth (actually class division), exploitation, oligarchy, a people deprived of rights and freedoms.

Q: At present, the legal status of the Communist Party of Ukraine has not been restored in the country. What measures has the Communist Party of Ukraine adopted to safeguard its legal rights?

A: In Europe, Ukraine today is the only country without left-wing representatives in its parliament. Shortly after the counter-revolutionary coup in 1991, the Communist Party was prohibited from carrying out activities in Ukraine. Thanks to the unremitting efforts and tenacious struggle of the Communists, the Constitutional Court of Ukraine finally acknowledged that the ban on the Communist Party was illegal and unconstitutional. However, the regime did not stop cracking down on the Communist Party of Ukraine. As a result of the coup in 2014, the militant nationalist extremists and successors to German fascists during the Second World War period came into power, wantonly trampling on the country's legal system. The regime implemented the harsh policies of neo-Nazism and was fascist in nature. The authorities' crackdown on the Communist Party was so brutal that the group of the Communist Party of Ukraine in the parliament was promptly expelled, the office of the Central Committee of the Communist Party of Ukraine was raided and the party's publications banned. In addition, the party's leaders, staff, ordinary members and even their families were unreasonably accused of "giving assistance to separatism and terrorism" before being imprisoned. Investigations and proceedings continued for many years while innocent people languished in prison. After the coup, the authorities demanded an immediate ban on the Communist Party by way of law and the so-called "ban on the Communist Party", which was obviously unconstitutional, was passed without giving any grounds or court hearing according to the law. The court made a decision to terminate the activities of the Communist Party. On this basis, the authorities effectively banned the communist ideology. In the past two years, the court has been reviewing the appeal lodged by the Communist Party of Ukraine, without putting an end to this absurd process. As a matter of fact, the Communist Party of Ukraine is denied the right given by the country's basic law. Moreover, this right has not been restored in the presidential, parliamentary and local elections. The Venice Commission of the European Council pointed out that the "ban on communism" adopted by Ukraine is not in line with the democratic practice of European countries and undermines the guarantee of the rights and freedoms of citizens in democratic countries. The Ukrainian authorities made a promise to amend the decree, but have not yet taken any action.

Presidential and parliamentary elections were held in Ukraine in 2019, but I don't think that the regime change has altered the situation faced by the communist organizations. In the presidential election, voters overwhelmingly rejected the former pro-Western presidential candidate, the political line of billionaire Poroshenko, and the parties and leaders with this tendency. After choosing politicians who are free from corruption and trusting the political parties they are forming, the Ukrainian people hope to fundamentally change their national policy to end the armed conflicts in the eastern part of the country. However, the wish of the people came to nothing. The new regime, instead of changing the main policies of its predecessor, was completely inclined to protect of the interests of the exploiting classes, follow a pro-Western and anti-Russian line, and continue to suppress the

Communist Party and other progressive forces. The regime has banned by law the newspaper, *Workers*, which is the only newspaper in Ukraine that reflects the lives, problems and needs of the working people. Western countries claim to abide by democratic principles and protect human rights and freedom, but turn a blind eye to flagrant violations of this principle in Ukraine. In European countries including Ukraine, the threat of fascism is growing. Under the aforementioned circumstances, the Communist Party of Ukraine is acting under semi-legitimate conditions and continues to struggle for the realization of social justice, the rule of law, people's genuine political power and socialism.

II. China's experience is worth studying and learning by Ukraine and other countries

Q: In your opinion, what specific achievements have been made in China's socialist development over the past 70 years since the founding of the People's Republic of China? What do you think are the main aspects of China's experience?

A: I sincerely congratulate China on her achievements in socialist development. Today's China has developed from a backward country to one of the most economically developed countries in the world through the path of development and innovation. China has successfully promoted scientific production and advances in science and technology and continued to search for advanced production techniques. China adopts effective local policies that take into account the interests of all parties concerned, pay attention to balanced local development, and improve the economic and living standards of the people in backward provinces. In terms of the issue of national reunification, China has courageously proposed "one country, two systems", solution which combines principle and innovation. China's solution to the issue of poverty that plagues many countries is an earth-shaking success because China has marvelously lifted hundreds of millions of people out of poverty in a remarkably short period of time. With the continuous improvement of its people's

China in the New Era

living standard and benefits, China has successfully cemented her international prestige. The Chinese people have made great contributions to world development, and the emergence and spread of the thought of "a community with a shared future for mankind" has further enhanced its international influence and appeal.

The successful experience of socialism with Chinese characteristics can be summed up in the following aspects. The first is the firm ideal and belief. Since its establishment, the Communist Party of China has taken the realization of communism as its highest ideal and ultimate goal. The Communist Party of China not only believes in and creatively develops Marxism, but also establishes and consolidates the dominant position of Marxism in the field of ideology. The second is to maintain the Party's progressiveness forever. As the vanguard of the times, the Communist Party of China always maintains its own advanced nature, and adheres to the Party's leadership in the process of socialist development. The Party is the backbone and core of the country. The third is that the CPC always puts the national and people's interests first, and constantly creates conditions to ensure national security and people's happiness. The fourth is that the Communist Party of China treats and evaluates the historical experience and lessons of its own country and other countries in an alert and cautious manner.

Q: Please talk about the international influence of China's experience and its reference to other countries.

A: China's effective and consistent domestic and foreign policies have had an important impact on the international order. China's success has shown the world that socialism is not only possible, but also the fairest and most effective social system capable of dealing with complex economic, social and ecological problems. In spite of its advanced productive force and traditional advantages, capitalism cannot solve these extremely acute problems in contemporary society. In addition, China supports handling international conflicts on the principles of justice and peace, and opposes the hegemonic policies of capitalist countries led by the United States, which is conducive to the establishment of a new international order of fairness and justice.

The progressive forces in Ukraine think very highly of the great Chinese people and their achievements in the field of national construction. Insightful people understand and agree that only by relying on the leadership of the Communist Party and embarking on the road of socialist development through revolution can these achievements be made. Although China and Ukraine have different political and economic systems, China's planning for its economic development as well as its prospects for social, national and world development is of great referential and practical significance to Ukraine. Because even today, nearly 30 years after the collapse of the Soviet Union, Ukrainian society has not found the answer to the important question of "what are we going to build?" The price of hesitating to press forward in the dark is extremely costly for both a country and its people. Ukraine's rulers are anti-communists and hostile to Russia. They have trampled on the rights and freedom of the people and driven the economy of Ukraine to collapse. They have deprived working people of the social security they enjoyed during the socialism period. The rulers of Ukraine seek the establishment of favorable economic ties with China. But their top objective is to secure huge investments. They do not object to making a positive assessment of China's achievements. However, they do not think that these achievements are just the result of the development of socialism and the efficient leadership of the Communist Party of China.

Q: With the rise of China's overall national strength and international status, some Western media keep on criticizing, accusing and even smearing China. What do you think is the main reason for this?

A: In view of the inherent bias of the Western media against China, I think this is not surprising, because the current world is still in the revolutionary stage of transition from capitalism to socialism, and the issue of socialism has become the most acute theme of political, ideological and class struggles around the world. Western media serving the interests of the ruling cliques of capitalist countries will not change their prejudice against socialism with Chinese characteristics and its achievements, and their smear of socialism and its history will continue. In spite of this, the achievements made by socialist China as well as the profound scientific connotation and practical significance of Xi Jinping Thought on Socialism with Chinese Characteristics for a New Era are still supported by Ukrainian socialist forces and progressive people.

III. China holds high the banner of socialism and leads the world socialist movement to march on

Q: Xi Jinping Thought on Socialism with Chinese Characteristics for a New Era is an important outcome of the CPC's theoretical and practical innovation since the 18th CPC National Congress. How do you evaluate Xi Jinping Thought on Socialism with Chinese Characteristics for a New Era? What do you think is the relationship between Xi Jinping Thought on Socialism with Chinese Characteristics for a New Era and the world socialist movement?

A: Communists and progressive forces in Ukraine attach great importance to Xi Jinping Thought on Socialism with Chinese Characteristics for a New Era, believing that its value and significance not only lie in the fact that it has armed the whole Party and the Chinese people with a specific and scientifically proven program of action, but also have opened up a broad prospect for the world communist movement. As the largest Communist Party in the world, the Communist Party of China has played an important role in the development of the world socialist movement. By holding high the banner of socialism, the Communist Party of China has creatively developed Marxist theory and kept abreast with the times by combining China's specific national conditions with the requirements of the new era, constantly updating and successfully implementing its socialist development program. As far as the fate of world socialism is concerned, China's unique construction experience accumulated in combining planning with market is of great significance. In the process of this construction, the creativity of the masses was unleashed and the most complex problems were solved. As a result, the face of the country changed rapidly. Possibly, some of the established economic and social management mechanisms need to be altered in order to eliminate the consequences that are not in conformity with the principles of socialism due to the increasing social differentiation and consumerism. So naturally, in President Xi Jinping's report to the 19th National Congress of the CPC and in the resolutions made by the Plenum of the Central Committee of the CPC, the CPC consistently focuses on how to improve the level of national governance, how to overcome shortcomings in the work of the Party and state organs, and how to effectively respond to emerging difficulties and challenges.

Under the circumstances of the failure of the socialism in the Soviet Union and Eastern Europe, the Xi Jinping Thought on Socialism with Chinese Characteristics for a New Era has aroused a heated discussion on the fate, path and chance of victory of socialism worldwide. The vitality of Xi Jinping Thought on Socialism with Chinese Characteristics for a New Era has been proved by the practice of Chinese socialist development, and shows to the world that socialism is still alive and that only by replacing the capitalist system that has run out of its positive potential with socialist society can the acute problems facing the humanity in the new era be solved. Today, there is every reason to draw a conclusion that, while taking into account the particularities of each country, the creative use of China's experience is very important for other socialist countries or countries that are about to embark on the road of socialist development because it is helpful for them to avoid errors and twists and turns.

Q: After the drastic changes in Eastern Europe and the disintegration of the Soviet Union, the world socialist movement has suffered a major setback. What are your views on the consequences of the social upheaval in Eastern Europe, the disintegration of the Soviet Union as well as the current situation and prospects of the development of the world socialist movement?

A: The aftermath of the anti-socialist coups in the Soviet Union and Eastern Europe in the 1990s was very serious because the return of capitalism provoked discontent and resistance from workers and the Communist Party in every country. People's living standards declined in a catastrophic way, and they lost all kinds of social security enjoyed in the socialist era. Today, mass protests and demonstrations take place in many countries, including the former socialist countries. These large-scale movements are a reflection of class contradictions, but they do not have the distinct character of class struggle. It will take time for the revolution to break out. As pointed out at the 21st Conference of the Communist Parties and Workers' Parties in Izmir, Turkey, in November 2019, a significant number of working people are unmoved by the idea of replacing capitalism with socialism. The reason can be attributed to the class enemy's long-term intensive anti-communist propaganda and subversive activities, but we cannot ignore the destructive acts that have harmed the socialist cause and violated the socialist principles in the process of fighting for the socialist victory and building a new life. The bourgeoisie, in addition to distorting the facts, cleverly takes advantage of this point. Communists are not always able to effectively deal with this problem and defend historical truth. Different from the period of the October Revolution a hundred years ago, the conditions for class struggle have changed and issues such as the seizure of political power by laborers, the replacement of capitalist private ownership by public ownership and the establishment of socialist democracy must be solved in different ways. This requires an in-depth theoretical study of the socialist transition and a deep reflection on how to guide the masses to realize that socialist fairness and justice must replace capitalism, and how to attract the masses to consciously take part in the struggle for socialism.

Under the current conditions, it is becoming increasingly important to strengthen international solidarity between the communist parties and working-class organizations (mainly trade unions) and to solve the problem of coordination of their actions in the fight against capitalism and the growing threat of fascism.

The necessity for communists around the world to formulate common strategies and exchange experience in revolution and socialist development has greatly increased. There is no doubt that China can offer valuable experience in this regard. In addition, the Communist Party of China, with its strong organizational capacity and rich experience, can take the lead in solving the problems arising from the organization and coordination of the international communist movement.

The Communist Party of Ukraine firmly believes that under the leadership of the CPC, the great Chinese people will withstand the ordeal of difficulties, realize the plan and strategy proposed at the 19th CPC National Congress, and build China into a prosperous, powerful, democratic, culturally advanced, harmonious and beautiful modern socialist country.

China's Rise Has Profoundly Changed the World Landscape
– An Interview with Zoran Jolevski, Former Defense Minister of Macedonia*

Interviewed by Zhou Miao[1], Liu Xiaolan[2]

Translated by Xie Shengzhe

Finalized by Wang Qiuhai

Zoran Jolevski

Zoran Jolevski has taught in the European University in Skopje, North Macedonia and also worked as vice president. He graduated from the Saints Cyril and Methodius University, where he received a Ph.D. in International Economy from the Faculty of Economy and a Master of Science degree in International Trade Law from the Faculty of Law. He published two treatises, edited a number of works, and also published over 50 papers.

Zoran Jolevski served as chief of staff to the late Macedonian President Boris Trajkovski from 2000 to 2004 and worked as the government's chief adviser on its

---

* Renamed The Republic of North Macedonia on February 12, 2019 and the original name "Macedonia" is still used in this book.

1 Zhou Miao, associate research fellow of the Academy of Marxism, Chinese Academy of Social Sciences.

2 Liu Xiaolan, doctorate candidate at the Graduate School of University of Chinese Academy of Social Sciences.

accession to the World Trade Organization. He held various posts in the Ministry of Foreign Affairs from 1988 to 1999 and was the chairman of the Boris Trajkovski International Foundation from 2004 to 2005.

He served as Macedonia's ambassador to the United States from March 2007 to June 2014. In November 2008, he was appointed as Macedonia's chief negotiator on the country name dispute with Greece. From January 2011 on, he worked as ambassador to Mexico and Brazil. From June 2014 to May 2017, he served as Minister of Defense of the Republic of Macedonia.

Zoran Jolevski is also the founder and first director of the Macedonian Institute of Economic Strategy and International Affairs. Zoran delivered speeches at international conferences, forums and seminars such as Halifax Security Forum, Brussels Security Forum, B2S Forum, Wroclaw Global Forum, Warsaw Forum, World Economic Forum, the World Trade Organization, the United Nations Economic Commission for Europe, United Nations Conference on Trade and Development, Sais Johns Hopkins, German Marshall Fund of the United States, and the Atlantic Council of the United States in Washington.

Interview Summary

Zoran Jolevski, former chief of the Macedonian Presidential Office, former ambassador to the United States, former Minister of Defense, and professor of the European University of Nortitsn Macedonia, mainly analyzes the reasons why China has become the most successful socialist country from the perspective of economic development effectiveness. When talking about the reasons for China's success in economic development, Zoran made a special comparison between Yugoslavia and Macedonia, pointing out the role of China's reform and opening up policy, demonstrating the positive influence China will have on the world order, and putting forward suggestions for China's future development. Of course, we should make a scientific analysis of some of Zoran's suggestions. His views that China's economy should focus on stimulating domestic demand, opening up to the outside world and further reducing poverty are worth learning from.

In January 2020, Zoran Jolevski, professor of the European University of Nortitsn Macedonia, former head of the Presidential Office of Macedonia, former ambassador to the United States and former Minister of Defense, analyzed the reasons why China has become the most successful socialist country from the perspective of economic development effectiveness, demonstrating the impact China will have on the world order. In addition, he gave his suggestions for China's future development.

I. The reasons why China has become the most successful socialist country in economic reform and development

Q: It's a pleasure to meet you, Prof. Jolevski! I am glad that you are so kind as to accept this interview. How would you comment on China's economic achievements?

A: After the Third Plenary Session of the 11th CPC Central Committee, the People's Republic of China began to implement reforms, which promoted the unprecedented growth and development of the market economy under socialist conditions. This is the second developmental stage of the People's Republic of China since 1949 when it was founded and won its political and economic independence. Some data have also proved the success of China's economy. By analyzing the changes of China's GDP in the period from 1978 to 2019, it can be concluded that China's GDP has doubled every eight years since the reform and opening up in 1978. According to the data from "World Economic Outlook" released by IMF in October 2019, China is the world's second largest economy, almost three times as large as Japan, the third largest economy, and four times as large as Germany, the fourth largest economy, as far as the size of economy is concerned. If GDP is measured by purchasing power parity, China is the largest economy.

With the rapid rise of the China's economy, China has also made remarkable progress in poverty reduction over the past three decades, indicating that economic growth has made a significant contribution to poverty reduction. Today, poverty in China is mainly targeted at the rural poor population because the urban poverty has been basically eliminated. It should be noted that China has contributed more to global poverty reduction than any other country.

Q: As a witness to the historical changes in Yugoslavia and Macedonia, how do you view the development and changes in Yugoslavia and Macedonia and what implications do they have for China?

A: People often analyze the disintegration of Yugoslavia from a political perspective, focusing mainly on the political and ethnic differences between federal entities (republics), thinking these are the reasons for the disintegration of Yugoslavia. However, there is relatively little analysis on the economic reasons that led to the disintegration of Yugoslavia and the Soviet Union. It can be said that Yugoslavia's untimely and inappropriate response in economic field is one of the factors that led to the disintegration of the country. After the Second World War, the economic development of the Socialist Federal Republic of Yugoslavia can be considered successful in its initial stage. The first stage began in 1952 with the introduction of the so-called self-governing economic system, which gave economic entities limited freedom in implementing their commercial policies. Subsequently, Yugoslavia opened up to the world market, mainly as a result of the deterioration of relations with the Soviet Union and other member states of the Council for Mutual Economic Assistance. In particular due to their market closure of Yugoslav products.

Although this economic opening was primarily caused by foreign policy, it had a positive influence on the economic development of the Socialist Federal Republic of Yugoslavia. From 1952 to 1965, the Yugoslavia's economy grew at an average rate of 9.5 percent annually. Such potent economic growth rapidly raised living standards of the people of the country. In order to maintain this rate of growth, the

Socialist Republic of Yugoslavia needed further reforms during the second half of the 1960s so as to enable market mechanisms to play a greater role in regulating the economy and to increase the openness of the national economy to the world market. In response to domestic demands for further liberalization of its national economy, Yugoslavia became a party to the General Agreement on Tariffs and Trade (GATT) on 25 August 1966. However, such foreign trade measures were insufficient, because it is necessary to gradually open the market of capital and technology to the world at the same time. Unfortunately, the leaders of the Socialist Federal Republic of Yugoslavia did not have enough courage to directly open the country to foreign investment which could bring both new capital and modern technology.

Yugoslavia also began to borrow money from abroad. Especially in the early 1970s, as interest rates were relatively low, so borrowing capital was cheap, hence attractive. But by the mid-1970s, interest rates began to rise and, in the early 1980s, reached their highest level since World War II. In addition, Yugoslavia allowed federal entities and republics to borrow money from abroad. For this sake, they (the republics) assumed that other republics (of the federation) would fulfill their due obligations. Although Yugoslavia's debt was not too high (about US$22 billion), the country was faced with challenges in repaying its foreign debt due to high interest rates on some loans and the lack of a strong export-oriented economy. In order to increase exports and provide hard currency, the dinar was devalued, which in turn led to the exacerbation of inflation in the 1970s. Inflation was already very high (about 10 percent a year) in the 1960s as a result of price liberalization. In the 1980s, inflation was quite high and steadily rising. During the second half of the 1960s and the first half of the 1970s, the momentum of economic opening in Yugoslavia waned. The lack of economic policy measures of creating and developing an export-oriented economy on the one hand and the sharp rise in interest rates in the late 1970s on the other led to economic stagnation in the Union of Socialist Republics of Yugoslavia. Under these economic conditions, the Socialist Federal Republic of Yugoslavia was disintegrated in the 1990s. The economic conditions of the Socialist

Republic of Yugoslavia have been inherited by the republics.

Besides, after gaining its independence, Macedonia was faced with external blows, both politically (delayed international recognition and accession to the United Nations due to Greece's opposition) and economically (United Nations sanctions against Serbia, and trade and transit embargoes from Greece). The conditions for change, or rather, the conditions for reform, were very complicated. The privatization model gave a few companies ownership. Some enterprises gradually disappeared as a result of external blows and privatization of the Macedonian economy. Another factor adversely affecting the situation of Macedonian enterprises was the interest rate policy of the banking sector, meaning that the main objective of monetary policy was to ensure low inflation and stability. It would have been a good economic policy if banks had been able to quickly adjust policy and cut interest rates when inflation fell. Macedonia brought inflation under control in 1996, but the banks had been delaying lowering lending rates, which seriously impeded the export-oriented economy. Because of the high cost of loans, the export-oriented economy became less competitive.

In a few years after Macedonia's independence, the country's leaders began to implement a policy of concluding free trade agreements with the aim of Bringing foreign markets into Macedonia. Thereupon, Macedonia concluded a number of free trade agreements, the most important of which is "the Stabilization and Association Agreement" with the European Union, a free trade agreement for foreign trade. Although Macedonia has kept opening its economy to foreign investors since its independence, there was little foreign direct investment in the style of green-field investment until 2006. In spite of the fact that since the mid-1990s, the country had begun its opening up to foreign direct investment, green-field investment has not developed on a large scale due to the situation in the region and its small domestic market. That is to say, the predominant foreign direct investment is in existing companies, which are in a privileged position in the domestic market. In 2007, the government began to carry out an aggressive or even a radical policy of attracting export-oriented labor-intensive foreign direct investment, with the purpose of boosting exports to reduce the trade deficit and historically high unemployment.

Q: You have reviewed the developmental history of Yugoslavia and Macedonia in a comparative way. What do you think are the reasons for China's great achievements?

A: The economic growth of the People's Republic of China shows that various reforms aimed at opening up the national economy have achieved the desired results. This is the outcome of China's policy of economic reform and opening up. These measures allow the market mechanism to play a greater role in economic aspect, making China more open to the world economy. An analysis of the changes that have taken place in the People's Republic of China over the past 40 years shows that these changes have been carefully designed and prepared, which are in line with China's social and cultural characteristics and, above all, the characteristics and potential of China's economy. Sound economic policy measures, careful planning and monitoring of implementation, which began in 1978 when the second developmental stage of the People's Republic of China was launched, as well as economic measures suitable to current conditions and needs are key factors for the economic prosperity of the People's Republic of China. All China's policies and strategies are aimed at boosting economic growth and changing the existing environment and culture. Reforms intended for increasing the role of the market have been well coordinated with the entities responsible for implementing them, thus providing support to individuals and organizations participating in implementing these reform measures.

II. How will the success of socialism in China influence the world economic order?

Q: In your opinion, China's economic development has made remarkable achievements. Then, what is its influence on the economy of the world?

A: Since China's reform and opening up, the country's status in the world economic landscape has been significantly enhanced, and the country has been deeply integrated into economic globalization. After the World War II, developed capitalist countries headed by the United States established international organizations such as the United Nations, the International Monetary Fund, the World Bank and the World Trade Organization, creating a world political and economic order dominated by the developed countries of the west. With the launch of the second developmental stage of the People's Republic of China in 1978, China opened to the world market to a greater extent, and the share of China's economy in the world is becoming bigger and bigger. In 1986, the People's Republic of China applied accession to the GATT and after the establishment of the World Trade Organization in 1995, the Working Group on Accession to GATT was formally reorganized into the Working Group on Accession to the WTO. After 14 years of negotiations, the People's Republic of China became a member of the World Trade Organization in 2001. Based on the analysis of the openness indexes of the 12 largest economies, the following conclusion can be drawn: it is 18.2 percent for Brazil in openness index, 20.2 percent for the US, 70.7 percent for Germany and 68.7 percent for South Korea. In recent years, China's economic openness index has been stabilized at the level of about 35 percent.

The most obvious manifestation of China's economic opening is the increase in exports and imports. When the second stage of China's development kicked off, the scale of its foreign trade was relatively small. However, after reforms aimed at opening up the Chinese economy and making market mechanisms more liberal, imports and exports increased sharply. A similar trend can be seen in foreign direct investment. Today China occupies an important position in both the inflow and outflow of foreign direct investments. In 2018, China attracted US$139 billion of foreign direct investment, up 4 percent year on year. The development of foreign direct investment in the People's Republic of China can be divided into three periods. The first period was from 1948 to the early 1980s, when China's economy was not opened to multinational companies. The second period began in the 1980s, during which the inflow of foreign direct investment was limited. In the 1990s, the People's Republic of China began to receive large amounts of foreign direct investment. The third period began in the middle of the first decade of the 21st century, when Chinese companies began investing heavily overseas. In 2015, the outflow of foreign direct investment exceeded the inflow for the first time which remained at a high level until 2017, when FDI in Chinese companies declined. As expected, both the outflow and inflow of China's foreign direct investment will increase.

According to the data from the United Nations Conference on Trade and Development (UNCTAD), in 2015, for the first time, the stock of foreign direct investment by Chinese companies exceeded the stock of foreign direct investment that China received. This indicates that a substantial change has taken place in foreign direct investment over the past decade. In the 1980s and early 1990s, China was a major recipient of foreign direct investment. As can be seen from the above, more and more Chinese enterprises are investing in manufacturing and service facilities overseas.

Q: What will be the influence of the increasing share of China's economy in the world economy on the world economic order?

A: China's influence on the world economic order can be analyzed from the perspective of the relationship between multilateralism and regionalism. Given the slow liberalization of international trade and the lack of progress in multilateral trade negotiations under the auspices of the World Trade Organization, a significant number of countries are taking alternative initiatives to address their international trade priorities. These initiatives are at the bilateral and regional levels and take the form of comprehensive free trade agreements and customs unions. To ensure the coordinated and parallel development of multilateralism and regionalism constitutes one of the most important issues in international trade. We are witnessing the emergence of the so-called mega-regional integration.

The People's Republic of China should actively participate in multilateral trade negotiations presided over by the World Trade Organization and in regional trade integration initiatives, which, as we have noted, will be broader in scope than traditional free trade agreements, including areas such as foreign direct investment, intellectual property protection and national trade. The People's Republic of China has begun to participate more actively in these regional trade initiatives. According to the statistics of the General Administration of Customs of China (GACC), in 2016, the trade volume between China and its FTA partners accounted to 38.8 percent of the total foreign trade volume of China (including Chinese Taipei, Hong Kong, and Macao), and 25.4 percent (excluding Chinese Taipei, Hong Kong, Macao). [1] The accession to the Free Trade Agreement is part and parcel of China's new strategy of trade liberalization, which is a very good one. According to the WTO's *Trade Policy Review Report of China*, "As the next step, China intends to construct a high-standard FTA network starting with neighboring countries, extending to the countries participating in the Belt and Road Initiative and opening up to the whole world. China intends, together with free trade partners, to continue to reduce tariff and non-tariff barriers, to mutually open up trade-in-goods and to strive for mutual benefits and win-win outcomes." [2] In addition, China has put forward the construction of "a community with a shared future for mankind" and the Belt and Road Initiative, established the Asian Infrastructure Investment Bank and concluded a number of free trade agreements.

The People's Republic of China should also pay attention to the new areas of multilateral trade introduced during the Uruguay Round negotiations. Given their influence on economic development, these new areas, such as trade in services, intellectual property protection, trade measures affecting foreign direct investment

---

1　WTO, *Trade Policy Review Report of China*, Report by the Secretariat, Geneva, June 6, 2018, p. 34.

2　WTO, *Trade Policy Review Report of China*, Report by the Secretariat, Geneva, June 6, 2018, p. 35.

and trade facilitation, are particularly important in the current global economy. China, Brazil and India are important large-scale economies, and companies of the People's Republic of China have already possessed the cutting-edge technologies of their own. It is particularly important to protect intellectual property rights at the international level, especially when modern economy is based on knowledge. Intangible assets such as technological innovation, design and patent are the key to determining an enterprise's position in the domestic and foreign markets. Compared with the Uruguay Round of multilateral negotiations, China's stance on IPR protection today is much closer to that of the industrialized countries.

III. Suggestions for China's future economic development

Q: What are your suggestions for the future development of China?

A: China's economic policy should include measures to allow for further liberalization of imports. Chinese enterprises have reached such a developmental level that they can compete with their foreign counterparts. Unless imports are further liberalized, the competitive pressure of imported goods and services on domestic producers will disappear. This pressure will make them more efficient and contribute to further improvements in production efficiency, product quality and design. The liberalization of the foreign trade system of the People's Republic of China should not only take the form of lowering tariff levels, but also relax other measures related to foreign trade policy. Given the characteristics of the China's economy, market and consumers, a prolonged period of unnecessary protection may adversely affect the efficiency and productivity of Chinese companies that are engaged in mass production for the domestic market. It is of great importance to the People's Republic of China to protect foreign direct investment and manage its overseas business activities. This indicates that it is necessary for China to become more actively involved in concluding agreements on protecting foreign direct investment at the bilateral, regional and even global levels.

China must further reform its economic system to maintain its high economic growth rate and change and reform its national economy in order to strengthen the role of market mechanisms and further integrate into the global economy. At the same time, China should transform its position in global political and economic relations. It is clear that China is no longer a developing country. The characteristics of China's national economy are close to those of developed countries.

For a country like the size of the People's Republic of China, thanks to its large domestic market, domestic demand is expected to continue to grow for some time to come. The increase in domestic demand is mainly attributed to the increase in disposable income of Chinese consumers, and domestic consumption has also become an important driver of economic development. If the second stage of China's development, which began in 1978, was mainly based on export-oriented production, the third stage, which began in 2012, will be dominated by domestic consumption. China should take advantage of the huge potential of its domestic market to improve the competitiveness of its domestic companies.

Although the China's economy has made remarkable progress, judging from its development level by per capita GDP, it can be concluded that there is still room and need for further improvement in Chinese people's living standards. China's per capita GDP still lags behind developed countries, and there is a need for China to achieve balanced growth for some time to come. The People's Republic of China needs to continue its successful policies, such as reducing poverty, improving health care and pension system. In addition, measures are needed to reduce inequality, especially among the rural population, where the Gini coefficient of rural residents' income distribution needs to be reduced. Measures intended for reducing inequality should be continued and strengthened, particularly among the rural population.

IV. Comments on Jolevski's viewpoints

(I) When talking about the reasons for the success of China's economic development, Jolevski pointed out the role of the opening-up policy by comparing Yugoslavia and Macedonia, but this should be analyzed scientifically. The reason why Jolevski measures the success of a country's economic development by openness needs to be scientifically analyzed and discussed. Since World War II, the United States has dominated the process of economic globalization through the establishment of international organizations such as the World Bank, the International Monetary Fund and the United Nations as well as the implementation of the Marshall Plan. Over the years, the United States has taken advantage of these mechanisms for its own gain. While opening up their economies, some developing countries have failed to establish mechanisms to safeguard their economic and financial security, resulting in the frequent occurrence of economic and financial crises that seriously affected their economic development. According to the so-called openness data, the openness of the US economy is also very low. China should also draw lessons from the economic development of Yugoslavia. Jolevski analyzed the reasons for the disintegration of Yugoslavia from an economic perspective. The disintegration of Yugoslavia was influenced by both international factors and overall crisis triggered by economic crisis. Moreover, the autonomy enjoyed by various local economies also fostered separatism. The contradiction between ethnic groups became intensified because of the conflict of economic interests. In a word, economic chaos eventually led to complicated problems such as political division. However, the economic problem was an important reason for the disintegration of Yugoslavia. In other words, Yugoslavia failed to properly strike the balance between international economy and domestic economy and borrowed too much foreign debt. Under the influence of western financial hegemony, its economic and financial security was seriously affected, which is worth our deep reflection. China should pay special attention to the protection of its financial sovereignty. While opening up its financial sector, China should attach great importance to its financial security.

Therefore, we should realize that the reason for the success of China's reform and opening up lies in the fact that China has carried out independent opening up, which is characterized by the adherence to the dialectical unity of independence and opening to the outside world. That is to say, while being able to make use of globalization to promote the development of its own, China always sticks to the dominant position of public ownership and control of its economic development for the purpose of safeguarding national economic sovereignty and security and avoiding the one-way dependence on developed capitalist countries, thus realizing independent growth and continuous industrial transformation and upgrading. The Fourth Plenary Session of the 19th CPC Central Committee also pointed out that adhering to the unity of independence and opening up, actively participating in global governance, and continuously contributing to the construction of a "community with a shared future for mankind" are the significant advantages of China's state system and national governance system.

(II) Jolevski saw the fact that China achieved great success in its reform and opening up by taking advantage of market mechanisms and suggested that China further strengthen the role of market mechanisms, which should also be correctly understood by us. Given the disadvantages of the previous planned economic system, China's economic system reform has been carried out in the direction of expanding the scope of market regulation and strengthening the role of market economy. The Third Plenary Session of the 18th CPC Central Committee adopted Decision on Some Major Issues Concerning Comprehensively Deepening the Reform, which pointed out that the economic system reform is the focus of deepening the reform comprehensively. The underlying issue is how to strike a balance between the role of the government and that of the market, and let the market play the decisive role in allocating resources. However, what has been established and is being continuously improved by us is the socialist market economy. Therefore, in his explanation of the above document, Comrade Xi Jinping specially noted: "Our market economy is socialist, of course. We need to give leverage to the superiority of our socialist system, and let the Party and government perform their positive functions. The market plays a decisive role in allocating resources, but is not the sole actor in this regard. To develop the socialist market economy, leverage should be given to both the market and the government, with differentiated functions." Therefore, the market is unable to play a "full role" and it is necessary for us to "give play to the role of the government in a better way". On the one hand, market regulation has short-term, one-sided, lagging, uncertain and other weaknesses and shortcomings. On the other hand, it cannot be solely relied on in some fields such as ideological and cultural, public services including medical care, health care and education, infrastructure construction, and major strategic industries related to the national economy and people's livelihood. We should dialectically look at the market economy, including its advantages and disadvantages. While emphasizing the decisive role of the market in the allocation of resources, we should give play to the function of the government in a better manner. This is one of the fundamental differences between the socialist market economy and the capitalist market economy.

China's achievements in economic development have also been made on the basis of adhering to the basic socialist system. China should be alert to the lessons of the privatization of Macedonia after the dramatic changes in Eastern Europe and the disintegration of the Soviet Union, and must adhere to the basic economic system with public ownership as the mainstay. Education, medical care, transportation, electricity and other sectors that affect people's livelihood should be dominated by public ownership, rather than the market alone. Efforts should be made to strengthen the oversight of private enterprises so that they play a role that benefits people's lives, instead of being dictated by capital interests.

(III) Jolevski's positioning of China as a developed country is not in line with the reality in China. Although China has made remarkable achievements in development and become the world's second largest economy and, based on this, many people in the world believe that China is no longer a developing country, yet the fact that China is still the largest developing country in the world has not changed. China is still in the primary stage of socialism and is a developing socialist country. The principal contradiction facing Chinese society is the one between unbalanced and inadequate development and the people's ever-growing needs for a better life. The report of the 19th CPC National Congress points out that the overarching goal of socialism with Chinese characteristics in the new era is to realize socialist modernization and the great rejuvenation of the Chinese nation. At the 19th National Congress of the Communist Party of China, the following strategic arrangements were made for building socialism with Chinese characteristics for a new era: From now to 2020, we will build a moderately prosperous society in three years. On this basis, after 15 years of struggle in the first stage, we will have basically realized socialist modernization; and then through the second stage of 15 years of struggle, we will build China into a powerful socialist modern country. Therefore, China still needs to make further efforts in its modernization drive.

(IV) Jolevski's view that China's economy should focus on stimulating domestic demand, and at the same time do a good job in opening up to the outside world, further reduce poverty and reduce inequality is worthy of our consideration. He stressed that China should attach importance to solving the poverty problem in the countryside and reducing the rural Gini coefficient. Take the COVID-19 pandemic as an example. Due to the unbalanced development in China, the medical resources in some regions and even cities are much more than those in other regions and villages. The outbreak of the pandemic has exposed the inadequacy of medical resources which shows that in the process of building a moderately prosperous society in all respects, we should vigorously address various problems of inequality and imbalance in development by seriously putting into practice the "five development concepts", and coordinating the synergic development of urban and rural areas and regions.

Socialism with Chinese Characteristics Has Brought Vigor and Vitality to World Socialism
– An Interview with Sylwester Szafarz, Former Polish Consul General in Shanghai

Interviewed by Qiao Ruihua[1]
Translated by Xie Shengzhe
Finalized by Wang Qiuhai

Sylwester Szafarz

Sylwester Szafarz was former consul general of Poland in Shanghai and an expert on international issues. He always has two small national flags, one Polish and one Chinese, in his briefcase. He said that studying China was his lifelong aspiration.

In the 1960s, Szafarz discovered a Polish translation of *The Analects of Confucius* in a university library, and was fascinated by the philosophical ideas in the book. The book became a seed through which Szafarz learned about China before gradually discovering the forest. For more than half a century, China became the focus of Szafarz's studies. He felt very honored to witness the development and revitalization of a great nation.

---

1 Qiao Ruihua, assistant research fellow of the Academy of Marxism, Chinese Academy of Social Sciences.

In the late 1970s, Szafarz visited China. According to his reminiscence, at that time, China was just beginning to reform and open up. The country was not rich yet, but there was a great enthusiasm for opening up and development among the people. Later, Szafarz worked at the Polish Embassy in France for many years, receiving many Chinese delegations visiting Europe and gradually increasing the cooperation with them. He once received a delegation of businessmen from Shanghai that planned to set up a factory for manufacturing coolers. They came from an enterprise engaged in multinational cooperation, with the Chinese side providing the plant and workers, German and French partners offering capital and equipment, and Polish side supplying raw materials like copper. According to Szafarz, it can be perceived that China had begun to integrate into the world market and is now part and parcel of the world economy.

Comparing the present with the past, Szafarz said that China's development and progress is surprising and what impressed him most is the change of the city skyline. When he went to Shanghai in the early 1990s, Pudong was an uncultivated land. More than a decade later, when he served as consul general of Poland at Shanghai, Pudong already had world-class buildings and Shanghai became a really international metropolis. China's foreign exchanges and cooperation keep on reaching new levels. More and more Chinese companies have become world's leading innovators and their status in the global economic industrial chain is on the rise. In the past, cooperation between China and foreign countries was mainly one-way import from China. Now, two-way exchanges are increasing and personnel exchanges are becoming more frequent.

Szafarz said that China has developed into the world's second largest economy from a weak nation at the beginning of its founding. It is worthwhile for the whole world to learn from the development experience of new China. Since his retirement in 2007, Szafarz has focused more on studying China's development experience. In recent years, together with his colleagues, he has translated books, including *Xi Jinping: the Governance of China*, into Polish. He is going to translate Xi Jinping thought on diplomacy and documents related to the Belt and Road initiative. He believes this will help Polish people to know more about today's China.

Szafarz holds that the traditional friendship between Poland and China goes back to ancient times. Poland is a bridge connecting China and the European Union. By participating in the joint construction of the "Belt and Road", Poland can better play its own advantages. Szafarz is a firm believer in the concept of "people share the same feelings". He has learned that many Chinese friends are interested in Polish cultural celebrities like Chopin and history, and that exchanges between young people in Poland and China are increasing. He believes that young people in Poland should learn more about China and the general situation and trend of the development and change of China and the world.

Szafarz said that China has always maintained a clear goal and direction in its economic and social construction and found a path really suited to its own development. The remarkable achievements China has made are admirable. Over the past 70 years, China has not only developed rapidly economically, but also played an increasingly important role in global politics and diplomacy. He is full of confidence in China's future development and sincerely wishes the Chinese people more brilliant achievements.

Interview Summary

Sylwester Szafarz, an expert on international affairs and former of Polish consul general in Shanghai, has made an in-depth analysis of the international situation since the dramatic changes in Poland more than 30 years ago. In addition, he has made a comprehensive and pertinent evaluation of the changes in Poland during its transition, believing that China's development can set a good example for the development of other countries in the world. At the same time, as a witness to China's development in the past and present, Szafarz fully affirmed the achievements made in building socialism with Chinese characteristics in the new era, sincerely praised the vigor and vitality China has brought to world socialism, and spoke highly of China's role in the construction of a new international order. In addition, Szafarz also talked about socialism and socialist China in the eyes of the Polish people, exposing and refuting the Western media's distorted reports on China out of ideological bias.

Sylwester Szafarz is a Polish expert on China and the former consul general of Poland in Shanghai. Both volumes I and II of *Xi Jinping: the Governance of China* have been translated into Polish by Mr. Szafarz and others. Mr. Szafarz is an important statesman who introduces China to the Polish people in an academic way. His research is of great theoretical significance for the Western world to overcome ideological bias and comprehensively and accurately understand China, especially its socialist development and new era.

I. The analysis of the situation in Poland since the dramatic change in 1989

Q: Mr. Sylwester Szafarz, nice to meet you! We are very glad that you are so kind as to accept our interview. The drastic changes in Eastern Europe and the disintegration of the Soviet Union was one of the major historical events that affected the course of human history in the 20th century. As a witness to the upheaval, how do you evaluate the development and changes in your country over the past 30 years?

A: Frankly speaking, it is premature to comprehensively evaluate Poland's development in the past 30 years because we must wait and see until the whole process of history, at least its first stage, comes to an end and brings complete results. As a matter of fact, Poland's development depends to a large extent on what is happening in other countries, especially global powers. Nevertheless, some preliminary assessments and conclusions appear to be possible.

First, it is necessary to know that the United States supported the ongoing transition process of the Soviet Union and its Eurasian allies, including Poland. In order to consolidate its regional and global position, the United States, starting from the Ronald Reagan era, decided to shift its global strategy from military means to the application of non-military means, especially in the Asian allies of the Soviet Union, Ukraine, Poland and other countries in Central and Eastern Europe, with the exception of Russia. Today, the Islamic Republic of Iran is considered the main enemy of the United States in Western Asia and the next source of potential "Maydan" revolutionary unrest that could lead to a dangerous increase in international tensions and major turmoil in the region and beyond.

In fact, we call this new global strategy of the US "maydan" in Ukrainian, meaning "square", "market" and the like. Therefore, we call it square revolution or tactics because the United States and its local allies often use this means to launch mass social movements to abolish the former pro-Soviet government and establish the legal system and pro-American regime. As you know, the first "revolution" of this kind, which was launched by Lech Walesa of Solidarity and his associates, took place in the Gdansk Shipyard in Poland. Similar incidents on a smaller scale have occurred in other communist countries in Eastern Europe. As a result, political and social systems such as "neo-liberalism", "neo-conservatism" and "populism" were established in these countries where new pro-American forces came to power.

The "neoliberal", "neoconservative", and "populist" countries in the world, including the United States, are very inefficient, which is well understood by their supporters. However, through these means, including paramilitary means, they are striving to maintain and expand their sphere of influence in the relevant countries and regions and regain their position of No.1 and hegemony in the world. This is not an easy task, if not impossible, because during this period, global power relations experienced fundamental changes, which paved the way for a new multilateral world order based on peace, security, justice, harmony, win-win cooperation, equality, partnership and so on. And none of these has anything to do with the outdated "neoliberal", "neoconservative" and "populist" rules and the neocolonialism that exploits people and their human and natural resources.

The above is the general background of our current situation. Poland, Afghanistan, Ukraine and other countries were used by the US to destroy and disintegrate the Soviet Union which achieved only a partial success, because post-Soviet Russia, the Russian Federation, proved to be much stronger than expected. The United States also underestimates the enormous potential of China's rise and its growing role in the development of our civilization under the new rules.

Socialism with Chinese characteristics for a new era is totally unexpected to those Americans who want to reshape the world order according to their own wishes and imaginations and continue to attempt to destroy China by way of the "Square Revolution". Being increasingly nervous and helpless, these people pose a more radical and dangerous threat to humanity than ever before. As a result, we now face two opposite global trends of development: one is the force of peace, progress and cooperation headed by the People's Republic of China and its allies, which constitute the overwhelming majority of the world. The other is the force of aggression, domination and exploitation, which is in the minority of the world. People are aware which one is more favorable to them. It must be pointed out that since China implemented its first innovative national strategy – reform and opening up, it has achieved great success, and as a realistic and feasible way of addressing the current development problems and building a new and better world, this strategy has won wide support in China and around the world which is an unprecedented opportunity for all nations. And we should make the most of this opportunity in order to achieve our goals!

As you've just said, how to evaluate the development of Poland in the past 30 years of a "dramatic" transition depends on, objectively speaking, correctly weigh the advantages and disadvantages, strengths and weaknesses and so on. The so-called "Solidarity Revolution" manipulated and financed by the United States and the American-style destructive neo-liberalism imposed on Poland are unexpected

China in the New Era

and unknown to the Polish people.

Politically, the new American-style Polish "twin brothers" and other countries following the American model have nothing special to offer Poland and other "transitional" countries because "neoliberal" standards have collapsed in the heartland of the United States and other countries that were previously forced to accept the "American Dream" and the policy of the peace under the rule of the US. In fact, even nowadays, we still do not know what a political, social and ideological system has been imposed in our country. What should we call it, "neo-capitalism", "neo-liberalism", "neo-Americanism", "neo-populism" or other names? The only point people can be sure of is that, whatever you want to call it, the word "system" was from the US, which should be responsible for its ultimate failure. Interestingly, Poland's constitution does not specify by name what kind of political system is practiced in the country. The Constitution mentions only in paragraph 20 that Poland's economic system is based on a "social market economy", which, however, is not really respected and implemented in practice. Therefore, there is an urgent need for a serious revision and modernization of the Polish constitution.

The Americanization imposed on Polish life has "imported" a large number of positive American models, such as good work/living standard, high production rate and cutting-edge innovation. However, the overwhelming majority of them including the two-party system, crime, money worship, the gap between the rich and the poor, corruption, discrimination, drug traffice and subcultures in the US are negative. As a result, the Polish political system at present appears to be a very strange mixture of all these elements combined with some of our fine historical traditions of national solidarity, cooperation, internationalism and patriotism. American and EU models and standards have not been deeply rooted in the soil of Poland, but show that these models and standards, such as corruption and crime, tend to undermine and anarchize our "system", thus turning it into a constant battleground for relevant parties and leaders. Therefore, candidates for domestic and European elections are nominated and supported by political parties and their leaders, while ordinary voters have only the right to put their ballots in the ballot box. In short, the Americanization and neo-liberalization of Poland have failed. On the contrary, we need a modernized socialism with Polish characteristics and a new foreign policy supported by the Polish people and reliable allies, old and new.

Finally, I firmly advocate the development of good-neighborly and friendly relations with neighboring and other countries in the world, including the United States, China, India, the European Union and other BRICS countries. Only by doing so will we not repeat our bloody history, and we should strive to open a new and better chapter in history on the basis of peace, security, cooperation and a brighter future for everyone.

II. Fully affirming the achievements made in building socialism with Chinese characteristics in a new era

Q: Thank you very much. Would you please tell us your views on socialism with Chinese characteristics?

A: The People's Republic of China is the genuine socialist country in the world, while other socialist countries, although wanting to serve their people as much as possible, are unable to do so due to severe material shortages. In addition, there are many socialist and social democratic parties around the world, as well as their "Socialist International", but they seem quite unable to adapt to the new reality and are strongly opposed to their enemies, such as France, Italy, Spain, the United Kingdom, Poland and other countries and regions. In this context, under the guidance of the powerful and united Communist Party of China with more than 95 million members, China's experience and example are a brilliant paradigm of theoretical wisdom and practical success.

Q: In your opinion, what specific achievements has socialism with Chinese characteristics made?

A: China's new achievements in socialist development not only have a good starting point and a solid theoretical and material foundation. Here is my personal ranking of what China has achieved over the past few decades:

-Positive economic results since 1978;

-Harmonious and sustainable development;

-Ambitious and realistic plans for the future;

-Rule of law, poverty eradication;

-Urbanization and agricultural modernization;

-Unprecedented development in education, science and technology;

-Integrated innovation and modernization trends;

-Significant and large-scale infrastructure investment;

-Building a green country;

-Consolidating social security;

-Combating terrorism, corruption and other crimes;

-Peaceful coexistence and win-win cooperation with foreign countries;

-Remarkable progress in space exploration as well as many other positive aspects of China's socialist development

We must also know that the People's Republic of China, a country rich in both natural and human resources, has laid a solid and unique global foundation for the long-term successful development of socialism to the highest level of our civilization.

Q: What do you think is the key to the success of socialism with Chinese characteristics?

A: China boasts about 1.4 billion well-educated, healthy and modest and prudent people. They work extremely hard and love their work, which is unmatched by other countries and peoples. The Chinese government adopts the famous "people-oriented" policy, a major initiative to motivate ordinary citizens and officials in a large socialist country to work hard, earn more money and live a decent life. Many overseas Chinese, including intellectuals, researchers, students, technicians and workers, will return to their motherland after going abroad for a period of time, because they are convinced that the living and working standards in their motherland are improving year by year. That speaks for itself.

III. Singing high praise for the vigor and vitality that China has brought to world socialism

Q: In your view, in the past 30 years since the drastic changes in Eastern Europe and the disintegration of the Soviet Union, has world socialism emerged from its low ebb? What is the basis for the revival of world socialism?

A: Toward the end of the 20th century, after the so-called "revolutionary" upheavals and "changes" in the Soviet Union and Central and Eastern Europe, "socialism" was in fact tantamount to Sovietism, which was abandoned by many countries and their people. As I said, Sovietism should be seen as a sarcastic version of socialism that fails to solve existing problems and help people to live and work decently. After the disintegration of the Soviet Union, there were no more vivid examples and practical applications of socialism. This is why it is so difficult for us to emulate a healthy and practical example from abroad, because it does not exist in the world. Moreover, the right-wing neoliberal and conservative elements are doing everything they can to prevent an ambitious revival of socialism, which, in any case, will prove inevitable sooner or later. Even now, international, political, economic and social conditions are more mature than ever before and are moving towards this prospect. At present, socialism in general is still only in theory and serves as an idealized vision of people dreaming of improving their hard lives and poor living conditions.

Under such circumstances, socialism with Chinese characteristics for a new era is the only positive criterion and model characterized by integrating theory with practice. It is indisputable that it can be used in other situations, in other countries, and even around the world. In fact, there are many universal components and principles in Chinese socialism, such as social welfare, sustainable development and peaceful coexistence, which may be easily and necessarily applied in other countries. The problem facing us, however, is that you call it "with Chinese characteristics". Does this mean that this kind of socialism only applies to China? Of course, it is not. My suggestion is that Chinese scholars and statesmen should work out a modern and balanced universal version of socialism as soon as possible. The neoliberals, conservatives, and factions of other right-wing movements have common ideas and principles that apply to all, even if they are not successful in putting them into practice. In short, your socialism, both in theory and in practice, is the solid foundation and symbol for the revival of socialism in the world. Let's give it a try in the future.

Q: In your opinion, what do you think is the significance of China's holding high the banner of socialism to world socialism? Or what role has China played in the development of world socialism?

A: China's modern socialist model has received more and more attention, welcome and support in many countries and regions around the world. Many American businessmen, researchers and managers are very interested in the experience and achievements of China. They want to know how to transplant some of them to the United States. That speaks volumes. More importantly, China's model of socialist system is more popular and feasible in many emerging and developing countries, because China itself is the largest and most important emerging and developing country in the world. This model, in law and procedure, has been successfully tested in your country and bears the hallmarks of China. In this sense, it is easier for these countries to follow this example to avoid potential errors and miscalculations in the sustainable development of their respective socialism. For many developing countries, such as the countries in Africa or Latin America, this will not be an easy task. The main reason for this is that they are very different from China in economic potential, intelligence and popular needs. This is why your help is of vital importance to them. Fortunately, China is sparing no effort to offer help in many ways.

IV. Speaking highly of China's role in the establishment of a new international order

Q: In your understanding, what impact has socialist China's achievements had on the international order?

A: Following the collapse of the bipolar and unipolar (the US) world order, a huge political and economic vacuum emerged in international relations, bringing about serious and dangerous consequences. The sooner the international community can cope with this paradoxical situation, the better. There are many powerful forces in the world willing to restore the former political and economic order and their global domination and hegemony. The first, of course, is the US and some of its allies. They seem to ignore an important lesson given by famous ancient philosophers, mainly the Chinese and Greeks, that "no one can step twice into the same river" or "lightning never strikes the same place twice". There are also important international organizations, such as the Freemasonry New World Order, whose purpose is to establish an order to rule the world according to their partisan interests. We must take these realities into account if we are to build a new order featuring peace, development, justice and prosperity for all the people.

Supported by its famous opening up policy, the People's Republic of China has begun to make big strides. Under the leadership of President Xi Jinping, the achievements of China's development are being greatly expanded and improved, which have nothing to do with the outmoded old models of the above-mentioned order, and stand in sharp contrast, if I may say so, to contemporary efforts to restore what has been consigned to the dustbin of history. A new order without a ruling or authoritarian state or organization is considered to be a global multipolar system, with each pole surrounded by several countries. This multilateralism already has had a solid foundation, i.e. BRICS, the Shanghai Cooperation Organization, the European Union, the African Union and the like, as well as numerous comprehensive strategic partnership agreements between China and other countries.

In addition, China's global projects, for example, the Belt and Road Initiative, are also helpful to building a really new world order based on new power relationships and the vital needs and interests of nearly 8 billion people in the world.

Q: As you have said, China is having a positive impact on the international order. So, how do you view the global significance and influence of Xi Jinping Thought on Socialism with Chinese Characteristics for a New Era?

A: President Xi Jinping's thought and works, published in many languages including Polish, have aroused great interest around the world, enabling billions of people to have an in-depth understanding of the political and social system of socialism with Chinese characteristics for a new era and the policy of deepening reform and opening-up and firmly support it. People have begun to understand that such important thought and unprecedented practical developments are in the interests of not only the Chinese nation but also the whole of humanity. It has once again proved that China is not a country seeking self-interest, but an important global power that takes care of all countries, acts for their vital interests and strives for their common bright future.

If our joint efforts are to achieve positive results and prevent a new world war or any other major disaster, the ultimate objective and precondition for such efforts is, of course, a stable and peaceful global environment. Therefore, China pursues a foreign policy of peace, security, cooperation, harmony, development, survival, equality and partnership, which is the most precious gift that China offers to the rest of the world. President Xi Jinping has also paid special attention to the modernization and combat capability of the armed forces. This is totally understandable because China has so much to defend. Therefore, China must have enough tools to defend Chinese socialism against all kinds of provocations and aggression. Moreover, as President Xi Jinping has pointed out many times in his works, China hopes to share with all other countries the rich fruits of its burgeoning socialism, innovation and modernization. In fact, it does mean that the goal of Chinese socialism is truly cosmopolitan, which may succeed in overcoming the

Socialism with Chinese Characteristics Has Brought Vigor and Vitality to World Socialism

existing defects, disparities and underdevelopment in large parts of our civilization.

V. Socialism and socialist China in the eyes of the Polish people

Q: The year of 2019 marks the 70th anniversary of the founding of the People's Republic of China and the establishment of diplomatic ties between China and Poland. As one of the first countries to establish diplomatic relations with China in the early days of the founding of the People's Republic of China, how do the Polish people view socialism and China?

A: With regard to socialism, our Polish Socialist Party was founded in 1892 and still exists today. Its main task is to build a pure and idealized socialism in the country. However, due to a number of major reasons and obstacles including the First World War, the Second World War, Sovietization, and Americanization of Poland and so on, it is impossible to complete the task. Therefore, there are great differences in the understanding and interpretation of socialism and China among different generations in our country. The people born in the post World War II period experienced the Soviet version of what became known as the "real socialism," namely, Sovietism, but this socialism has nothing in common with the later socialist reality. Our country was ravaged and destroyed by Nazi Germany. Therefore, the government and the people think it extremely important for Poland to be engaged in reconstruction, so they are less concerned about other political and social systems and factions.

In Europe, there are quite strong socialists or social democratic parties such as the Italian Socialist Party, the French Socialist Party, the British Labor Party, the German Social Democratic Party and the Spanish Socialist Workers' Party. But they all failed to establish real socialism in their respective countries. Therefore, there are no good examples and clear guidelines for us to follow. On the other hand, the correct understanding or application of Mao Zedong Thought was too far away and vague. Yet things look different now, because socialism with Chinese characteristics for a new era has made many positive and amazing achievements in China and around the world. It is a truly universal solution that can successfully and flexibly be adapted to other countries and save our civilization.

On the whole, our people speak highly of China, its civilization, culture, art and foods, and its great contribution to world development. The Polish people respect China even though they don't know much about it. Poland is grateful for your support and assistance in our time of need. For example, Chairman Mao Zedong opposed and prevented the imminent military intervention of the Soviet Union in Poland during the revolutionary turmoil in 1956 and ordered food from Poland. As far as we know, Poland is one of the first countries to establish diplomatic ties with China at the beginning of the founding of the People's Republic of China. It set up the first China-Poland joint airline company – China-Poland Company. It supported China to join the United Nations and adheres to the one-China principle. It presided over ambassadorial level talks between China and the US in Warsaw, making a great contribution to the normalization of China-US relations. Poland also did not criticize China and Mao Zedong Thought on the China-Soviet dispute and other issues. This is an important and real achievement made by the leaders and peoples of the two countries in the early days of friendly coexistence.

But at the same time, in spite of various modern media, tourism, transportation, business, cooperation between friendly cities, exchanges and even intermarriage between people, Confucius institutes in Poland and Polish cultural institutes in China as well as better cooperation within the multilateral frameworks, such as the Belt and Road Initiative, 17+1, Asia-Europe Meeting, China-EU Consultation, Asian Infrastructure Investment Bank and UN peace-keeping operations, there is still a serious information and knowledge gap between our two peoples, although the gap is gradually narrowing. Both sides still have a lot of work to do to eliminate the aforementioned information and trade deficits in order to better understand each other and pave the way for the common ultimate goal of a new multilateral world order and a fruitful China-Poland-Eurasia cooperation.

There are generational differences in the attitude of the ordinary Polish towards China, but on the whole, as I mentioned above, it is friendly and positive. Of course, the old and middle-aged know China better than the young. Anyway, in the eyes of the young Polish, China is becoming more "fashionable" in terms of culture, language, traditional medicine, food, electronic products, cars, bicycles, clothing, household items, and sports and so on. Our businessmen and young people are increasingly inclined to build partnerships with China. They are becoming more and more interested in investing, studying and working in China. The steady and substantive advancement in the cooperation between our two countries will undoubtedly provide more favorable conditions for better mutual understanding, which is both possible and necessary for we both look forward to more positive outcomes in the future on the 100th anniversary of the founding of the People's Republic of China and the 100th anniversary of the establishment of diplomatic relations between our two countries. To the tune of a famous Polish pop song: "Sto lat niech żyje nam...," I congratulate the People's Republic of China beforehand on its happy 100th birthday. Long live the friendship between the People's Republic of China and Poland! Come on! Come on! Come on!

Socialism with Chinese characteristics in a new era has achieved many exciting results in China and the world at large. It is a truly universal solution that can be successfully and flexibly applied to other countries and save civilization. It is an important model of combining theory with practice for the success of national development. Chinese leaders have a long-term vision for China's development and their policies are consistent. At the same time, the Chinese people are hard-working and united as one. I am full of confidence in China's future. I am fully convinced that China knows better than any other country what it needs to do and how to do it in the future.

The CPRF's Interest in and Research and Evaluation on Xi Jinping Thought on Socialism with Chinese Characteristics for a New Era
– An Interview with Dmitry Novikov, Vice-chairman of the CPRF

Interviewed by Kang Yanru[1] , Li Xiaohua[2]

Translated by Xie Shengzhe

Finalized by Wang Qiuhai

Dmitry Novikov

Dmitry Novikov was born on September 12, 1969 in Khabarovsk, Soviet Union (now Russia). During his youth, Novikov lived with his family in a village 25 kilometers from Belogorsk, Amur Oblast. He received education there and graduated from the No.1 Middle School. He left there in 1986 and studied in the Department of History at Blagoveshchensk State Pedagogical University. Then he was recruited into the army the next year and served in the Soviet Air Defense Forces.

In 1989 Novikov returned to university for further study. In 1992, he graduated

---

1   Kang Yanru, assistant research fellow of the Academy of Marxism, Chinese Academy of Social Sciences.

2   Li Xiaohua, assistant research fellow of the Academy of Marxism, Chinese Academy of Social Sciences.

with honors from the department of history, sociology and law in Blagoveshchensk State Normal University, the Soviet Union. After graduation Novikov began his career in the department of cultural studies at Blagoveshchensk State Normal University. He was first an assistant teacher, then a senior teacher. In the meantime, he pursued his study in graduate school and was engaged in scientific work.

In 1992 Novikov joined the Communist Party of the Russian Federation (CPRF). He took an active part in the reconstruction of the Amur Oblast branch of the CPRF and was elected the member and secretary of the CPRF Blagoveshchensk Municipal Committee and the CPRF Amur Oblast Committee for many times. In the same year, Novikov worked as the leader of the organizing committee for the reconstruction of the Communist Youth League in Amur Oblast.

From 1995 to 1997, Novikov served as a part-time assistant in the Federation Council of the Russian Federal Assembly. From 1997 to 2001, he was in charge of the Youth Affairs Committee of Amur Oblast. In 2001, after Novikov completed the defense of his associate doctoral thesis in the department of history at Moscow State Normal University, he went on to work as an associate professor at Blagoveshchensk State Normal University.

From 1992 to 2001, Novikov was at the helm of the Communist Youth League of the Amur Oblast and was elected member and secretary of the Central Committee of the Communist Youth League of the Russian Federation. In the autumn of 2001, he participated in the by-election of Blagoveshchensk Single Member Constituency (Amur Oblast) for the Duma of the Russian Federation. In 2004, he was elected member and secretary of the Central Committee of the CPRF. Moreover, in 2005, Novikov was elected representative of the CPRF in the local assembly of the Amur Oblast. During his tenure, he severely criticized Nikolay Kolesov, governor of Amur Oblast, accusing the latter of putting pressure on the Communist Party and preventing it from organizing its election campaign. He even appealed to the Russian president, demanding to remove Kolesov from office. Communists said the governor's policies had "weakened the power of the state". In 2008, Kolesov was relieved of his post. From 2007 to 2011, he served as a deputy to the State Duma of the Russian Federation. In 2011, he was elected deputy to the 6th State Duma of the Russian Federation, member of the Party Group of the CPRF, and the first vice-chairman of the Science and Technology Committee. Since 2016, he has served as a deputy to the 7th State Duma of the Russian Federation and first vice-chairman of the Duma Committee on International Affairs.

On February 24, 2013, Novikov was elected vice-chairman of the Central Committee at the 15th Congress of the CPRF. At the same time, he was appointed head of the Center for Political Education of the Central Committee of the CPRF. On May 27, 2017, he was elected a member of the Central Committee of the CPRF at the 17th Congress of the party and a member of the Presidium and vice-chairman of the Central Committee of the CPRF at its first plenary session.

Interview Summary

The CPRF believes that China's tremendous achievements in development have overturned the assertion that socialism is bound to suffer a historic defeat in the competition with capitalism, and the left-wing political parties and movements in the world have regained confidence in China's experience and achievements. Xi Jinping Thought on Socialism with Chinese Characteristics for a New Era is a profound and detailed ideology aimed at realizing socialist modernization and the great rejuvenation of the Chinese nation, and the realization of this goal will make important contribution to the prosperity of the mankind. Since the 18th CPC National Congress, Xi Jinping has not only put forward a series of major ideas on governance, but also supervised the formulation of very effective principles and policies. Communist parties of other countries should learn from the CPC's measures and experience in boosting the modernization of its governance system and capacity. The globalism dominated by Western countries is today's version of imperialism, from which ordinary people do not benefit. The concept of "a community with a shared future for mankind" emphasizes fairness and justice. It embodies the unique principle internationalism of the communists and represents the direction of the development of mankind in the future.

I. Xi Jinping Thought on Socialism with Chinese Characteristics for a New Era is a major achievement in deepening our understanding of the law of socialist development

Q: Mr. Dmitry Novikov, nice to meet you! The Communist Party of China (CPC) and the CPRF have a good relationship. Both parties always pay close attention to each other's policy and activities. Could you please talk about the research of the CPRF on Xi Jinping Thought on Socialism with Chinese Characteristics for a New Era?

A: The CPRF always pays close attention to the theoretical and practical work of the socialist development of the Communist Party of China. The CPRF has carefully studied the documents of the 18th and 19th CPC congresses and other meetings, following with interest Xi Jinping Thought on Socialism with Chinese Characteristics for a New Era. The reports of General Secretary Xi Jinping and other leaders of the Communist Party of China have been successively published in *Pravda* and *Soviet Russia*, the TV program of the CPRF, "Red Line", the journal *Political Education* and the local newspapers and websites of the CPRF. Activists of the CPRF from all over the country have also learned about Xi Jinping Thought on Socialism with Chinese Characteristics for a New Era while receiving training at the Center for Political Study of the Central Committee of the CPRF. On the initiative of the party group of the CPRF in the Duma, Xi Jinping Thought on Socialism with Chinese Characteristics for a New Era was discussed and studied at the hearings and the round-table conferences held by the Russian Parliament.

The congress and the plenary session of the Central Committee of the CPRF also pay close attention to the work of the Communist Party of China. Gennady

Andreyevich Zyuganov, chairman of the CPRF, pointed out at the plenary session held in March 2019 that China has achieved a unique historical leap by carrying out economic reform under the red flag. Such achievements can only be matched by the great achievements of modernization under the leadership of Lenin and Stalin. China has consolidated its economic strength and defense capability and enhanced its influence on international affairs. Today, Russia is moving closer to China's socialism than to the capitalism in the West. This situation has laid a foundation for economic, political, cultural and security cooperation between the two countries. The CPRF maintains solid and close ties with the Communist Party of China. In addition, it is using its influence to bring the two countries closer to each other, deepen the friendship between the two peoples, and increase the constructive role of the two countries on the world stage.

The CPC has proved to the world that in the new era, the building of socialism with Chinese characteristics is not just a slogan and a beautiful declaration, but a profound and detailed ideological system. For example, in the field of national construction and Party building, Xi Jinping Thought on Socialism with Chinese Characteristics for a New Era proposes to build a socialist country under the rule of law. In the field of national defense, it emphasizes the consolidation of the Party's leadership over the armed forces and the modernization of the people's army. In aspects of diplomacy and international relations, Xi Jinping Thought on Socialism with Chinese Characteristics for a New Era calls for the construction of a new-style international relation and a "community with a shared future for mankind." The core issue of the Thought for a New Era is the people and their interests and needs, as well as the all-round development of each individual.

Q: How do you evaluate the achievements and experience of the People's Republic of China in building socialism over the past 70 years?

A: Over the past 70 years, the great achievements of the People's Republic of China have, first of all, been attributed to the work done by the Communist Party of China in upholding Marxism-Leninism, creatively developing socialist thought, continuously improving the theory and practice of socialist development, and paying close attention to the needs of the people. In particular, adhering to Marxism-Leninism and ideological principles is the main experience of the Chinese people under the leadership of the Communist Party of China. On the one hand, the CPC carefully studied and summarized the lessons that led to the collapse of the Soviet Communist Party and the disintegration of the Soviet Union. On the other hand, the CPC abides by the basic principles of communist ideology and takes a keen attitude toward all phenomena and events in today's world. On the basis of these principles, the ideological system of socialism with Chinese characteristics has been formed.

Q: While China is developing rapidly, it is also faced with a variety of new challenges. Could you talk about them in detail?

A: While China is developing at a high speed and has made great and remarkable achievements, it is facing increasing challenges, including environmental deterioration and ecological problem caused by the rapid development of industry, the dependence of Chinese economy on advanced science and technology of western countries, corruption and negative phenomena within Party and state organs and the like. At the international level, as the global crisis of capitalism intensifies, the exploitation of laborers and natural resources has led to an increase in the number of poor people, serious social differentiation and ecological disasters. At the same time, in order to compete for resources and markets, the internal struggle of imperialism is becoming more and more intense, and the contradiction of imperialism is aggravating. Under such conditions, the CPC, based its deep understanding of the law of socialist development in China and the development trend of capitalism in the world, has creatively put forward Xi Jinping Thought on Socialism with Chinese Characteristics for a New Era with an attempt to realize socialist modernization and the great rejuvenation of the Chinese nation. The realization of this goal will make an important contribution to the prosperity of mankind as a whole. Zyuganov pointed out in his book that the whole Russian society should study the experience of socialist development in China, for China has achieved success, while Russia is still suffering the "punishment" of liberal reform and refusing to carry out socialist modernization like China.

II. China's reform and opening up policy has scored remarkable achievements

Q: Could you please comment on how the CPRF views the main experience of China's reform and opening up policy and its influence on the world over the past 40 years?

A: The CPRF speaks highly of the achievements China has made in the past 40 years since the implementation of the reform and opening-up policy, believing that China's rapid development involves all aspects and fields of Chinese society and has in effect eliminated extreme poverty. All sectors of society in Russia have paid a lot of attention to China's impressive achievements. But unfortunately, during the same period, Russia has descended from the world's second largest economy (the Soviet Union) to the 11th economy in the world, accounting for less than 2 percent of the world economy. In contrast to Gorbachev's policy, China's reform is carried out in stages after prudent consideration, with the state retaining its leading role in the economy. The state ownership in key strategic sectors and the national economic planning system are preserved and play an important role, and the social security of the people is steadily improved. The CPRF believes that the reform and opening up policy is the greatest achievement of the Chinese people and its experience can and should be studied and applied by other countries. China's achievements debunk the argument that socialism is bound to suffer a historic failure in the competition with capitalism. Left-wing political parties and movements around the world have regained confidence in China's experience and achievements.

The CPRF holds that China's reform and opening up are closely related to the process of economic globalization. When the world's largest country is part and parcel of the global economy, it is unlikely not to affect the speed and nature of globalization. In the past few years, China has made eye-catching achievements in economy, society, culture and international relations. The proportion of China's exports in the world's total is 13 percent and ranks first. According to economists, without China, the average annual growth rate of the world economy would be 0.6 percent lower and its fluctuation range would increase sharply. These figures show that China's role in the global economy is steadily increasing and that China is making an increasingly important contribution to world development. At the same time, China always insists that the global economic development should follow fairer and more open rules that reject radical protectionism, sanctions, trade wars and other forms of pressure that the United States routinely uses. China represents a globalization that serves the interests of all peoples and nations and opposes discrimination and inequality. Directly proportional to the growth of China's economic influence, China's influence in international affairs is also growing accordingly. China is working with Russia and several other countries in the world to make efforts to establish a new order of international relations that is more harmonious.

III. The CPC's measures in boosting the modernization of governance system and governance capacity are of useful reference

Q: In your opinion, what measures taken by the CPC have played an important role in modernizing state governance system and capacity?

A: The reason why China has made such enormous achievements today is the political system established after the founding of the People's Republic of China, in which the Communist Party plays a crucial role. The role of the CPC is manifested in the following two aspects. On the one hand, the Party formulates necessary domestic and foreign policies. On the other hand, it has branches all over China. The CPC formulates work objectives before achieving concrete results through key members. In fact, it is because of the leadership of the Communist Party of China, which takes Marxism as its guide to action, that China has been able to get rid of its semi-colonial status, pursue an independent foreign policy, make great economic achievements, and become one of the world leaders in economic development. Practice is the only criterion for testing truth. China's practice has proved that it is precisely because of holding high the red flag and following Marxism as a guide to action that China has made today's brilliant achievements and ensured its steady, firm and efficient development. Since the 18th National Congress of the CPC, Xi Jinping has put forward a series of major ideas on governance and formulated very effective guidelines and policies. I believe that China is fully capable of accomplishing all the tasks he proposed, such as completing the building of a moderately prosperous society in all respects and fighting corruption. The policies implemented by China on the international stage are also very dynamic.

A scientific and mature attitude holds the key to the success of socialist development cause. The Communist Party of China thoroughly studies and analyzes every issue in social life before making a decision. The five-pronged overall plan for China's development put forward by the Communist Party of China covers the construction of economic, political, cultural, social and ecological civilization. The modernization of the governance system and governance capacity and the improvement of the work efficiency of government agencies at all levels are the necessary conditions for realizing this grand plan. The Communist Party of China always emphasizes a people-centered philosophy and takes the people's aspiration for a better life as the focus of its efforts. Since reform and opening up, 740 million people in China have been lifted out of poverty, with the rural poverty rate dropping from 97.5 percent in 1978 to 1.7 percent in 2018. This achievement has attracted worldwide attention. In addition, the CPC also strives to promote the all-round development of social field and citizens, and plans to complete the building of a moderately prosperous society in all respects by 2020, basically realize socialist modernization by 2035, and build a great modern socialist country that is prosperous, strong, democratic, culturally advanced, harmonious and beautiful by the middle of this century.

The CPC has the courage to criticize and reform itself. After the 18th CPC National Congress, the Party's work style has been significantly improved. The correction of formalism, bureaucracy, hedonism and extravagance has eliminated the obstacles in the relationship between leading cadres and the masses. The leaders of the party and the state have constantly stressed that the fight against corruption should adhere to the principle of no forbidden zone, no ground left unturned and zero tolerance, and not only taken punitive measures to promote the fight against corruption, but also set up preventive mechanisms to prevent the occurrence of it. China's fight against corruption has been approved by the world.

The CPC's measures and experience in modernizing its governance system and capacity are worth studying by the communist parties in other countries including the CPRF. The Communist Party of China is keenly aware of the process of social development, public opinion and world development trends, and makes timely and significant adjustments to the country's governance structure and policies in light of new developments at home and abroad. The experience of the Communist Party of China in this regard has inspired the CPRF and communist organizations in other countries to explore new forms and methods of work.

IV. Xi Jinping's thought of "the Community with a Shared Future for Mankind" represents the development trend of the globalization in the future

Q: Today, globalization has become an irreversible trend sweeping across all countries in the world. How does the CPRF understand the globalization at the current stage? In the context of globalization, how do you evaluate Xi Jinping's thought of building a "community with a shared future for mankind"?

A: I'd like to expound on the CPRF's understanding of the issue of globalization. Firstly, globalization is the inevitable result of scientific and technological progress and economic development of human society, and it is an irreversible process. With the advent of the first industrial revolution in the middle of the 18th century, the international division of labor came into being. In the middle and late 19th century, the second industrial revolution gave birth to the first wave of economic globalization. The scientific and technological revolution that emerged in the mid-1970s further promoted the process of economic globalization. Secondly, the globalization dominated by western developed countries threatens human society. Globalization at the present stage is still in the imperialist stage, which does great harm to mankind. For example, under the imperialist system, with the continuous division and refinement of social division of labor, economic expansion is no longer limited to one country, and the scale of speculative economy is constantly expanding. There is a serious gap between the rich and the poor in society. Globalization led by the west is threatening human security, as exemplified by the turmoil in Libya, Afghanistan, Yugoslavia and other countries. In terms of culture, the core idea of the globalization promoted by European countries and the US embodies the inherent way of thinking and values of Western civilization characterized by emphasizing the superiority of Western civilization and despising other civilizations. In short, Western-led globalism is the present-day version of imperialism from which ordinary people cannot benefit. Thirdly, there are three main types of thinking about globalization including Xi Jinping's thought on "the community with a shared future for mankind", the religious globalism characterized by relying on some special spirit (some Muslim countries) and anti-globalization thought (the United States under the leadership of Donald Trump). Of the three above, the concept of "a community with a shared future for mankind" puts stress on the fairness and justice without imposing the will of China on other countries. It is aimed at creating a wonderful world in which "countries respect each other's interests while pursuing their own and advance common interests of all". Such a wonderful world of universal harmony is the direction for the development of mankind in the future. Trump's idea of anti-globalization is rigid, conservative and isolated, and has no prospects for development.

V. The US starts a trade war to maintain the global dominance of its domestic monopolies

Q: Please share your ideas about the trade war launched by the United States against China.

A: The fundamental purpose of the US in launching a trade war is to maintain the global dominance of its domestic monopolies. Trump's policy is not based on the fabricated "unfriendly China", but on the fear of a rapidly developing China on the part of the ruling clique of the US. Western capital is terrified of what China has achieved, especially the "Made in China 2025" strategy, which aims to make China a world leader in the high-tech field. Advocating the so-called "America First" slogan, he is the representative of the richest bourgeois elites in the United States, relying on the military industrial group and financial capital group. Therefore, when talking about US interests, Trump actually refers to the billionaires and owners of big companies in the US. "America First" is in effect the slogan of a handful of most reactionary forces in the United States.

As for the trade war launched by the United States, the CPRF believes that China should make use of every opportunity to engage in dialogue with the United States, giving consideration to both flexibility and toughness in its policy about its economic and trade relations with the United States and actively developing economic ties with other countries. In addition, China should also vigorously promote the establishment of a new order of international relations based on justice and equality, which should, in the first place, start from consolidating the position of the United Nations in the contemporary world. The idea of building a "community with a shared future for mankind" proposed by President Xi Jinping is very attractive. At the present stage, this thought embodies the unique internationalist principle of the Communists.

China Seeks a Just Global Order in the New Era
– An Interview with Srgjan Kerim, Former Foreign Minister of Macedonia*

Interviewed by Zhang Li[1]
Translated by Xie Shengzhe
Finalized by Wang Qiuhai

Srgjan Kerim

Srgjan Kerim was born on December 12, 1948 in Skopje and got a Ph.D. at the University of Belgrade. In 1972, he became an assistant professor in the Faculty of Economics of the university and later a professor in the Department for International Economic Relations.

From 1986 to 1991, he served as the chairman of the Sub-Committee on Foreign Economic Relations under the Order Council of the Socialist Republic of Macedonia, and concurrently as the assistant minister and spokesman of the Ministry of Foreign Affairs of the former Federal Republic of Yugoslavia. In 1990, he was a member of the team responsible for preparing for and participating in the first OSCE Conference on Economic Cooperation, which was held in Bonn.

From 1994 to 2003, he was ambassador of Macedonia to Germany,

---

* Macedonia was renamed as Republic of North Macedonia on February 12, 2019.

1 Zhang Li, an associate research fellow of the Academy of Marxism, Chinese Academy of Social Sciences.

Liechtenstein, Switzerland and the United Nations.

From 1999 to 2000, he served as Special Envoy of the Coordinator of the Stability Pact for South-Eastern Europe.

From 2000 to 2001, he was Minister of Foreign Affairs of the Republic of Macedonia.

On September 17, 2015, he was nominated by the Macedonian government as the UN Secretary General, becoming the first official candidate to be nominated.

From 2007 to 2008, he worked as president of the 62nd Session of the United Nations General Assembly. In 2008, he served as the Special Envoy of the UN Secretary General on Climate Change. In 2009, he became a member of Committee of Presidents of the United Nations General Assembly.

From 2003 to 2012, he was General Manager of WAZ Media Group in Southeast Europe and Director of Media Print Macedonia News Group. In 2012, he acted as chairman of Media Print Macedonia News Group.

Interview Summary

As the former president of the 62nd Session of the UN General Assembly, Srgjan Kerim witnessed the drastic changes in the Central and Eastern Europe and the rising international status of China that is playing an increasingly important role on the international stage. He has closely observed and pondered over China's rapid development since it entered the new era as well as its role as a promoter of world peace, a contributor to global development and a defender of international order. He believes that the Belt and Road Initiative put forward by Comrade Xi Jinping is a new form of promoting new regional cooperation, and the diplomatic thought of "a community with a shared future for mankind" and the strengthening of the status of the United Nations are very important for the pursuit of a better world and a more just global order.

Professor Srgjan Kerim, former Minister of Foreign Affairs of the Republic of Macedonia, served as President of the 62nd Session of the UN General Assembly in 2007 and Special Envoy of the UN Secretary General on Climate Change in 2008. In the field of diplomacy, he is regarded as the "world president" in this era. *Globalization and Diplomacy-In Search of a Better World* is Kerim's memoirs and diplomatic manifesto, which clearly reflects the reality of the world, namely, the amazing problems and dilemma we are facing. In this book, he speaks highly of China's development achievements in the new era, pointing out that China's unremitting effort to make the world a better place than it is now is a major contribution to the new global discourse. In diplomacy, he holds that China has embarked on a historic new journey guided by Xi Jinping Thought on Socialism with Chinese Characteristics for a New Era. In recent years, China has played a more proactive role in international affairs, becoming a promoter of world peace, a contributor to global development and a defender of international order.

I. Praising China's tremendous achievements over the past 70 years

Q: It's a pleasure to meet you, Mr. Kerim. We are very glad that you accepted our interview. The People's Republic of China has made great achievements since its founding. In particular, the military parade marking the 70th anniversary of its founding attracted the attention of the world with a new look. As a witness of socialist practice, how do you understand and evaluate China's achievements over the past 70 years?

A: I watched the celebration of the 70th anniversary of the founding of the People's Republic of China and the military parade. I was deeply impressed by the tremendous achievements China has made over the past 70 years and the development and changes that have taken place in your country. President Xi Jinping has formed the theory of socialism with Chinese characteristics for a new era to ensure that a stable, prosperous and strong China plays a key and more important role in today's world. China's opening up strategy is not only an inevitable process of adapting to globalization, but also to the vigorous development of China's economy and trade. Over the past 40-odd years since the policy of reform and opening up was implemented, China has played an important role on the world stage. As the world's second largest economy, it is active in almost every area of the international business community.

Q: As a witness to the drastic changes in Eastern Europe and the social transformation in Macedonia, how do you view the development and changes of world socialism in the past 30 years after the drastic changes in Eastern Europe?

A: First of all, let's review the development history of socialism, especially in the past 100 years. At the beginning of the 20th century, communism, which was based on socialism and subsequent Marxism-Leninism, emerged on the historical stage. The Bolshevik Revolution of 1917 gave birth to the Soviet Russia, the first socialist country ruled by a Communist Party. After the Second World War, socialist countries emerged in Eastern Europe, Asia, Africa and South America. There were a total of 25 such countries, including China. However, with passage of time, many countries abandoned the socialist system and took the path of capitalism. Currently, only five countries including China, Laos, Cuba, Vietnam and North Korea adhere to the socialist system.

The drastic changes in Eastern Europe and the disintegration of the Soviet Union brought great harm to the world socialist movement. As a value system, socialism is multifaceted and there is no unified model. One of the key factors for the failure of the Soviet Union's socialist model is the neglect of this problem. On the one hand, simply exporting the socialist model to other countries did not work and was counterproductive, which has been proven by history. On the other hand, Francis Fukuyama, an American political scientist, was wrong to say that the collapse of communism in the Soviet Union and Eastern Europe was "the end of history". The rivalry between the West and the East still exists. The US and the EU belong to the former while Russia and China belong to the latter. This is not simply

China in the New Era

a matter of geography, but of significant differences in the perception of different national institutions and fundamental values. Although the process of globalization, based on the rapid development of information and communication technology, is in full swing, there are huge differences in values between the East and the West due to differences in history, culture and other aspects. To overcome these differences, countries need to tolerate and respect each other. The great development of socialism with Chinese characteristics has enhanced China's political status in the world.

Q: You have also recognized and spoken highly of the path of socialism with Chinese characteristics that China has blazed over the past 70 years to achieve the great goals of national prosperity, rejuvenation and people's happiness. This path is of great significance. Do you think the path of socialism with Chinese characteristics is of world historical significance to the world socialist movement?

A: Yes, China's socialist path has been the most successful. It is a perfect combination of socialist political system and market economic measures. One of the most successful reasons for China's socialist path is that opening up its economy to the world has played a crucial role. In 1995, when China joined the World Trade Organization, its trade share accounted for only 2 percent of the world's total. In 2004, China ranked fourth in the WTO with US$516 billion, accounting for 5 percent of the world's total trade. In 2018, China's trade accounted for 10 to 20 percent of the world's total and ranked first in the world with US$26 trillion, followed by the United States with US$25 trillion. For many countries, China is now a more important trading partner than the United States, and much of Asia is centered on China, especially because of its development model that has made poor countries rich. Since the 16th century, a country's strength and prosperity have been measured by its exports and its balance of foreign trade. The performance of economy and trade today is very important for geopolitical influence and power.

The more important reason for the success of China's socialist path is the leadership of the Communist Party of China. As the largest political party in the

264

China Seeks a Just Global Order in the New Era

world, the CPC, with more than 95 million members, plays a decisive role in maintaining the cohesion of Chinese society. This is no easy task for a country with 1.4 billion people. Therefore, on the one hand, President Xi Jinping has insisted on strengthening the role of the Communist Party of China. Corruption is a major problem that must be addressed through a combination of reasonable means, such as the rule of law and taxation. On the other hand, the CPC has to correctly address the issue on how to better combine socialism with the advantages of capital, which is necessary to function at the national, provincial and local levels. The guiding principle of socialism is one of the greatest achievements of the People's Republic of China which has provided an effective means to eradicate poverty.

II. China in the new era has made contributions to the global order

Q: Thank you very much! Economic globalization is surging forward, and the new scientific and technological as well as industrial revolution is rapidly developing which means that globalization has provided potential benefits for all countries. Both developed countries and developing countries can benefit and enjoy an equal status in the global economy, especially the rapid rise of emerging economies such as China and India in a relatively short period of time. Since the 18th National Congress of the CPC, the most important theoretical and practical innovation of the CPC is that it has put forward Xi Jinping Thought on Socialism with Chinese Characteristics for a New Era. Please share your views on China in the new era under the leadership of Xi Jinping.

A: China's achievement in development is not only intended for helping hundreds of millions of its people out of poverty. More importantly, its rising revenue and wealth have provided huge new business opportunities for developed countries. China's greatest achievement in the past 70 years, namely, the experience of lifting more than 700 million people out of poverty, is based on the implementation of a people-centered and sustainable development strategy. This and other concrete achievements in the economic, social and technological fields have increased China's reputation and credibility as a reliable and ideal partner all over the world.

China's reform and opening up has achieved fruitful results. Today's economic and trade performance has a very important impact on world geopolitics. In 1995, before China joined the world trade, it accounted for only two percent of the total world trade. In 2018, China accounted for 11 percent. China ranks first with US$26 trillion, while the United States ranks second with US$25 trillion. Germany, Japan and France rank third, fourth and fifth, respectively. These figures show the strength of a country. Therefore, the rise of China is a normal and rational development in the current globalization process. The main reason is that the reform and opening up policy of socialism with Chinese characteristics in the new era formulated by Xi Jinping has promoted the continuous rise of China's competitiveness in the world economy. For many countries, China is now a more important trade partner than the United States, and most countries in Asia regard China as a cooperative partner, especially because the socialist development model with Chinese characteristics has moved from poverty to prosperity.

Q: As you said, China's development achievements have enhanced its status in international politics. It is true that China is a popular trade partner. In the past two years, the United States has been in constant friction with China over the Huawei issue. What do you think is the underlying problem behind this?

A: In my view, economic globalization and the emerging "digital age" are the leading forces representing a major shift from the "Cold War" period characterized by emphasizing the ideological disputes to a technology-dominated and thriving era of peace and development. By fostering and supporting new sources of growth through innovation, emerging economies such as China are greatly changing the picture of global innovation. High-tech and its controllers have gained the status and discourse power in the process of globalization. China's R&D expenditure ranks second in the world and holds many cutting-edge technologies in the world, as evidenced by Huawei's success as a global telecommunications equipment provider.

This issue is of great significance for President Xi Jinping to launch the modernization process in the new era. Focusing on quality rather than quantity in development means more and more investment in innovation and advanced technology. Therefore, scientific research is becoming the driving force for the sustainable development of the national economy. In his keynote speech at the opening ceremony of China's second International Import Expo on November 5, 2019, President Xi Jinping proposed building an open and innovative world economy, and "promoting integrated development of science and technology and economy, and the sharing of achievements in innovation". What President Xi Jinping has said is entirely in line with a world that is moving toward a scientific and technological economy. Governments around the world will redouble their efforts to ensure they are not left behind. The results of research should be of beneficial to the people of the world and promote peace and stability. It is very interesting to look at the statistics of research and development from different perspectives. The top five countries with the highest R&D spending as a percentage of GDP are Israel (4 percent), South Korea (15 percent), Japan (49 percent), Finland (32 percent) and Sweden (30 percent), with China (12 percent) in the sixth place.

In the age of globalization, we actually live in a "digital world" or a world of the fourth industrial revolution. Globalization is an unstoppable process, which is driven by rapid advances in innovation, research and technology, especially in the field of information and communications. We should rethink the emergence and development of industrialization in the early 19th century. It's a process that has been going on for more than 200 years, starting in the United Kingdom and Germany, continuing in the United States and Japan, and taken over by the so-called Third World countries including China, India and other emerging economies. Globalization will decisively shape the 21st century, and will show a new dimension of the digital society. However, in a just society based on the equality of the people, how to solve and establish new social relations and a balanced distribution of wealth are still the key issues. The first two industrial revolutions fundamentally altered the relationship between the individual and the state, and the ongoing "digital revolution" has inevitably brought a fourth giant leap forward. In the context of economic globalization, Economic globalization needs to give technology more freedom to control the change of production mode, which may lead to the creation of a new framework for implementing global technology rules, i.e. how to control the flow of high-tech technology. The tension between China and the United States around Huawei 5G system and its distribution and China-US trade friction are the best examples.

Q: You mean we are going through the fourth revolution in production technology. Will that have an impact on international relations, or change the existing international relations?

A: The innovative power of technology forces us to re-examine our understanding of international relations. The world economy is entering an era in which global governance needs to play an increasingly important role to ensure that the benefits of global economic cooperation and integration can be maintained. As the embodiment of globalization and the fourth industrial revolution, the digital world is not the only great challenge of the 21st century. The impact of climate change should not be underestimated. The same is true of demographic changes and migration trends. All these deserve our full attention, at least because they are global. International institutions, including the United Nations, must adapt to this profound change in world affairs. They need to go through an important process of reform. China should play a very important role in this regard. At the same time, it should make contribution to the necessary changes in international institutions to steer the political and economic systems towards sustainable and harmonious development for whole human society, including the poorest 50 percent of people who live at the "bottom of the pyramid".

Global governance makes sense only if it is inclusive of all countries, regardless of their size, strength and geographic location. Since the 1970s, China has undergone a comprehensive reform of its economic system, especially Xi Jinping Thought on Socialism with Chinese Characteristics for a New Era, in which the Belt and Road Initiative and the concept of "Community with a Shared Future for Mankind" have opened up a whole new vista for China as a developing country to play a vital role in promoting the world economic system. It is necessary to promote the building of a new type of international relations and a sustainable global future for mankind. In terms of diplomacy, under the leadership of President Xi Jinping, China has completed a historic journey. It is more active in international affairs and is a promoter of world peace, a contributor to global development and a defender of international order.

III. The Belt and Road Initiative is a new form of promoting neo-regionalism cooperation

Q: Since the dramatic changes in Eastern Europe and the disintegration of the Soviet Union, Western neo-liberalists have advocated and cheered the "end of history" and the beginning of a "new world order". Since you witnessed this process, what do you think is the essence of the new order they are talking about?

A: The Balkan region has an important political and strategic position in the Eurasian corridor. After the dissolution of Yugoslavia, the Republic of Macedonia became an independent state. Because it has chosen this kind of democratic transformation, it has experienced many setbacks, which has seriously hindered economic growth and development.

The last decade of the 20th century was marked by turmoil in Eastern Europe. Two federal states, the Soviet Union and Yugoslavia, disintegrated. The former went thought it peacefully while the latter through armed conflict and war. All Eastern European countries, including the new ones that emerged from the ruins of Yugoslavia, began to experience the process of transition from socialism to capitalism. In other words, in terms of geopolitics, a structural transformation took place in Eastern Europe. In this historical context, the Republic of Macedonia became an independent state, which opted for the Western model of democracy established after the Second World War in 1945. This implies the country takes the respect for the rule of law, freedom of expression, human rights and market economy as the fundamental values of society. However, it is easier said than done. The transition from socialism to capitalism is a rather complex process with many setbacks and relapses. For a country with per capita GDP of between US$10,000 and US$50,000, the transition from state ownership to private ownership ended in a slippery slope of de-industrialization, which hindered economic growth and development. As a result, imports continued to exceed exports, indicating an enormous trade deficit created by Macedonia.

Macedonia's diplomatic strategy is based on its successful accession to the EU and the NATO. However, its fragile economy does not qualify it for a membership. The process is long and very complex. Ethnic tensions, particularly between Macedonians and Albanians, are constantly on the political agenda with serious consequences. This has created serious political problems in the country. The country name dispute with Greece, which has only recently been resolved, was once a major obstacle to the achievement of the desired diplomatic and political objectives. Macedonia's progress towards joining the European Union and NATO is long and has been repeatedly delayed, which is really frustrating.

Q: The transition in Eastern Europe in the past 30 years is really a sad thing. Could you further analyze the reasons behind this problem?

A: The removal of Berlin Wall in the late 1980s and early 1990s was hailed as the "end of history" and the start of a "new world order" by the people in the West. The new order, they argued, was based on a balance of interests rather than power. In other words, geopolitics would be replaced by liberalism on a global scale. The global financial crisis is a sure sign that this order is no longer suited to the developmental needs of today's world. Now, the role of geopolitics should not be underestimated any longer because it has become the foundation of foreign policy and international relations, which has been proved by the conflicts in the Balkans in the 1990s and in the Caucasus in the first decade of the 21st century. Western scholars point out that the focus of geopolitics has experienced an important shift from the Atlantic Ocean to the Pacific Ocean. Emerging economies such as China and India have begun to rise. These structural shifts in the balance of power have obviously had a significant impact on the ways and means of the international community to deal with the global crisis.

Q: Yes, China has put forward the Belt and Road Initiative to strengthen regional cooperation. But there are also different voices claiming that China is trying to "split Europe" and challenge the Western liberal world order with its economic investment and political infiltration. What do you think of such remarks?

A: Under the leadership of President Xi Jinping, as a new framework for better regional economic governance, greater worldwide development, and enhancement of the international cooperation among Asia, Europe and Africa, the Belt and Road Initiative has served as a means of establishing a special cooperation mechanism called "China + 17" with CEE and Southeast European countries. All of these cooperation models are aimed at building global connectivity partnerships. From 2013 to 2019, 136 countries and 30 international organizations signed cooperation documents with China on Belt and Road Initiative. The Belt and Road Initiative is a new form of cooperation for promoting new regionalism. It is a multilateral and bilateral regional economic cooperation model based on equality that does not seek ideological export, geopolitical bloc or military alliance through economic cooperation.

The Belt and Road Initiative follows the principle of extensive consultation, joint contribution and shared benefits to achieve common prosperity. This new model of regional cooperation offers hope to the Balkan countries. I agree with President Xi Jinping's speech at the Boao Forum for Asia that "we should abandon the outdated mindset, break away from the old confines that fetter development and unleash all the potential for development." China is Macedonia's partner within

China in the New Era

the "17+1" cooperation framework. As a permanent member of the UN Security Council, China is a staunch supporter of Macedonia and bilateral relations have been booming. China is investing in infrastructure and transportation in Macedonia, and the political cooperation between the two countries is in an excellent state.

IV. "Community with a Shared Future for Mankind" and new international order

Q: In this increasingly globalized world, the global problems we face, such as climate change, terrorism and sustainable development, require a new internationalism. What do you think is the new internationalism?

A: A new internationalism services the new global society. It is based on principled pragmatism and common responsibility, and is a new way of thinking about our common destiny, because it can reflect the complicated situations of contemporary human and economic relations. In addition, it pays attention to the well-being of the individual. We are now witnessing two major changes in world affairs that bring hope for current international relations and culture.

Q: What are the two major changes? Please analyze them in detail.

A: The first one represents a gradual shift from state-centered policies to people-centered strategies. China should play a very important role in this regard and contribute to the necessary changes in international institutions. The "community with a shared future for mankind" proposed by Xi Jinping means that the destiny of each nation and country is closely linked. It has turned the aspirations of people around the world for a better life into reality. The initiative of building a "community with a shared future for mankind" has been repeatedly written into UN documents, thus exerting an increasingly extensive and far-reaching international influence. It has become a bright banner for China to guide the trend of the times and the progress of human civilization. The goal of UN reforms and adjustments is to lead the construction of a new culture of international relations by building an interculturalism in international relations based on greater emphasis on mutual trust and cooperation and more equitable economic consensus. The promotion of a new culture of international relations requires a new global civil society in which all nations are partners and actively create a better, more sustainable and more just future that benefits all.

The second change is to pay special attention to the rights of the state and the individual, and to accept and recognize the responsibilities of the state and the individual that accompany these rights. We must be willing and able to take action against the threats to human security and fulfill our responsibilities. Accepting the people-oriented security concept requires us to take on greater responsibilities based on mutual respect, not only for ourselves, our own goals, but also for "others".

As President of the 62nd United Nations General Assembly, I believe that the United Nations, including the Security Council, must protect individuals and groups from threats and challenges. As the largest developing country, a permanent member of the UN Security Council and the UN's major donor, China firmly supports and pursues mutually beneficial and win-win multilateralism. China adheres to the multilateral cooperation mechanism and is a staunch supporter of the establishment of an international order around the United Nations. China advocates the establishment of the multilateral trading system with the World Trade Organization as its center.

Q: As a staunch supporter of human progress, the United Nations must adapt to the new environment. How can it increase its operation and prestige and enhance its effectiveness?

A: The role of the United Nations is focused on managing the challenges in the future. There must be a radical reform targeted at international relations. The following three points must be implemented. The first is broader democracy. As the speech delivered by Xi Jinping at the fifth BRICS Summit, promoting democracy in international relations and peace and development should be defined as "noble causes" which China should take an active part in and play a constructive role in so as to push international order in a more just and reasonable direction and provide institutional guarantee for world peace and stability. The second is to develop more equal relations with developing countries. As Chinese Foreign Minister Wang Yi pointed out when he chaired the UN Security Council's open debate on maintaining international peace and security in New York, this strategy is based on the principle of win-win situation rather than zero-sum game. The third is the willingness to conduct experiments. To achieve these goals, we must be more courageous and transcend our own limitations. Without the creation of a new culture of international relations, it would be impossible to address these global issues in an inclusive manner.

Q: What do you think of the global significance and impact of Xi Jinping Thought on Diplomacy?

A: The reason why am I quoting and emphasizing the thought of Chinese leaders here is that I firmly believe that we cannot translate these noble goals and causes into reality without affirming the primacy of multilateral cooperation mechanisms and their tools in the entire United Nations system. For me, it's all about the pursuit of a better world. For China, it's all about the pursuit of a more just global order, and we're all heading in the same direction.

The Unique Advantage of Socialism with Chinese Characteristics and Its World Significance
– An Interview with Vladimir Petkovski, the First Macedonian Ambassador to China

Interviewed by Song Lidan[1]
Translated by Xie Shengzhe
Finalized by Wang Qiuhai

Vladimir Petkovski

Vladimir Petkovski was from the former Socialist Federal Republic of Yugoslavia. Now he lives in the Republic of Macedonia (the present-day Republic of North Macedonia). He was the first Macedonian ambassador to China.

Vladimir Petkovski earned his master's and doctor's degrees in economics from the University of Belgrade in Yugoslavia in the 1970s. After graduation, he taught at a university. From 1980 to 1984, he was assigned to the Yugoslav Embassy in Washington, D.C., as a scientific and technical advisor. After a four-year stint at the embassy, Petkovski returned to a university to teach. At the end of 1989, he was appointed Yugoslavia's last ambassador to Sudan. In March 1992, with the disintegration of the Socialist Federal Republic of Yugoslavia and the independence

---

1 Song Lidan, associate research fellow of the Academy of Marxism, Chinese Academy of Social Sciences.

of Macedonia, Petkovski resigned from his diplomatic post in Yugoslavia and returned to Macedonia to teach in universities. Two years later, he became the first ambassador of Macedonia to China after it became an independent country. Petkovski's diplomatic career is full of legendary stories. According to him, he is not only the last ambassador of the Socialist Federal Republic of Yugoslavia but also the first ambassador of Macedonia as a new country in the world.

Interview Summary

Socialism with Chinese characteristics is an effective weapon for social and economic transformation and all-round development of a country. The Chinese political model offers an alternative to the existing governance system in the world. The main reason for the Western media's bias against socialism with Chinese characteristics lies in ideology. At the same time, ideology is also a major reason why the West regards an increasingly powerful China as a rival. The Communist Party of China is capable of meeting future challenges, and the international influence of socialism with Chinese characteristics will further increase.

I. Consequences and lessons of privatization in Macedonia

Q: Thank you, Professor Petkovski, for accepting our interview. The drastic change and disintegration experienced by the Socialist Federal Republic of Yugoslavia were not only a major geopolitical event, but also a major setback for the international communist movement. How do you evaluate the influence of the drastic change in Yugoslav on Macedonia?

A: Various republics lived together in the former Socialist Federal Republic of Yugoslavia as a prosperous European country for nearly 50 years. The disintegration of the federal republic was shocking, especially in the economic sphere because economic interconnectedness and interdependence were suddenly torn apart. A single market with a population of 23 million was reduced to one with a population of only 2 million in Macedonia. The task of re-establishing new economic links is not an easy one, for it has proved to be a costly and time-consuming task, requiring the establishment of vast new regulations and organizations from scratch. Most important of all, it is extremely painful.

After its independence, Macedonia abandoned the socialist system and embarked on a path characterized by private ownership (capitalism). At the same time, a pluralistic political system was introduced. Privatization has been going on in Macedonia for the first 10 years since it became independent in 1991. Infrastructure such as industry, service industry, most of telecom and banking facilities and electric power sector and other major national resources were massively privatized, incurring large-scale unemployment and negative growth of national economy. As a result, Macedonia lost the most crucial industrial production capacity (heavy industry and machine building industry). During the socialist period, Macedonia was able to export industrial refrigerators and public buses to China, and to undertake large-scale infrastructure projects in the Middle East, Africa and many other countries. However, after the disintegration of Yugoslavia, with the implementation of privatization, these industrial capacities disappeared. Macedonia's economy and society as a whole underwent a difficult and long process, taking almost two decades to reach the level of gross domestic product (GDP) before its disintegration in the 1990s. For this reason, many analysts have called Macedonia's privatization process "wild" and the decade of the 1990s a "lost decade".

In contrast to Macedonia, China's strategic principle of reform and opening up is both rational and stable, and the steps taken are both well-considered and progressive. According to the policy, "learning by experience" is allowed (a typical example is the establishment of the first special economic zones in China's coastal areas). Obviously, the political elite of the former Yugoslavia failed to learn from China's experience in implementing reform and opening up policies. They knew nothing about the saying that one can cross the river only when he has a clear understanding of the stepping stones. By the same token, only by getting a clear picture of the overall situation should people ask themselves whether it is worth doing something, or what the social and economic transition is and how to cross the river.

In Macedonia, people have suffered too much from the painful consequences of privatization and become disillusioned with liberal capitalism. During the same period, the continuous progress made by China made people interested in why the socialist system could generate such great achievements. They realized that all of China's achievements are the result of appropriate reform and transformation. It is the integration of socialist socio-economic and political system with Chinese society that has produced such a result.

II. Socialism with Chinese characteristics is an effective weapon for socio-economic transformation and all-round development of the country

Q: I agree with your understanding of China's reform and opening up. What do you think are the reasons for China's great achievements?

A: Modern social systems (whether "capitalism-oriented" or "socialism-oriented") are bound to possess many prerequisites before becoming successful and endure thereby. These prerequisites are, in the long run, stable economic and social systems that provide sustainable social and economic development. Throughout the period after Deng Xiaoping, China's leadership has displayed a strong ability to ensure a predictable, planned and regulatory transition of the whole society, the especially the economy, to a new level of development and social progress. Equally important, The Chinese leadership can ensure a smooth intergenerational succession of power. The system of "socialism with Chinese characteristics" is very congruent with this framework. The comprehensive progress and prosperity that China has achieved in recent decades is rare in human history. In particular, under President Xi's leadership over the past few years, the Chinese leadership has demonstrated its ability to cope with the tasks and challenges in the new era.

Historically, China is a country belonging to the third world, characterized by low per capita income, backward industrial structure, low agricultural productivity, outdated technology on the part of state-owned enterprises, insufficient infrastructure including roads and railways, low degree of world economic integration, low level of international trade, and big regional disparities. But now, judging from the scale of economic development, China is not only "the most successful socialist country" but also one of the most successful countries in modern human history. Just as important as its economic achievements is the establishment and development of such a social system in China that has demonstrated that admirable achievements can be made not only in the country's economic development but also in the development of society as a whole. Such is the system of socialism with Chinese characteristics.

In my opinion, there are at least four main reasons why China has such a great influence in the contemporary world. The first reason lies in the size of the country, including its vast territory and large population as well as its colossal cultural and civilizational heritage for thousands of years. The second reason lies in achievements in art, philosophy and education, including the ethical principle of harmonious relationship between society and family life, major technological innovations such as gunpowder, the compass, paper-making, printing technique, rudders, fortifications and stirrups. The third reason lies in the great achievements in social and economic development and economic growth that have made the China's economy the main engine of the world economy. The fourth reason lies in the characteristics of China's social, economic and political system – socialism with Chinese characteristics, which can achieve impressive outcomes in the social and economic transition and the country's overall development.

Q: After the profound changes in Eastern Europe and the disintegration of the Soviet Union, bourgeois scholars were optimistic that "history has come to an end". However, since 2008, the West has fallen into something of a chaos. The achievements made by China in the past 40-plus years of reform and opening up have become the subject of much discussion and research around the world. What do you think is the global significance of socialism with Chinese characteristics?

A: Xi Jinping Thought on Socialism with Chinese Characteristics for a New Era can be seen as a continuation of Marxism-Leninism, Mao Zedong Thought, Deng Xiaoping Theory, the Theory of Three Represents and the Scientific Outlook on Development. They are all the guiding principles based on "adapting Marxism to China's national conditions".

In my opinion, the great value and significance of Xi Jinping Thought on Socialism with Chinese Characteristics for a New Era is not only because it has been written into the Constitution of the Communist Party, but also because it is a document of strategic importance for China's social and economic development. This thought touches on the most important areas in China today, including the position of the CPC as the leading political force in Chinese society, thus providing guidance for the future development of Chinese society and the well-being of the country and its citizens. The scope of Xi Jinping Thought on Socialism with Chinese Characteristics for a New Era is comprehensive, because it covers the most important areas, not only involving the role and status of the Communist Party, but also going deep into the country's social and economic structure. This thought, which reflects the country's actual situation, has been developed on the basis of impressive achievements in the economic and social fields and has a clear view on the tasks and challenges facing China in the years and decades to come.

Xi Jinping Thought on Socialism with Chinese Characteristics for a New Era can help explain the prerequisites and background for China's impressive achievements in economic and social development to date, including the principal features of the unique role played by the CPC as the country's leading social and political force. At the same time, this thought has clear a view on the tasks and challenges China will face in the coming years and decades. While pondering over the world significance and international influence of Xi Jinping Thought on Socialism with Chinese Characteristics for a New Era, we should keep in mind the relationship between ideology and real life. In other words, the dominant ideology (thought) should not only inspire and correctly guide the future, but also mobilize people from all walks of life, not just Party members.

Xi Jinping Thought on Socialism with Chinese Characteristics for a New Era points out that "the dream of the Chinese people is closely connected with the dreams of the peoples of other countries". Therefore, it is necessary to adhere to "the building of 'a community with a shared future for mankind'". In this sense, Xi Jinping Thought on Socialism with Chinese Characteristics for a New Era is of worldwide significance not only to the socialist countries but also to the globe. Besides, President Xi's views and initiatives on diplomacy including peaceful development, a new model of major-power relations, diplomacy with neighboring countries, cooperation with developing countries and multilateral relations also have an international influence. And the size of China's economy, especially its level of integration in the entire world economy, has paved the way for its decisive role on the international stage, thus allowing China's influence in international relations and diplomacy to grow greater.

What has happened in China – ranging from the Silk Road in ancient times including the Middle Ages, the national democratic revolution in the 20th century, the founding of the Communist Party of China and the great people's revolution, to reform and opening up, as well as the development and achievements related to the building of socialism – is of worldwide significance. Now, the influence of socialist China encompasses the whole of international relations, including foreign policy and diplomacy, international development assistance, bilateral and multilateral world security and military cooperation. Contrary to the interventionist policy practiced by some Western countries, China pursues a policy of non-interference in the internal and foreign affairs of other countries (including the countries in which China has made immense investments), respecting the existence of different social systems and development paths, and not exporting socialism with Chinese characteristics. This is clearly recognized and respected and appreciated by other countries. It can be expected that the influence of the socialist system with Chinese characteristics on the international order will increase further.

Socialism is drawing greater attention from people in the world, especially the younger generation. In the US, different social groups, including the "middle class", are deeply disappointed with the growing social inequality, stagnant growth in real wages of workers and the further accumulation of wealth by the top 1 percent of richest Americans. On the other hand, China's huge achievements in social and economic development based on the policy of reform and opening up and led by the Communist Party of China have provided the world with a good example of the legitimacy, capacity and vitality of the socialist system with Chinese characteristics. Leaders of the Communist Party of China and the state have made a great contribution to socialist thought and practice. Therefore, socialist China is making its mark on human history in the late 20th and early 21st centuries.

The contemporary world is witnessing a pluralism of social and economic systems. As a successful governance model, the Chinese socialist model is also of great significance. Is China's "successful story" likely to be replicated? Yes, but the key is to keep economic development model and reform successful and sustainable for a long time, and accordingly, it is also necessary for the political system to be stable and predictable in the long run. The success of socialism with Chinese characteristics cannot be separated from the social and political system developed under the leadership of the Communist Party of China. China's political model offers an alternative to the existing governance system in the world. It is a political system under the leadership of a single party that has achieved tremendous success in economic and social reform, including the lifting of hundreds of millions of people out of poverty and the formation of a massive middle income group of hundreds of millions of people.

III. The Communist Party of China is capable of meeting the challenges in the future

Q: We know that the Western media always have a very unfriendly attitude toward China, and there are many distortions and misinterpretations of China. What do you think is the cause of this phenomenon?

A: There are many examples of Western media being biased against socialism with Chinese characteristics, and the main reason for this lies in ideology. Except the Scandinavian countries with a tradition of social democracy, in other Western countries, socialist thought is labeled as "totally inappropriate" and "unacceptable". It is because of the bias against socialism and China (this bias can be traced back to the October Revolution and the years after the founding of the Soviet union) that some western media face a knotty task – how to explain to the public why a socialist country with a hidebound, undemocratic social political system ("single-party system") can achieve such impressive achievements in economic and social development and become a strong and respected country in the world in a short span of several decades. However, ideology alone is not the only fundamental cause of such prejudice. The political orientation (class stance) of the founders and owners of these Western media as well as their interests and attitudes may also be the reasons to be considered.

The fact that the West regards an increasingly powerful China as a rival is also the reason for the media's bias against China. China's huge market and the prospects it offers for international trade and development make it a strong competitor to the West in sectors that have long been monopolized by developed economies, such as telecommunications, information, space and military technology, which is also a cause of their bias. To some extent, the achievements of the socialist system with Chinese characteristics have had a feedback effect, because they have begun to influence and even, to some degree, shape the strategic thinking of the world's "leading circle", the media included. Various international "circles" and powerful countries are actively observing and studying China. Proceeding from dealing with the national interests of particular countries, these countries often see China as a potential or real competitor on the world economic stage or even as a threat to their geostrategic interests and to transnational organizations such as the World Bank, the IMF, the WTO, the IFC and the United Nations. In the past few years, this competition between interest has focused on China's achievements in science and technology and high-tech innovation systems.

An increasing number of experts from around the world will study issues such as China's contribution and influence in the near future in terms of shaping the world and the destiny of mankind in the 21st century, the relationship between China's social and political system and its social and economic development, the transition of Chinese society to a modern and efficient system. These analyses and studies, assuming that they are completely independent, impartial and unbiased, are bound to prove the efficiency of the socialist system with Chinese characteristics.

Most Western media find it very difficult to acknowledge the fact that China's political system is a success, believing that a country's all-around development can only be achieved on the basis of a bourgeois democratic system. However, the financial and economic crisis in 2008 showed that the western countries failed to supervise the financial sector, which was a warning to the limitations of "democratic system".

Q: Historically, since the founding of the People's Republic of China, many Western media have been badmouthing China. In your opinion, is it possible for the CPC to tackle the problems and challenges it faces?

A: China has a crucial experience in its success from revolution to construction and then to reform and opening up. That is to say, the Communist Party of China always leads the progress of China's various undertakings. Under the leadership of the CPC, China is able to establish a stable and efficient political system to ensure the stability and predictability of the governance structure.

According to some foreign media, compared with the multi-party political system in "western democratic countries", the "single-party system" in China means that China's political system is not democratic. But this criticism ignores the fact that the Communist Party of China takes democratic centralism as the fundamental decision-making principle within the party. Under the principle, Party members can express their views on specific issues. However, once the Party has made a decision, its members should carry it out completely and indisputably. At the same time, the other side of the "single-party system" is reflected in the system of people's congress and the multi-party cooperation and political consultation under the leadership of the Communist Party. Anti-corruption is a very important aspect which embodies the governance ability of the Communist Party of China. Cracking down on corruption can also serve as a criterion for measuring the efficiency of the political system. In addition, while fighting corruption ("zero tolerance" to corruption), strictly adhering to rule of law policy (everyone is equal before the law), "law-based governance of the country" as well as deepening judicial system reform becomes another pillar of institution-building and a part of the country's overall policy for social development. In this regard, the Communist Party of China is determined to further create necessary institutional conditions, political and social requirements for the construction of the rule of law in China.

The Communist Party of China is capable of dealing with the problems and issues that have emerged in the past decades, especially in the past ten years, and meeting the challenges in the future. These issues and challenges are a direct consequence of rapid economic growth and cover a wide range of areas. For example, to ensure the integration of further economic growth with overall development means not only economic development, but also the development of the whole society, for "improving the livelihoods and well-being of the people is the overarching goal of development", so constant efforts should be made to ensure that economic growth and overall social development are sustainable in the long term. At the present level of China's economic and social development, the national economy needs to realize a new transformation from investment driven growth to consumption driven economy.

I'm confident of China's development. China's per capita GDP still lags far behind that of developed economies, which provides enough room for China's economy to grow steadily at a relatively high speed in the next several decades.

Comments on the Failure of European Socialism and the Success of Socialism with Chinese Characteristics

– An Interview with Frank Schumann, Director of the Edition Ost Verlag in Berlin

Interviewed by Li Ruiqin[1], Wang Jianzheng[2]

Translated by Xie Shengzhe

Finalized by Wang Qiuhai

Frank Schumann

Frank Schumann is director of the Edition Ost Verlag in Berlin, a renowned German publishing house.

Frank Schumann was born in the German Democratic Republic (GDR) in 1951. In 1966, he joined the German Workers' Union (Freier Deutscher Gewerkschafts-Bund, FDGB). From 1970 to 1973, he was in the people's navy of the German Democratic Republic, was promoted to lieutenant. During this period, he joined the Socialist Unity Party (Sozialistische Einheitspartei Deutschlands, SED).

From 1973 to 1974, Schumann worked as a journalist intern with the *World Youth Newspaper (Junge Welt)*, the official newspaper of the central committee

---

1 Li Ruiqin, research fellow of the Academy of Marxism, Chinese Academy of Social Sciences.
2 Wang Jianzheng, senior advisor of China Institute for International Strategic Studies.

of the World Youth Union (Freie Deutsche Jugend, FDJ). From 1974 to 1978, he studied journalism in Karl-Marx-Universität in Leipzig and obtained master's degree in journalism.

From 1978 to 1991, Schumann worked at the *Junge Welt*, acting as director of department of science/publicity, editor-in-chief in charge of cultural column and managing editor of the newspaper. With a circulation of 1.60 million, the newspaper was the largest at that time in the German Democratic Republic.

After German reunification in October 1990, the Ost Verlag Press was established in 1991. From then on, Schumann became a publisher and critic in politics. He published works of the general secretaries of the former SED including Walter Ulbricht, Erich Honecker and Egon Krenz as well as Hans Modrow, former premier of East Germany and leaders of The Left (Die Linke) Gregor Gysi and Sahra Wagenknecht.

In November 2019, at the invitation of the World Socialism Research Center of the Chinese Academy of Social Sciences, Frank Schumann came to China for the first time to attend the international symposium, "Belt and Road Initiative and the 'Building of a Community with a Shared Future for Mankind'".

Interview Summary

In Schumann's view, an important reason why China has effectively avoided repeating the failure of socialism in Europe is that the top priority is given to the development of productive forces. After more than 40 years of reform and opening up, China is playing a first-class role in the world economy, exerting a remarkable influence on the current situation and development of the world economy. China has successfully avoided the Gorbachev policy that led to the disintegration of the Soviet Union. In the course of reform and opening up, China always adheres to the leadership of the Communist Party, ensuring the socialist goal and nature of overall social development. In the contemporary era, a strong socialist China guided by

Comments on the Failure of European Socialism and the Success of Socialism with Chinese Characteristics

Marxism with Chinese characteristics can completely change the world political map. China will become the main actor in the second act of the drama of world history and stand at the center of the stage of the socialist world for a long time.

Schumann spent his youth in the period of the GDR. After German reunification, he became a famous publisher. He once was closely associated and cooperated with the leaders of the ruling party, the government and the armed forces of the former GDR. From the perspective of a left-wing publisher, he reflected on the history of world socialism and the dramatic changes in Eastern Europe, and seriously pondered over the historical process of the development of socialism with Chinese characteristics. Based on the fruitful achievements of socialism with Chinese characteristics, he put forward insightful thinking and views with distinctive theoretical and dialectical characteristics.

I. China has effectively avoided the important factors that led to the failure of European socialism and put the development of productive force as the first priority

Q: Thank you, Mr. Schumann, for accepting our interview. The year of 2019 marked the 30th anniversary of the drastic changes in Eastern Europe. As a publisher who grew up in the period of the GDR, you now live in the capitalist Germany. How do you view the failure of European socialism?

A: Although European socialism failed in 1989, it was not the socialist ideal but the Soviet-style socialism that failed. The socialism of the Soviet Union was the result of the adoption of the model of the Soviet Union in social and economic organization as an example for its Eastern European allies after the end of the Second World War. After the establishment of the socialism of the Soviet model in Eastern European countries, the Cold War began, leading to the change in the international situation. Therefore, for a long period of time, the socialist camp headed by the Soviet Union did not attempt to revise and reform the political and economic system according to the actual conditions of its respective countries. At that time, the reforms in socialist countries were suppressed, including the use of military force. The Soviet side believed that counterrevolutionary forces might be behind the attempts to change the Soviet model.

Under the circumstances at that time, attempts to change the Soviet model might be a counter-revolutionary conspiracy. In fact, such concern and understanding are not unreasonable. During the Cold War period after 1945, the imperialism led by the United States adopted a comprehensive strategy of containment and peaceful evolution of European socialism. It is necessary for communist party leaders to remain politically and ideologically firm and vigilant so as to concentrate resources and strength in response to such containment and strategy. However, the European Communists in power apparently lacked courage and fortitude in seeking new approaches and implementing them. Perhaps the most important thing is that they ignored one of Lenin's most important points of view that productivity is the most important and critical criterion for the success of a new social system. Capitalism will eventually be defeated by socialism, and the ultimate way to defeat it is to create a newer and higher productive force. The level of productivity is the main embodiment of overall economic strength, and it is just in this regard that there was a gap between European socialism and capitalism.

Q: How do you view China's reform and opening up policy and understand socialism with Chinese characteristics?

A: I think that as a Chinese leader, Deng Xiaoping understood Lenin's thought and made a correct decision that the core issue of developing socialism is to develop its economy. The reform and opening up policy initiated by Deng Xiaoping included the following two key measures. Firstly, China was to experience a transition from a single planned economy to a market economy. Secondly, it was necessary for China to make use of foreign investment to develop its economy. A strong economy is not only the most effective force to resist the imperialist attack, but also the most powerful proof of winning the trust of the people. Attractive and vibrant socialism is the best advertisement for the socialist cause. Such is my understanding of the policies of the Communist Party of China.

China's achievements in economic development since the reform was launched by Deng Xiaoping have indicated that a socialist country can greatly change its backwardness in a relatively short period of time after it actively participates in the world market and the international division of labor. It is through such efforts and spirit of enterprise that China, which used to be an underdeveloped country in industry, has now grown into the world's largest exporter and exerted remarkable influence on the world's economic and political development. China has become a top actor in the world economy, and has had a great influence on the current situation and development of the world economy.

Deng Xiaoping's thinking was incorporated into the resolution of the 14th National Congress of the Communist Party of China. On the basis of "socialist market economy", "socialism with Chinese characteristics" has been developed. It can be said that Marx developed his understanding of socialism in the process of criticizing capitalism. Lenin planned to build socialism by utilizing capitalism. According to Deng Xiaoping's theory, socialism can be achieved by way of studying capitalism. It follows that socialism with Chinese characteristics and Marxism are compatible with each other.

II. China has successfully avoided Gorbachev Line that led to the disintegration of the Soviet Union

Q: How do you see the conflict and struggle between capitalism and socialism in the 20th century?

A: When we look back, the hostilities of the imperialist powers against European socialism constituted a very important factor which will have a huge influence on its future direction. In 1918, imperialist powers supported the tsarist

China in the New Era

counter-revolutionary forces through military intervention. In the 1920s, they continued to initiate numerous hostile operations, especially British imperialism. Later, Nazi Germany launched a surprise attack on the Soviet Union. After the Second World War was over, the imperialist powers led by the United States continued this hostile action. The above-mentioned long-term and continuous actions of encirclement and suppression of socialist countries put the socialism led by the Soviet Union under double or even multiple pressures of national construction and preparation for war with the foreign enemy.

Therefore, the Soviet leaders should not be accused of making every effort to maintain a military balance with the West because they learned their lessons from the Second World War. However, the Soviet Union paid a high price. The huge military expenditure brought a huge burden, blocked the pace of social progress, and put excessive pressure on the Soviet economy.

The strategic goal of the United States and its allies was to wear the Soviet Union down through arms race. Leaders of the Communist Party of the Soviet Union took many actions in an attempt to put an end to this fatal arms race and to improve relations with imperialist powers including the United States because the policy of peaceful coexistence is completely in line with Lenin's idea. In the 1980s, however, the Communist Party led by Mikhail Gorbachev deviated from this policy by increasingly emphasizing the so-called "universal human interests", which, sadly, embraced Western values. But it did not stop the imperialist attack on socialism. The West has always been engaged in a desperate struggle against socialism with a hostile system. Moscow at this point clearly has forgotten the history of the disintegration of the anti-Hitler alliance in 1945.

Q: After Gorbachev became the leader of the Party and state of the Soviet Union, he initiated perestroika in the Soviet Union. How do you evaluate his perestroika?

A: In my view, as a leader of the Communist Party of the Soviet Union, Gorbachev's intention was to move in the direction of the Social Democratic Party, which had a special impact. Most people and members of the Soviet Communist Party had never been exposed to the idea of social democracy in their political lives, so they mistakenly believed that this position was a democratic form of socialism, and that a greater level of welfare could be achieved quickly as long as the integration of the domestic economy with the market was realized.

This is an intentionally misleading act. Gorbachev probably knew that instead of being able to defend "pure democracy" and socialism, social democracy was intended for guarding the foundation of a "petty bourgeois and bourgeoisie state". It was merely to cover up the nature of the state with "social democracy" and to use "social market economy" to cover up its capitalist production mode. Gorbachev's practice was an emergency response to the transition from crisis to social democracy at the end of perestroika. Judging from its social nature, such a country was actually under the economic and political rule of oligarchic capital and financial capital.

Socialism should be a democratic form of organization, or else it is not socialism at all. Democracy is of vital importance to socialism. However, the path of democratic socialism often leads to the abuse of Marx's relevant basic points of view. There is no "pure democracy" independent of class and state. "Freedom" is not a general phenomenon that can be introduced in accordance with resolutions, but has its concrete and objective content determined by history. This "freedom" is closely related to the interests of various social forces. The abstract propaganda of "freedom" and "democracy" by the so-called "reformists" in the CPSU proved to be a catalyst for leading to social-democratic ideas and policies. As a result, reform policies eventually resulted in the CPSU being outlawed and self-disbanded.

While the perestroika weakened the Soviet Union, Gorbachev's popularity in the West and the Western media was on the rise, which made him increasingly filled with vanity. Therefore, it was very easy for the West to boss him around and the imperialist politicians to tactfully exploit the weakness of the Soviet Union. Whether to most socialist supporters or to bystanders, the reason why such a colossal country as the Soviet Union collapsed so quickly was closely related to the incompetence of the CPSU.

III. A strong socialist China under the guidance of Marxism with Chinese characteristics can completely change the political map of the world

Q: Thank you very much for sharing with us your evaluation on the history of world socialism and perestroika in the Soviet Union. What do you think of the prospect of future socialism?

A: Thank you!

I'm full of confidence in socialism in the future.

In the 20th century, the victory of the Chinese revolution, the founding of the People's Republic of China and the progress of China's socialist development greatly increased the strength of the socialist camp. In the early 1960s when the socialism became a worldwide system, people gained firm confidence and believed that socialism would overcome difficulties, achieve successful development, and eventually beat the capitalist social system and keep on making progress.

In the 1980s, China's path of reform and development was fundamentally different from that of the Soviet Union. Are all the sizable achievements of China's economic development sufficient to ensure the socialist objectives and nature of overall social development? Deng Xiaoping had a thorough understanding of this difficult problem and ensured the prospect of socialist development mainly through two aspects. The first is to emphasize the leading role played the Communist Party of China in the overall development and maintain the Communist Party's absolute control over the regime. The second is to ensure the leading role of state ownership in crucial means of production. Now president Xi Jinping also stresses the Communist Party's leadership over all work and emphasizes China's leadership and influence in the country. This is a successful practice and historical experience, which are indispensable for socialism with Chinese characteristics in the new era to accomplish its goals and tasks at this stage.

Q: In your opinion, what impact will the development of socialism with Chinese characteristics have on world socialism in the future?

A: I believe that a strong socialist China can not only completely change the political map of the world, but also give a strong impetus to other countries and regions on earth which are pursuing socialism. It will sufficiently prove that the failure of socialism in the Soviet Union and Eastern Europe was not the end of socialism, but merely a small episode in the long history of socialism when people look forward into the distant future.

The success of socialism in China has successfully proved that Marxism has spread from Europe to countries, regions and cultural circles with completely different social, political and spiritual traditions. China has a long history, and its social, cultural and spiritual experience is very different from the European tradition, which is based on ancient Greek and Roman history, the Renaissance and the Enlightenment. China is diametrically different from Europe as far as way of behavior and thinking are concerned. For these reasons, the process of mastering and applying Marxist theory in China is much more complicated. The combination of Marxist theory with Chinese culture and spiritual tradition must demonstrate Chinese characteristics. The localization of Marxism in China, or the socialism with Chinese characteristics, has expanded the horizon of European Marxist theory.

From the perspective of the world history, the 70 years between the establishment and development of socialism in Europe were only the first act of a long drama in which capitalism is decaying and perishing and being replaced by a new social form. China will play a leading part in the second act of this long drama and stand in the center of the socialist world stage for a long time. No one can be allowed to hurl abuses at the glorious 70 years of the People's Republic of China!

This book is the result of a co-publication agreement between Contemporary China Publishing House (China) and Paths International Ltd (UK)

Title: China in the New Era: Interviews with Politicians and Academics from the Former Soviet Union and Eastern Europe
Editor-in-Chief: Jiang Hui
Associate Editor-in-Chief: Xin Xiangyang
Compiled by Li Ruiqin, Yu Haiqing, etc.
ISBN: 978-1-84464-696-8
Ebook ISBN: 978-1-84464-697-5

Copyright © 2022 by Paths International Ltd, U.K. and by Contemporary China Publishing House, China

All rights reserved. No part of this publication may be reproduced, translated, stored in a retrieval system, or transmitted in any form or by any means, electronic, mechanical, photocopying or otherwise, without the prior permission of the publisher.

The copyright to this title is owned by Contemporary China Publishing House, China. This book is made available internationally through an exclusive arrangement with Paths International Ltd of the United Kingdom and is permitted for sale outside China.

Paths International Ltd
www.pathsinternational.com
Published in the United Kingdom

Ingram Content Group UK Ltd.
Milton Keynes UK
UKHW052111090323
418225UK00007B/352